D0374970

KING OF THE COWBOYS

KING OF THE COWBOYS

THE LIFE AND TIMES OF JERRY JONES

JIM DENT

ADAMS PUBLISHING
Holbrook, Massachusetts

Published by Adams Media Corporation
260 Center Street, Holbrook, MA 02343

ISBN: 1-55850-527-X

Printed in the United States of America.

J   I   H   G   F   E   D   C   B   A

Library of Congress Cataloging-in-Publication Data
Dent, Jim.
King of the Cowboys : the life and times of Jerry Jones / Jim Dent.
p.   cm.
Includes index.
ISBN 1-55850-527-X (hc)
1. Jones, Jerry, 1942–   . 2. Football team owners—Biography. 3. Dallas
Cowboys (Football team) I. Title.
GV939.J64D46   1995
796.332'092—dc20
[B]   95-34426
CIP

Photographs on first page of insert courtesy of University of Arkansas Media Relations.
All other photos by David Woo ©1995 *Dallas Morning News*.

This book is available at quantity discounts for bulk purchases.
For information, call 1-800-872-5627.

To Leanna and Jimmy Dent,
My Heroes

TABLE OF CONTENTS

ACKNOWLEDGMENTS

JIM DONOVAN IS MY AGENT, EDITOR, AND FRIEND. IF NOT FOR HIS passion for *King of the Cowboys*, this book never would have made it into print. I thank him for his patience, insight, and tireless support. His immense editing skills were greatly appreciated.

Edward Walters, the editor-in-chief of Adams Publishing, made this book possible. His unwavering belief and patience inspired me to keep going. Reading the final edited manuscript was a great joy. I can't imagine there being two better editors anywhere than Walters and Donovan.

Friends are so important when you're trying to make sense of something this complex. Not everyone believed. But Roddy O'Neal saved me from an emotional collapse late one night with the greatest impromptu pep talk ever delivered. Thanks to Roger Carruth for repeatedly telling me I'd get it done.

"Big Al" Fossler of Southern Methodist University provided superb research as my intern for the book. He is destined to be a great journalist. Thanks to my sister, Janice Dent, and to Ernie Dumas, a great reporter, for their contributions from Little Rock.

To all of the folks at Prime Sports Radio who had to live with a tired, tense, and cranky talk show host in the mornings, you are the best. Special thanks to PSR program director Allen Stone and my producer, Greg Sher, for their patience and understanding.

More than three hundred people were interviewed for this book, some at great lengths. Thanks for your time and insight and, in some cases, your courage.

Not to be overlooked is Rolly "Big Cat" Dent who sat at my feet for the countless hours while I wrote this book. Thanks for keeping my chair warm, big boy, during the coffee breaks.

CHAPTER 1

Ground
Zero

THE ALARM IN JERRY JONES'S HEAD CLATTERED AT 2:30 THE MORNING of January 15, 1995, just as it had so many other times during the last six years. Worrisome nights were nothing new to Jones. Once awakened by the slightest noise, he could never get back to sleep. After a lifetime of high-stakes gambling Jerry Jones has learned to walk that anxious floor.

His presidential suite was located on the twelfth floor of the downtown San Francisco Marriott, an odd structure that looks a lot like the world's largest jukebox. On a clear day, you could see the Golden Gate Bridge in the distance. Just beyond Fisherman's Wharf, Alcatraz Island sat perched in the bay.

For the past few months, though, San Francisco had been cloaked by fogs and low clouds, and views of its famous tourist attractions were virtually nonexistent. The constant downpour had turned thirty-four of the state's counties into federal disaster areas. Northern California had been transformed into a giant sponge.

Yet beyond the earthquakes, the mud slides, and the rivers rising in the wine country, another uprising was underway. In about ten hours, the Dallas Cowboys would play the San Francisco 49ers at Candlestick Park—in their third consecutive National Football Conference championship game. Dallas had won the first two. San Franciscans had been saving their venom for this day, for the Cowboys, and for Jerry Jones.

Jones had been waiting for this day since buying America's Team on February 25, 1989. Sure, there had been other days when everything had seemed to be on the line. Days like January 31, 1993, when the Cowboys won their first Super Bowl of the Jerry Jones/Jimmy Johnson era, humiliating the Buffalo Bills 52–17. Then, a year later, when the Cowboys won a second straight NFL title, again crushing the Bills, this time by the lopsided score of 30-13, and setting the stage for the hellish pressure of the 1994 season.

Would the Cowboys become the first team to win an unprecedented third straight Super Bowl? And would fans and critics blame Jerral Wayne Jones, formerly of Dogtown, Arkansas, if they didn't?

★ ★ ★

Jones's mood had been upbeat all weekend around the hotel. On Friday night, he had taken twenty close friends and family members to a private room at one of San Francisco's elite gourmet restaurants. He sat next to his long-time friend Don Tyson, known as the Chicken King. Tyson is one of America's wealthiest men, having built his chicken empire from scratch more than forty years ago in Springdale, Arkansas.

"When Jerry gets wound up talking about the Dallas Cowboys—and he was doing some talking Friday night—I don't hardly get a chance to talk chickens," Tyson said later. "This is one of the most driven men you will ever want to meet. Here is a guy who, by God, made it by himself. He planted his own crop and he harvested the damn thing."

After six years of owning the Dallas Cowboys, Jerry Jones may be the most ambitious man in America. Surely, he has become one of the most outspoken and powerful men in all of sports. In 1994, he was chosen as one of the ten most fascinating people of the year by an ABC-TV program. Outside of Commissioner Paul Tagliabue, no one wields more power in the NFL than Jones. He was the driving force behind the Fox Network deal that brought the NFL a $1.6 billion television bonanza at a time when most executives were expecting TV revenues to decline. He is the most quoted and the most visible of all owners in American sports. NFL owners like to joke that Jones never met a TV mini-cam that he didn't like.

Beyond the back room joking, though, some hard feelings are starting to spread towards Jones and the way he does business. Given the opportunity, he would rewrite the NFL's sixty-year old policy on revenue sharing—so that the lion's share of the Cowboys' lucrative licensing business would come his way. There is a growing perception that Jones is in the NFL to line his own pockets at the expense of the other teams. His cocky swagger has rubbed more than a few of the other owners and executives the wrong way. Carmen Policy, the general manager of the 49ers, doesn't smile when he refers to Jones as a "snake oil salesman" or a "gunslinger."

Jones's critics predict that he will self-destruct before his grandiose schemes are complete. They call him a control freak. They point to his thirst for power and control and to his seemingly compulsive behavior. They point to the sudden gear-changes in his personality. They point to the night in Orlando when he hatched his intoxicated plot to fire Jimmy Johnson. They wonder if Jones is truly "harvesting the crop he planted," as Tyson might say? Or did he take a machete to the field when he dumped Johnson, considered by many to be the best coach in the NFL?

Five years earlier, just hours after he had bought the Cowboys, Jones had battled to survive a public relations disaster after firing Tom Landry, the legendary coach of the Cowboys for twenty-nine years, and one of the most respected and beloved figures in Texas. At the time, the former Arkansas oilman was nicknamed "Jethro" because he reminded fans and media critics of the bumbling character from the *Beverly Hillbillies*.

Now, if possible, he had an even bigger concern on his hands. Replacing Landry with his long-time friend Johnson had been a major-league gamble, but replacing Johnson with college football outcast Barry Switzer was different. The Cowboys had suffered a long decline during Coach Landry's final seasons, but Jimmy Johnson had just won the Cowboys their second consecutive Super Bowl.

Issues of control, disloyalty, and respect led to this celebrated divorce. Both Jones and Johnson are avowed control freaks. Because Jones had drained his life's earnings and taken enormous risks to buy the Cowboys and the Texas Stadium lease for $140 million, he expected loyalty and respect from Johnson. Conversely, Johnson believed that he should have sole control of the football operation. He wanted no meddling from Jones.

Jones believed that Johnson was fostering an "us-against-Jones" attitude among the players. The tension between the two was never higher than one afternoon after practice when the owner and the coach got into a shoving match just outside of the Cowboys' locker room. Johnson had asked Jones not to bring his friends to closed practices. Jones had reminded Johnson that he might "just fire his ass" any time he felt like it. Guard John Gesek had to step between the two to break up the fight.

"I laid every dime on the line to buy the Dallas Cowboys," Jones said. "I personally guaranteed his contract. He would have gotten his money if he had never won a football game. Therefore, I expected more respect from Jimmy when we got to a level of success."

Later that day, Johnson shot back, "Jerry can say all he wants about my disloyalty. But I worked sixteen hours a day to get this team to the level that it is. If he thinks that's disloyalty, then he is screwed up." Jones responded, "Well, if he worked sixteen hours a day, then I worked twenty. There were a lot of people who worked the long hours around our offices. But they didn't do half the bitching."

Jones knew that firing Johnson would make him the most hated man in Cowboyland. A letter to the *Dallas Morning News* summed up many fans' feelings, saying simply, "Jerry Jones is a goober." One of the paper's columnists, Randy Galloway, called the breakup the "biggest soap opera in the history of sports, even bigger than the O. J. (Simpson) thing."

While Jones's action knocked the wind out of many of the Cowboys' fans and followers, family members and close friends weren't surprised. The hatred between the two had been festering for some time. Jones had told Tyson that he "hated the son of a bitch" nearly two years earlier. Just a few days after the Cowboys' Super Bowl XXVII win, he had confided to Tyson and several other friends that he was thinking about firing Johnson.

All over the country, football fans were wondering if the Cowboys could take the final step to their third Super Bowl without Jimmy Johnson. All of Jones's chips were now on Barry Switzer, who had coached the team to a 12-4 regular season record and an easy win over Green Bay in the divisional round of the playoffs.

Just before the kickoff of the title game, Jones would admit the risk he had taken: "From the day I fired Jimmy Johnson, and from the day I hired Barry Switzer, I knew that I would have to cross this bridge and face this day. I started planning for this day emotionally a long time ago. You do that when you roll the dice. You don't necessarily think about losing. But you have to think about what it will be like if you do."

One of Jerry Jones's biggest concerns on that January morning would have been whether Dallas fans would remember him as the football genius who had taken them to three consecutive Super Bowls, or as the compulsive gambler who couldn't leave a winning hand alone.

COMPETITIVE FORCES HAD ALSO BEEN WORKING AGAINST THE Cowboys. After losing their second straight NFL championship game to the Cowboys in 1994, San Francisco owner Eddie DeBartolo and general manager Carmen Policy slumped against an elevator wall inside Texas Stadium. Policy hung his head and wondered about the future of the franchise. "We can't repeat this," DeBartolo said in a hushed tone. "I know," Policy said. "We would be better off getting worse than standing still. We have to do whatever it takes, even if it means getting worse in the process." Pounding the wall, DeBartolo said, "The attitude has to change. Everyone has to commit themselves to winning again."

The team's chartered flight back to San Francisco was as quiet as a library. The 49ers had been humiliated by their seventeen-point loss. Quarterback Steve Young had suffered a rare loss of composure in the face of the Dallas pass rush.

"There was a fire burning on that airplane as it headed west," Policy said. "I was trying to frame a process by which I would address the next season. I had lots of difficulty doing that. So I really sat there and wallowed in my own self-pity."

It didn't take long for his depression to pass. The 49ers approached the 1994 season with a fire in their gut. Policy was soon on a flight to Youngstown, Ohio, where he asked Edward DeBartolo, Sr., to open his vaults. He returned to San Francisco with an extra $10 million to fuel the free-agent market. Existing contracts were shredded and rewritten to fit the 49ers spending spree within the league's rules. Amid protests throughout the league—and howls from Jones—they pried loose enough money to get Deion Sanders under contract. Meanwhile, the Cowboys were losing eight quality players to free agency.

For the sole purpose of finally beating Dallas, the 49ers' front office had moved relentlessly, exploiting loopholes in the NFL salary cap to replace and rebuild the core of their defense. Jones was openly critical of what he considered a massaging of the rules. He predicted that the 49ers' credit card mentality would wreck their future.

Forty-niners' center Bart Oates, a veteran of eleven NFL seasons, put it bluntly: "This organization isn't hiding its intentions. We've been built with one intention in mind: Beat Dallas." This single-minded commitment had taken root on an elevator at Texas Stadium. Now the 49ers were ready to try their new attitude out on the hated Cowboys.

★ ★ ★

BESIDES FOOTBALL, JONES HAD ALSO HAD FAMILY CONCERNS ON HIS mind over the previous three months. One of the most pressing involved the health of his father—one of his strongest supporters. Over the Thanksgiving holiday, 74-year old J. W. "Pat" Jones had suffered a heart attack while the family was duck-hunting near Stuttgart, Arkansas. Pat Jones almost didn't make the trip. Even though he had felt fatigued for the previous few weeks, he was concerned that this might be his last opportunity to spend Thanksgiving with his family, and he went anyway.

Jones's hunting lodge is located in the White Water Refuge. Each Thanksgiving, about thirty family members cram into a lodge with only fourteen beds. For three taxing days, they participate in the annual World Duck-Calling contest, the Wings-over-the-Prairie festival, and a duck gumbo cook-off. On Saturday, a parade is held for the duck-callers. Twelve Cowboys cheerleaders, dressed in bird outfits, cavort, smile, kick, and shimmy down Main Street.

Jones had awakened at four in the morning to find his father getting dressed for the drive back to his home in Springfield, Missouri. Pat Jones was pale and stooped and complained of severe indigestion. Alarmed by his father's appearance, Jones hustled him onto his corporate Lear Jet and flew him directly to a hospital.

Doctors in Missouri were perplexed over the elder Jones's condition. They feared that surgery would be fatal. Two weeks later, he was moved to Dallas. Doctors there told the family that heart surgery would provide no more that a fifty-fifty chance of survival. Later, as Pat Jones clung to life, Jerry Jones leaned over his father and gave him a pep talk. "Fight. Try hard. Don't give up. We all love you so much." Tears in his eyes, he hugged the man he calls "the most influential man in my life."

As the Cowboys prepared for the trip to the Bay Area, Pat Jones was resting comfortably in Dallas. But his son knew that there would be a void in the family's box above Candlestick Park at kickoff.

★ ★ ★

As Jones stood at his hotel window and stared into the damp and foggy San Francisco night, two wishes came to mind. First, he silently hoped for a healthy Emmitt Smith, the Cowboys' star running back, who had been playing since December 19th on a badly pulled hamstring muscle. Second, he wished for firm footing on the playing field at Candlestick Park. A muddy and treacherous field would nullify the Cowboys' speed advantage, especially in the defensive line.

At six o'clock, as the sun peeked over a cloudless horizon, Jones wondered if his wishes were already being granted. Amazingly, you could actually see the blue sky for the first time in days.

Preparing for the team's pre-game breakfast, Jones worked the knot on his lucky blue tie with white dots. It was the same tie he had worn during the previous two NFC championship games and the last two Super Bowls, making it an unblemished 4-0 in big games. In the midst of a San Francisco sunrise, he was already feeling the adrenaline start to kick in. Pulling on his sky-blue jacket, he sped through the doorway, revving his engine for a full day of rush-hour traffic.

In a banquet room deep in the basement of the Marriott, Cowboys' players made their way through a buffet of waffles, pancakes, sausage, bacon, pastries, biscuits, and scrambled eggs. At another table, two cooks hurriedly prepared omelets.

The players moved in near silence. Defensive end Charles Haley wore a cap that read ZULU—and an angry expression. Haley had informed both Jones and Switzer of his intention to retire after the game. Haley had retired more than once during his years with the 49ers, only to return for more money.

Earlier in the season, Coach Switzer had been concerned about his team's level of motivation. But not today. He had told friends that it was the best week of practice since he'd become the coach of the Cowboys.

"I'm telling you, Jerry," he said. "I've never seen a football team more focused. If it means anything at all, we'll win this damn football game."

Troy Aikman, the team's star quarterback, would say later, "There wasn't a single doubt in anyone's mind when we got on that airplane to go to San Francisco that we were going to win the football game. I know it sounds like a cliché. But with everything we had gone through all season—all of the struggles—we really felt there was no way we were going to lose that game."

Aikman, like many of the players, had an added motivation. The night before, he had said, "To me, this is the most important game of my whole career. With all of the changes we've been through, you want to just show people that you win because of the players, not because of the coaches. I guess a lot of the players want to prove that we can win without Jimmy."

WHEN THE TELEVISION CAMERAS CALL, JERRY JONES IS OBLIGED TO answer. He arrived at Candlestick Park three hours before kickoff to film a segment of *Up Close* with ESPN's Roy Firestone. It would be part of an hour-long show to be aired the following Saturday. Among the other guests was San Francisco quarterback Steve Young.

Standing near the 30-yard line, Firestone pointed out a temporary wooden balcony erected in the end zone for the Fox Network's pre-game, half-time, and post-game shows.

"Jimmy will be sitting right there," Firestone said.

"You can see," Jones replied, "that they had to widen the booth just to get Jimmy in there."

Jones had been listening to Johnson's jabs all season, and he wasn't above landing a blow or two himself. Johnson's diet consists mainly of imported beer, nachos, take-out Mexican food, and barbecued ribs—but he hates references to his girth.

The week before the championship game, Jones had sent a letter to the league office demanding that Johnson be banned from the field before kickoff. He didn't want Johnson visiting with his former players at such a critical time. Jones knew that Johnson had been calling some of the Cowboys' players, especially Troy Aikman, on a regular basis. He worried that the shadow of the former coach had become an unsettling distraction.

"We just didn't feel it would be appropriate for Jimmy Johnson to have a homecoming at our expense," Jones said. "We didn't think it would be right for him to come by and shake hands and see all of our ball players down on the sideline. It was time to get ready to play a ball game. We just didn't need that."

Instead, Johnson sat like a prisoner in the makeshift Fox studio from 8 A.M. until 5 P.M. His broadcast partners, Terry Bradshaw and Howie Long, watched the first half from the field and the second half from a dressing room located next to the Cowboys' lockers. Johnson didn't go to the dressing room, hoping to avoid an unpleasant collision with his past.

TWO HOURS BEFORE KICKOFF, JONES'S MOOD REFLECTED THE SUNNY morning. Even the squishy playing surface couldn't dampen his spirits. One of the first players to step on the field for pre-game warm-ups was backup quarterback Jason Garrett, who took one look at the mid-field muck and declared it "kitty litter." The Cowboys' players were wearing three-quarter-inch cleats to provide better footing in the mud. But Jones had spent the better part of Saturday, calling all over the country trying to find rare inch-long cleats. When safety James Washington and running back Lincoln Coleman got into a pre-game shoving match with a group of 49ers, Jones knew that Switzer's assessment of the team's mood was accurate.

Hand outstretched, crooked grin fixed to his face, Jones swaggered towards Rupert Murdoch, the owner of the Fox Network and a media kingpin. Two weeks earlier, *The Sporting News* had dubbed Murdoch the most powerful man in sports. Jones had driven home the $1.6 billion deal that had brought the NFL to Fox. One of the deal's stipulations was that Fox could carry a hefty roster of Cowboys' games on a national basis. Jones fixed his eyes of Murdoch and said, "Rupert, doggone it, I told you I'd deliver the Dallas Cowboys today. And I'll tell you something else—we're going to win this ball game today!"

Jones was in one of his "peak-on-peak modes." Others might call it an overdose of adrenaline. His eyes glistened like a cat in pursuit of a canary. It was the same look he'd had in his college days at Arkansas, when as a undersized 190-pound guard he'd not only started, but led his team to a national championship.

"There was this swagger to him on the field," Firestone remembered later. "His attitude was like the attitude of a gambler walking up to the craps table. It was like a guy betting on a horse race that he knows he just can't lose. It was like a gambler saying, 'I've got my lucky shoes and my lucky tie. I'm just setting myself up for a lucky day.' Jerry Jones *knew* he was going to have a great day. He was jabbing people in the ribs and saying, 'Yessir, we're going to win this ball game.' He even said, 'We have more at stake in this game than in any other game we've ever played.' It was just that big to him. He was talking like winning the game was a done deal."

As the Jones entourage of twenty began the trip up to their box at Candlestick Park, Tyson took one look at the random configuration and the snaking halls and said, "You'd have to be a well-trained mouse just to get around in this thing." In just a few minutes, it would be clear just how badly the Cowboys had lost their way.

JONES AND HIS FRIENDS HAD BARELY FOUND THEIR SEATS IN THE DRAFTY box when the Cowboys fell behind 7-0. On the third play of the game, 49ers' tackle Bryant Young over-powered guard Derek Kennard and was standing nearly in quarterback Troy Aikman's face as he released a pass. With two Cowboys' receivers running through the same area, 49ers' cornerback Eric Davis was able to leave his coverage of Michael Irvin, step inside Kevin Williams for the pick, and return it 44 yards for a touchdown.

Feeling antsy and slightly hexed, the Jones clan started swapping chairs, hoping to change the Cowboys' luck. A fumble by Irvin three plays later led to another 49ers' touchdown. Williams then fumbled the ensuing kickoff. When 49ers' fullback William

Floyd scored from the 1-yard line with 7:33 left in the first quarter, there was more chair-swapping. Now the Cowboys had run six plays and were behind 21-0.

Jones closed his eyes and made his third wish of the day. "I told myself that when I opened my eyes all of the bad things that had been happening to us would start happening to them," he remembered later.

Sitting in the Fox booth, Jimmy Johnson sat with his eyes glued to the TV monitor. His only display of emotion came when the Cowboys tried a third-down draw play from the 49ers 10-yard line while trailing 21-7. (The Cowboys had scored on a 44-yard touchdown pass from Troy Aikman to Michael Irvin.) In trademark Johnson style, he raised his arms and dropped his jaw. "A draw play, huh!" was all he said.

Jones, on the other hand, was getting more and more angry with Switzer. As Emmitt Smith slipped in the Candlestick mud, gaining only two yards on the draw, Jones jerked up in his seat and yelled, "What the hell is Barry doing out there? What the hell is going on here? We've got a chance to win this ball game and he's fucking it up."

In fact, offensive coordinator Ernie Zampese was calling the plays as he had all season. But Switzer had called a time-out to discuss the play before it was run.

Jones wasn't the only person puzzled by the draw. Fox analyst John Madden commented, "I don't know where that call came from. That was a give-up call." Jones, pointing at the TV monitor, nodded in agreement. "You are right, John Madden. We blew it there. That was a bad call."

When the Cowboys eventually attempted a field goal, Johnson turned to Barry Horn of the *Dallas Morning News* and said, "You gotta try and get a touchdown down there. A field goal is no sure thing on a field in this condition." Sure enough, kicker Chris Boniol slipped in the mud and shanked the 27-yarder.

The Cowboys earned another touchdown on a four-yard run by Emmitt Smith, which followed a 34-yard field goal by the 49ers' Doug Brien. Down 24-14 with just over a minute to play in the first half, the Cowboys got the ball back at their own 16-

yard line. Given the condition of the field and the lack of time, Jones figured that Switzer would try to run out the clock. He didn't. Troy Aikman attempted three long passes, all incomplete. The first was batted at the line and nearly intercepted by Toi Cook, who would have scored easily. The three plays consumed only twenty seconds, giving the ball back to San Francisco at the Dallas 39-yard line with thirty seconds left. John Jett's 23-yard punt didn't help.

"What the hell is wrong with Barry?" Jones asked, to no one in particular. "It's the same old problem that we've had with clock management all year. Why can't he figure it out?"

With thirteen seconds left, no time-outs, and the ball on the Dallas 28-yard line, everyone in the stadium knew that 49ers' quarterback Steve Young would either throw the ball to the sideline or into the end zone. As the teams lined up to run the play, Cowboys' players on the sideline realized that cornerback Larry Brown was in man-to-man coverage with Jerry Rice. They scrambled to the edge of the field, yelling, "Back up, Larry! Back up, Larry! No shit, Larry, they're going to throw to Rice. They're going to the end zone, Larry."

San Francisco had lined up in a two tight-end formation, leaving Brown alone with Rice. With predictable ease, Rice's out-and-up pattern burned Brown badly. Rice caught Young's heave in the left corner of the end zone with eight seconds to play. Instead of a ten-point deficit, the Cowboys were now down seventeen at half-time.

Chaos broke out on the Cowboys' sideline. Players started yelling for coaches to pull Brown from the game. "Get his ass off the field," several shouted. Wide receiver Michael Irvin got into a face-to-face shouting match with defensive assistant Mike Zimmer, who helps coach the secondary.

"God damn it," Irvin yelled, pointing his finger at Zimmer. "How can you leave somebody like Larry Brown in man-to-man coverage with somebody like Jerry Rice? That just doesn't make any fucking sense. Get these guys fired up! This game ain't over!"

Up in the Fox booth, Johnson threw up his hands and laughed.

"It is just conventional coaching wisdom that you run out the clock with the ball at the 16-yard line," he said. "They didn't *try* a single running play to take time off the clock. Every other coach in the league would have run the ball in that situation."

In his box, Jones nodded in agreement. It was painful to hear Johnson's criticism, but Jones was forced to admit, "You're absolutely right, Jimmy. You are absolutely right."

Then Jones turned quiet, a sign that often worries friends and relatives. It can be a signal that an explosion is coming. Firestone sensed the uneasiness in the box.

"The touchdown to Jerry Rice just blew his mind," Firestone said. "It was clear that he was very angry right then. The one thing that really bothered him was the bad clock management."

JERRY JONES COULD FEEL THE WALLS CLOSING IN AS THE PLAYERS trotted off the field. He wanted to get out of the box and into the locker room at half-time, but he didn't want to create the wrong impression.

More than a year earlier, Jones had opened a can of large worms when he told writer Frank DeFord, "Hey, I could coach the shit out of this team." And about ninety minutes before kickoff he had admitted, "I am a frustrated football coach. No doubt. But I paid $140 million for this. The interest on that is $45,000 a day. Think about trying to get back to the Super Bowl and then strap that action on right there."

All season long the question of who was running the team had been a major issue. Switzer, for obvious reasons, was very upset with the talk around the locker room that Jones was calling the shots. At one point, in a rare display of anger, he tossed a Coke can across the team's meeting auditorium and shouted, "I'll cut any of you fuckers who thinks that Jerry is coaching this team." And his only half-time outburst had come during a game against Washington at Texas Stadium. After hearing Charles Haley chiding younger players for preferring Jimmy Johnson's whip-cracking motivational methods, Switzer's face seemed ready to explode. "Fuck Jimmy Johnson!" he shouted.

Some of the players thought the time might be right for another outburst. But Switzer didn't. He still sensed a high energy level among his players, and a calm determination to come back. Preparing for the second half, Michael Irvin stood at the dressing room door, slapping shoulder pads and yelling, "Don't give up! Dammit, don't give up!"

★ ★ ★

THE 49ERS' ADAM WALKER FUMBLED THE SECOND HALF'S OPENING kickoff, and the Cowboys recovered. At least temporarily, Jones was able to put the painful prospect of reporters asking the inevitable Barry versus Jimmy questions out of his mind. When Emmitt Smith scored from the 1-yard line, Tyson said, "Jerry almost jumped out of the box." The 49ers' lead had been cut to ten points.

Throughout the second half, there was the continuous promise of a Cowboys comeback, even though the 49ers did push their lead back to seventeen points at one point. Aikman and Irvin were moving the offense, and connected for a 10-yard touchdown pass with 8:29 to play to cut the lead back to ten points. Seventy-one seconds later, hard-rocking Candlestick Park turned restless and quiet when Dallas got the ball back.

After spotting the 49ers twenty-one points, a Dallas win was now within reach. A quick score would have cut the lead to three points with plenty of time to go in the game. The game turned on a controversial play that featured a tangle of arms that somehow escaped the officials. Running stride for stride with Irvin at the 6-yard line, cornerback Deion Sanders reached across the receiver's body and held both of his arms as the pass fell incomplete. Back judge Bill Carollo had a perfect view of the play. He was seven yards in front of the players, just inside the end zone. He actually reached for the flag in his right back pocket twice. But Carollo finally waved the pass incomplete.

Up in the Fox booth, Pat Summerall put it bluntly, "There should have been a flag." A week after the game, NFL supervisor of officials Jerry Seemon would admit, according to Jones, "We blew that call very badly. I mean, very badly." More than a month later, Switzer still had a *Sports Illustrated* picture of the non-call on his desk at Valley Ranch. Waving the picture over his head, he yelled, "Just look at this. This is all you have to see." Sanders's left arm is draped over Irvin's right arm as the receiver grasps for the ball. It appears to be a classic case of pass interference.

Unfortunately, what had been merely a setback quickly turned into a disaster for the Cowboys. Switzer had barely raised his voice on the sideline throughout the season. At times, he appeared to be nothing more than a spectator wearing a headset. But now he found the nearest official, head linesman Sid Semon, and began spewing expletives. Standing a few inches from Semon, Switzer raised both arms, trying to demonstrate how the infraction had occurred. He was dancing like a barefoot man on hot coals. Without warning, Switzer rammed his right hip into Semon. The two men looked like they were doing "the bump," a popular disco dance move from the eighties.

The flag for unsportsmanlike conduct cost the Cowboys fifteen yards. NBC analyst Dan Hampton said, "It was like the hood ornament [Switzer] decided to wake up all of a sudden. He just picked the wrong time to do it."

Instead of third-and-ten from the San Francisco 43-yard line, the fifteen-yard penalty created a third-and-twenty-five from the Dallas 42-yard line. It was a hill Aikman couldn't climb, although he did complete a fourteen-yard pass to Alvin Harper on third down.

On fourth down, Aikman was victimized by another coaching decision that had been nagging at the Cowboys all day. Rookie tackle Larry Allen, playing on a badly sprained ankle, had been getting whipped around like a rag doll by 49ers' linebacker Ricky Jackson. Cowboys' defensive players yelled at the offensive coaches to get Allen out of the game. In the Fox booth, Madden was openly critical of Switzer's decision to stick with Allen. On this play, defensive end Tim Harris took advantage of Allen's limited mobility to sack Aikman and end the Cowboys' final drive.

Without question, Switzer's untimely outburst had cost the Cowboys an opportunity to convert on third down, and a chance to move into scoring territory. A touchdown would have brought Dallas within three points with five minutes to play. But Switzer couldn't control himself.

Six weeks later, Aikman would say, "I haven't said anything to Barry. But I'm sure that if somebody did, Barry would openly admit that it was a foolish thing. It hurt the football team."

But the first words out of Switzer's mouth in the crowded post-game interview room were that the Cowboys had been wronged by the officials.

"I've been in this league for one year. But I can tell already that officials protect Deion Sanders more than NBA officials used to protect Michael Jordan. Deion's a great player. But he makes mistakes, too."

As Switzer criticized both the condition of the field and the officials, Jerry Jones stood outside beneath a TV monitor, listening to Jimmy Johnson's analysis of the game. Again, he nodded in agreement as Johnson stated that poor clock management before half-time was the turning point of the game.

"I can tell you without equivocation that Jerry was very disappointed in the performance of Barry Switzer that day," Firestone said. "He was very disappointed in the way that Barry handled himself in the heat of battle. He seemed very surprised at how Switzer impacted the game. Switzer bumping the official was just inexcusable to Jerry. What might seem odd is that the bad call on the Irvin interference didn't bother him at all. It bothered everyone else in the booth, except for Jerry. He was not shouting or screaming. By then, he had said it was not to be. He just looked at it like a symbol of the whole game. It was as if he thought the Cowboys already deserved to lose because of Switzer's mistakes."

As the players dressed in their cramped locker room following the loss, Jones braced himself against a wall just inside the door. For more than an hour, he fielded dozens of reporters' questions. At times, the crowd around Jones was larger than the one around Troy Aikman.

In spite of what he had said to Firestone and others during the game, Jones was still trying to sell his coach to the media.

"I will not tell him anything," Jones said. "I will not get down on him. So I think it would be an overreach to blame Barry Switzer right now for any of this. If Jimmy had been here, it still would have been a long shot to make it to the Super Bowl. Right now I'm not going to second-guess the decision I made to hire Barry Switzer. I know that I will get a lot of criticism. But you have to remember there was a helluva lot of finger pointing going all the way back to 1989 when we went 1 and 15."

His eyes were still bright. He still carried much of his pre-game enthusiasm, at least on the outside.

"This is not one of the top ten disappointments in my life," he said. "And nobody had better think that this is the end of the Dallas Cowboys' dynasty."

★ ★ ★

NINETY MINUTES AFTER THE TEAM HAD LEFT THE FIELD, THEIR chartered flight was ready to leave San Francisco International Airport. Unlike the 49ers' flight from Dallas to the Bay area of a year ago, this one didn't seem like a morgue. There was laughing and plenty of beer-drinking on the way home. Players walked the aisles without fear that Barry Switzer might come roaring out of first class—Jimmy Johnson-style—to take them apart.

"I think that for three years this team has been heavily scrutinized," Aikman said later. "I think there was really a little bit of relief when it was over. We said, 'Hey, it's not us this year. It's over, and now we can go back and just do what we do best—and that is play football.' It's been a great three years. But it has been a long three years."

Jones spent most of the evening shaking hands and slapping backs. The Switzer experiment hadn't clicked. But Jones was not about to admit that he was unhappy with the coaching that day. Weeks later, he went as far as to state, "I don't really mean to be smug about it. But I really felt like we had the best team on the field. I thought we were better than San Francisco."

★ ★ ★

JONES STILL OPERATES ON THE OIL PATCH MENTALITY HE PICKED UP during his early business years: Roll the dice until your knuckles bleed, and never, ever do what the traditionalists would do. Jones is determined to succeed on his own terms and in his own way—

even if it means firing two of the most popular and successful coaches in the history of the National Football League, even if it means giving up a chance at winning a third consecutive Super Bowl.

And there's no reason to believe that Jones will stop taking risks now. He doesn't mind taking a wrecking ball to traditions and traditionalists. For example, even though he's stated that the Cowboys' standard home jerseys are as traditional as "Yankee pinstripes," he changed those jerseys for new ones for seven of the last eight games in 1994. Jones may have been angling for a few more dollars—the jerseys were worn throughout the Christmas shopping season, starting on Thanksgiving.

He has many more ambitious plans on the drawing board. Before the turn of the century, Jones plans to transform the land around Texas Stadium into a kind of football Disneyland. He plans to add a retractable roof, raise the height of the roof by fifty feet, and lower the field by twelve feet—increasing seating capacity from 63,000 to 104,000. The eighty acres around the stadium will be converted into virtual reality theaters, hotels, restaurants, executive offices, and anything else that pops into Jones's mind. It is easily the most ambitious blueprint in the sports world.

Jerry Jones thinks big and rolls the dice. Anyone who thinks that his splendid run in the NFL was over that day in San Francisco needs to check Jones's pedigree—going back to his humble beginnings in a tiny railroad community just across the river from Little Rock, Arkansas. Just measuring how far the self-made owner of the Dallas Cowboys has come should convince you that, for him, the game has just begun.

CHAPTER 2

Dogtown

At five o'clock one September afternoon in 1959, traffic began its evening flight from downtown Little Rock, Arkansas, clogging the Broadway and Main Street bridges heading into North Little Rock. Two seventeen-year-old boys gazed across the Arkansas river. They were fresh from the barbershop, sporting flattop haircuts with "whitewalls" down the sides. They wore pressed blue work shirts and blue jeans rolled up at the ankles, along with white socks and penny loafers.

Over the work shirt, the larger boy wore a blue and gray jacket with the letters N-L-R emblazoned over the heart. What better time than in the middle of the football season to wear your high school football letter jacket—with "All-District" and "Co-Captain" stitched on the sleeves. Both boys were members of the North Little Rock High School football team. The larger one played in the backfield and, in spite of his lack of speed, had been making headlines with his powerful running style.

The boys stood at the edge of the Broadway bridge, their knees braced against the railings. The river swirled more than sixty feet below. They presented an unusual sight to passers-by as they wrestled with more than three hundred feet of steel cable, with one end already tied to the Main Street bridge to the east. The Main Street bridge would later be torn down and rebuilt several city blocks up the river, but during the 1950s the bridges were close enough together that the boys were able to connect them by wrapping the line around the steel girders. Working the cable, they grunted like two studs colliding head-on during the Friday night high school clashes at Wildcat Stadium, just a few miles away across the river.

The job required muscle, timing, and a halfback's footwork in order to avoid the long plunge into the dark river. While one pulled the steel cable taut, the other wrapped it around the steel girder of the Broadway bridge. The line bobbed and danced on the wind. The two teenagers prayed that they wouldn't make a fatal misstep. If the river didn't get them, they'd be heroes by nightfall.

"Are you sure you wanna do this?" one yelled above the wind.

"Right now," responded the boy in the letter jacket, "I don't think we have much of a gol-durn choice, do you? Can you figure a way to get out of this now?"

With the steel cable tied securely to both bridges, the real work was just beginning. Huffing and puffing, the boys had also dragged pieces of an old septic tank up the side of the bridge. Now, they planned to attach the large concrete tank to the steel line, sending it floating over the river like a gondola over a ski resort. Attached to the sides of the tank were crudely painted signs that read, "Pat Jones for State Senate." The idea was to hang the huge campaign "poster" directly between the two bridges, where commuters from both directions couldn't help but notice. These folks might even vote for Pat Jones, the boys thought.

Traffic along Broadway was grinding to a halt. Rubbernecking motorists wondered what the two crazy kids were doing. With a loud grunt, they hoisted the tank onto the line, sending it swooping down the cable. The sliding steel on steel created a burning sound as the tank rushed outward, then downward, shooting sparks over the river.

"God almighty," one of the boys yelped. "We're going to make it—if the damn cable doesn't break."

According to their plan, the tank should reach a midpoint between the bridges, where it would find a balancing point. There it would stop and hang freely, rocking back and forth about fifty feet above the river. As the huge tank rocketed down the steel line, the boys cheered wildly. The tank seemed headed for some kind of place in history, maybe even the front page of the Arkansas *Gazette*.

Suddenly, their concrete cable car dipped and began to dive toward the gray river below. Their hearts sank with it. They gripped the steel girders of the bridge more tightly and leaned far out over the river, trying to balance themselves against the wind.

Perhaps the first miracle was that the cable didn't break under the heavy load of the septic tank's fall. But with the surface of the river now licking the tank, and with the swirling current washing high over the sides, they heard the dull collisions of concrete smacking water. Then, a loud sucking noise as the river tried to swallow the tank. Still, the cable held together.

With the bridge now quaking from river's pull on the cable, they almost didn't have time to react as the girders shook, loosening their grip on the railings. The sensation was like a crosswind violently buffeting a small airplane. Their hearts sinking, they braced themselves for the long fall. Seconds later, they recovered their balance as the line snapped. They watched as the tank slowly sank into the river. Pat Jones would never make it to the chambers of the Arkansas senate. Quietly, but with their hearts still pounding, they began the long walk back across the bridge, wondering what they would tell their friends.

"That thing looked just like the Titanic going down," the larger boy gulped. Walking on rubbery legs, trying to calm his shaking body, Jerry Jones told himself that he would never, ever try anything that crazy again.

★ ★ ★

DURING THE 1950s THE ARKANSAS RIVER CRAWLED LIKE DARK CORN syrup through the heart of the state—neatly dividing the state capital, Little Rock, from its poorer cousin, North Little Rock. The river produced a foul smell, as raw sewage rolled in for miles from the tiny farming communities upriver. The main artery through the state was truly in need of bypass surgery.

If one dared to swim the river, the obstacles included brown whirlpools and powerful undercurrents that might drag your body more than one hundred miles into the Mississippi River. Boys diving from the sandbars knew all of the hazards. On the North Little Rock side, they walked far up the bank, measuring the powerful current that would pull them more than a half-mile off course as they struggled to reach Little Rock.

Rising twelve stories above the river near the Little Rock bank were the Marion and Grady Manning hotels, leftovers from the turn of the century, now decaying. Late in the afternoon, guests would gather on the long covered porches to drink iced tea. They wagged giant fans, chasing away the mosquitoes that bred in the river's backwaters. Ceiling fans kept the air busy.

The Marion was more than just a fading brown relic. With its lavish parlors and ornamental lobby, it was the most elegant of Little Rock's architecture. Towering above the Old Statehouse, the Marion was considered the unofficial state capital during sessions of the legislature. Brown whiskey was poured. Votes were purchased. Deals were struck in the Gar Hole, a saloon and dining hall, overlooking a river going nowhere fast.

North Little Rock, just across the river, enjoyed the distinction of having one tavern for every six citizens. Originally known as Huntersville and then Argenta, and renamed North Little Rock in 1917, its primary employers were railroad and machine shops, along with the saloons on nearly every street corner. To its neighbors across the river, North Little Rock was nothing more than "Dogtown," a name hung on the place back in the 1940s. Little Rock folks showed their lack of respect by loosing their unwanted dogs into North Little Rock from the bridges that connected the two cities.

Rose City was a jagged slice of North Little Rock with no clearly defined boundaries. East Broadway was the blacktop fourlaner that ran parallel to the river, and still carries the thundering eighteen-wheelers from Memphis into Little Rock. It is generally accepted that Rose City began to the east at the junction of Highways 61 and 170, where the roads converged to create Protho Junction. It spread west along East Broadway about one and a half miles towards the England highway, where, on the edge of the river delta, the swampland began to slope towards the Arkansas river.

During the 1950s, the clatter and thunder of the big trucks and the railroads as they traveled through Rose City never stopped. The trucks rolled in from Memphis, and from Hope to the south, where watermelons were harvested. The coal-blowing steam engines of the day with their high stacks kept the blue-collar town dirtied from layers of black soot. Curving west from the roundhouse at Baring Cross, the Missouri-Pacific rail line rumbled through Rose City before heading east into the land of cotton, to places like Cotton Plant and Des Arc, and farther north to Bald Knob and Mountain Home. Likewise, the Cotton Belt line carried soybeans and hauled wood pulp from the south. The Rock Island line completed the puzzle by linking the transit hub to New Orleans and St. Louis.

Pat Jones is a stump of a man, distinguished by a red face and the energy of a locomotive. With a large pinkish nose that is somewhat askew, he looks like a lightweight boxer. In truth, he has rarely stopped bobbing, weaving, and jabbing.

A born promoter, Pat Jones was raised in a tiny farming community, about twenty miles southeast of Little Rock and just twenty-five miles southeast of Rose City. Like many others, the boy from the Arkansas farmlands had grown up on fear. The Great Depression hit the farmers with a haymaker. Share-cropping turned to dust with the drought of 1931. The Jones family lived in a leaky, poorly painted shack in England. Their nightmares were realized when the food ran out in the early days of the Depression.

England made national headlines during the "Food Riot" of 1931. Believing that the Red Cross was hoarding food, more than five hundred farmers loaded into flatbed trucks and rolled into downtown England. They threatened to invade one of the local grocery stores set up as a distribution site. "We're not going to let our families starve," the farmers shouted. The incident was cited for several months during debates in Congress and the press about President Herbert Hoover's relief policies. Some time later, cowboy sage and humorist Will Rogers got involved, traveling to England to visit the farmers in the shacks along the Arkansas river bottoms. He donated $5,000 to the relief effort.

After the Depression, Pat Jones relocated to Rose City to do what he did best—sell. His sales career had begun back at Lasater's Corners with buckets and buckets of peas that he would tote up the dusty roads from the farm. Most days, the peas were sold before he even made it into town. By the age of fifteen, he had money invested in Postal Savings, a government-backed program, and was making car loans to men twice his age.

Even as a teenager, though, his vision carried him far beyond the rice and soybean country, and Pat Jones moved west to the land of opportunity—Los Angeles—to work for an aircraft manufacturer during World War II. On October 13, 1942, Jerral Wayne Jones was the first child born to Pat and Arminta Jones in Los Angeles. Soon, however, Arkansas started calling Pat Jones home. More than two years later, just after the birth of a daughter, Jacque, he had the family packed and back on its way to Dixie.

He settled his family right in the thick of the action, at the corner of East Broadway and the England Highway in Rose City. Jerry Jones grew up in a tiny second-floor apartment that stood fifteen feet from the edge of East Broadway, just above Pat Jones's drive-in fruit stand. Next door was a feed store that, with the wind from the south, could bring a tear to a cattle drover's eye. The fruit stand was accessible to the tenant farmers to the east, and for black and white folks alike who lived in Rose City. It was this mixing of all kinds of people that, at first, made Pat Jones happy about his store.

Day and night, Rose City was a never-ending center of loco-motion. Young Jerry was soon entranced by the constant buzz of the busy four-lane highway and the rumble of the trains. The family of four lived in the small apartment for over seven years, nurturing the store downstairs by working day and night.

NOT LONG AFTER PAT JONES OPENED HIS FRUIT STAND, BUSINESS along East Broadway boomed. Just as the rail companies were thundering into economic prominence, so was little Pat Jones. After starting with fruits, he added a meat market and a bakery. Groceries became the heart of the business, and almost overnight, the place became Pat's Supermarket, a bustling centerpiece for the Rose City economy. The Jones family moved out of the second floor apartment and into a stone house next door.

It seemed that everyone knew Pat Jones, the hustler who had come out of the delta farmlands to bring a rhythm and a new spirit to Rose City. On Saturdays he would dress up like a rhine-stone cowboy, drink a few beers, and head down to the store. By the late 1950s, he was bringing the Light Crust Doughboys into the store, converting the place into a dance hall. Every Saturday was reserved for a country and western band, and the customers danced in the aisles between the fresh okra and the pork chops.

Pat even put together his own country-and-western act—Pat's Supermarketeers. "I couldn't play or sing, but had my own band," he recalls.

His next promotion was nearly unheard of in 1954: live on-site radio shows that mixed music with heavy endorsements for the store. "Brother Hal" Webber did his hillbilly act from the back of Pat's Supermarket and the parking lot was jammed before noon.

"They came from fifteen counties," Pat Jones remembers. "One of the damnedest things I've ever seen. They came won-dering what the heck was going on in that store. And once they got there, they always came back for more. We showed them that you could have a lot of fun."

Pat's Supermarket was young Jerry Jones's first exposure to hard work and showmanship—and he took to his father's example like a duck to water.

His first lesson in succeeding was to work harder than anyone else.

"I worked everything," Jerry said. "I learned to do everything in the store. I was up at the crack of dawn, or I'd be working until midnight on something. My dad was a driver. But he was also a teacher. He just somehow knew where he was going."

More than sixty years after the Great Depression, Jerry Jones still feels its influence.

"It was that mentality from that era that drove him [Pat Jones]. When I was a kid, it was all he could talk about—the Depression. It scared the hell out of the people who grew up then, especially the ones on the farms. My dad passed that fear along to me. That's why I always worked when I was a kid. They never put their foot on me to bring books home from school. I never took a book home from junior high or high school, and I always wondered about that. I asked them later why they didn't make me study. My dad knew I had a lot of buddies who were not that serious about working. He'd say, 'I'm going to teach you to work so that you won't mind working and it'll be a part of your personality when you grow up.' God dog, if I wasn't down there working at the store every day, I was found guilty of something. I knew that my butt was going to be in trouble."

By the age of seven, he was plugging watermelons in front of the store on East Broadway, carving an inch or so from the outer core to let customers peek inside. The red innards indicated the melon was ripe. From selling watermelons, the young huckster graduated to pumpkins, then to Christmas trees. He learned to move quickly at the scent of a sale. A deal-maker had been born in Rose City.

"I knew that Jerry had the instincts," Pat Jones remembered more than thirty years later. "Even when he was a kid, he could talk to people just like he was an adult. It was a gift. I guess he got it from me."

Arminta Jones agrees. "Jerry heard nothing but business talk during breakfast, lunch, and dinner. He understood that he wanted to make money and get ahead."

Leave it to the mother to know if a child will become a pitcher or a concert pianist, a saxophone player or a surgeon. It didn't take Arminta Jones long to know in which direction young Jerral Wayne was heading.

"He was born to be a showman," she says of her only son. "He wanted attention from the very beginning. That was very, very clear about Jerry right from the start. He went out and worked to get it. I happen to think he deserves all of the attention he's getting now. The boy worked hard to get there."

As more and more shoppers began shopping at Pat's Supermarket in Rose City in the early 1950s, Arminta would dress her nine-year-old son in a dark suit with a white shirt and a bow tie. With his hair neatly slicked back, the young salesman would stand at the front door, greeting customers with an angelic smile on his face. "Help you find somethin', ma'am?" the boy would ask brightly. Then the little showman would drop his right arm below his waist and bow.

"Those women just loved him," Arminta Jones remembers fondly. "One woman I knew would drive thirty miles just to see Jerry. Those women would buy, buy, buy just because Jerry was standing there at the door."

THE OTHER REAL DRAWING CARD ALONG EAST BROADWAY—BESIDES Pat's Supermarket—was the White Pig Inn, a tiny barbecue joint where the chopped beef sandwich still spills over the side of the bun and the beer is colder than the Buffalo River in the heart of an Arkansas winter. Pat Jones could be found on a barstool at the White Pig Inn day and night.

From the day the White Pig Inn was opened in 1940 it was a white man's domain. "Colored folks" couldn't even stop to use the phone. Owner Vance Seaton, a tough character, ruled the Inn with an iron fist and a large cleaver. He openly sold cases of beer to a roadhouse next door whose owner, a beefy woman named Bessie, chain-smoked Roy-Tan cigars. Bessie couldn't get a liquor license, so she leaned on the White Pig Inn.

Around noon the regular customers, including the local police, would arrive. They were armed with racing forms and the inside scoop from Oaklawn Park, a hot little thoroughbred racetrack in Hot Springs, just fifty miles to the south. Vance Seaton took cash bets over the counter, even from the cops, then turned the wagers over to his bookie by phone.

While enjoying barbecue, customers would listen to live races over the large RCA radio, pounding the bar with clenched fists and drinking the cold Falstaff. Vance paid the winners in cash at the end of the day. Even legendary gambler "Titanic" Thompson, who ran with the likes of Nick "The Greek" Dandolos and became a legend for his con games, made a few whistle stops at the White Pig Inn, enjoying the cards and playing the ponies.

More than an entrepreneur, Pat Jones became a kind of cult hero up and down the main drag, shaking hands and savoring the taste of cold beer and barbecue. He had a fun-loving side and played as hard as he worked. He often drank until last call at the taverns along East Broadway. Those late nights of revelry frequently spilled over into the coffee shop at the Broadway Motel, located along a row of used car lots in the 2400 block of East Broadway. After hours, the hotel coffee shop was the center of action in North Little Rock. Folks stood in line for the booths and for a seat along the long row of barstools. Pat was a regular visitor, regaling the customers with jokes and one-liners over breakfast.

Early one morning, according to a coffee shop regular, after failing to make it home the previous night, Pat Jones looked up from a booth in the coffee shop to find Arminta staring coldly into his bloodshot eyes. (He also happened to be in the company of two ladies.) By his mother's side was young Jerry, who stared blankly at the floor, wishing he were somewhere else.

"Jerry Jones," Arminta shouted. "I want you to take a good, long look at your father. Jerry, if you were wondering where your father was last night, he was right here, with these you-know-whos. Son, I don't want you to grow up to be this way."

Then she walked out with her son. Some said the slamming of the screen door could be heard all the way across the river in Little Rock.

Pat Jones had a soft spot in his heart, and he often reached out to the poor and unemployed in Rose City. Over the airwaves, he asked his customers to bring clothes for the needy into the store.

One afternoon, when Jerry was little, a small boy walked into Pat's Supermarket,

"My mother is dying and we have no money," he told Jerry's mother, Arminta. "She said that maybe you could help us."

Pat Jones loaded a station wagon full of groceries and drove the boy home.

On another occasion, a regular customer walked into the supermarket and began to explain his latest predicament to Pat Jones. His wife had passed away that morning and there was no money for a burial. Pat asked Arminta to open the cash register and count the money.

"Seventy dollars," Arminta said.

In truth, it was all the money the family had at the moment.

"Give it to him," said Pat. "He needs it more than we do."

"To the people who lived in some of those burned-out houses, there was nobody like my dad," Jerry Jones remembers. "He would give them anything. In a way, that's why he thought he might have a chance to make it to the Arkansas senate. Shit, *I* might have had a better chance of getting voted in. But just like anything else, he just got that wild hair up his ass. In our hearts, we knew he wouldn't win."

Jerry Jones often acknowledges his father as the most influential man in his life. Many factors have bonded the two Jones men over the years. At the Jones dinner table, Pat Jones would lecture Jerry almost every night on his business philosophies. He instilled a sturdy Puritan work ethic in his son. And, whether through genes or through constant instruction and example, he also instilled his taste for flamboyant risk-taking and a fearless compulsion to do things his own way. Like his father, Jerry Jones has those qualities in spades.

"There's just twenty years' age difference between them," Arminta Jones points out. "They are as much brothers as they are father and son. They both have the courage and the drive to accomplish what they set out to do. They're both workaholics. But they also happen to love their work. They make it their life. They are just alike—almost like twins."

UNTIL SEPTEMBER 4, 1957, LITTLE ROCK WAS A QUIET AND undistinguished southern city known primarily for its Bible Belt fervor and its reputation for cleanliness. Before the federal order for the desegregation of Central High School incited Governor Orval Eugene Faubus to call out the Arkansas National Guard, nothing had ever happened to put the sleepy town in the public eye.

The federal plan called for nine black students to enter Central High on the first day of school. Several other schools in rural parts of the state had already been quietly and successfully desegregated. But on Labor Day, just forty-eight hours before integration at Central High was to begin, Faubus delivered an ominous message to local television viewers, claiming to have information that several carloads of white supremacists were headed towards Little Rock. "Blood will run in the streets," he said, if the black students were allowed to enroll.

For several weeks, reporters from across America portrayed Little Rock as a volcano of hate. Grown men with slicked-back hair glowered from the covers of *Time* and *Newsweek* magazines as they tried to break down the barricades outside of Central High. Black students were spat on by white students as they tried to enter the school, which was closed until September 23rd, when a white mob numbering in the thousands encircled the three-block campus. The next day, President Dwight D. Eisenhower sent 1,100 members of the battle-tested 101st Airborne Infantry into Little Rock to enforce the federal desegregation order. The nine students were successfully escorted into the school, and desegregation officially began in Little Rock.

Still, the city had received a permanent black eye. Thanks to the angry persistence of Faubus, who had supported desegregation just two years earlier, the state of Arkansas was branded with an image of intolerance and bigotry that still endures. In the eyes of the nation, the Civil War had been restaged in the streets of Little Rock in 1957 over the issue of whether nine black children could enter all-white Central High.

The Arkansas *Gazette* would win a Pulitzer Prize for its coverage of the riots. Editor Harry Ashmore was also awarded a Pulitzer for his editorials supporting desegregation. Now retired in California, he recently reflected on his twelve years in Little Rock, and says that the city and state got a bad rap in 1957—when Faubus fanned the embers of hate.

"Anywhere you go now around the world, you hear that Little Rock had so much racial strife that the federal government had to send in the troops to shut it down," he says. "But that whole picture is wrong. It was simply a case of Faubus getting a phony populist movement going. In essence, this was like the governor of the state wanting to fight the Civil war all over again. This was a case of defiance that hadn't happened since Fort Sumter. It was a case where Eisenhower eventually had to show that he had more guns than Orval.

"I don't think there would have been any kind of protest that couldn't have been handled by the city police and backed up by state police. When Orval called out the Arkansas National Guard, that was the summons for the mob to come in."

THE OLD SMOKE-BELCHING CITY BUS STOPPED TO PICK UP YOUNG Jerry Jones every morning at 7:30 at the corner of Lynch and East Broadway. He made his way to the front of the bus, trying to distance himself from the tension in the rear.

In the heart of Dixie in the 1950s, Jim Crow laws were still king, and for a young man growing up the rules were clear and simple. Until Little Rock Central High was grudgingly and painfully desegregated, few challenges to the traditional order ever arose. Lines were clearly drawn when it came to public transportation, hotels and restaurants, which were marked either "colored" or "whites only." Blacks and whites were separate and unequal. Nowhere was this more evident than on the streets of Rose City.

"There could be a hundred black people crammed into the back of that bus behind that door," Jones said. "You could get some action on that bus. There would be some talking up. There would be a little interaction between the blacks and the whites. There would be some fighting. They would get a little irritated with us. Try to picture, the back third of the bus crammed full of black people, and about four white people in the front two-thirds of the bus. Back then, people didn't use the word 'colored.' They didn't use the word 'black.'"

No, they used other words—harsher, hostile, derogatory words—like "coon," "spade," "jigaboo," and "nigger."

"It is still hard for me to believe that black people had accepted for all time that that was the way to do things," Jones said. "It is just hard for me to fathom today that that was the type of situation we were in back then."

Three blocks from Pat's Supermarket, Dixie Street angled to the northeast into a tightly wound section of white clapboard houses that were known as the Dixie Addition. On the other side of the Cotton Belt tracks, the Dixie Addition was mostly government-subsidized housing where blacks could live side by side without intruding on the white domain of North Little Rock.

Just as the farmers from Scott and England came to Pat's Supermarket, so did the blacks from the Dixie Addition. It was a rare mixing of the races in Rose City. Out back, where the kids played, there were no Jim Crow laws.

"I was just very comfortable around black people," Jerry Jones remembers. "Oh, comfortable is not the word for it. I spent a lot of my life seeing the black moms and the dads and the kids and recognizing their lives, just as I would my own life. But, really, I had a total acceptance of black people, and black people as friends.

"My buddies back then were all black. We would hang around the back of the store in the trash area and on the gravel road right out back. The biggest time I ever got my ass whipped, me and one of my black buddies found a bunch of oranges and grapefruits that had been thrown out. We got on the blind side of Dad's store and we bombed the tails of the cars coming by on East Broadway with grapefruits and tomatoes. We were knocking the shit out of the cars coming down through there. Boy, it was a real scandal. We just hung in there too long and somebody got us by the nape of the neck."

When he left the gravel playground behind Pat's for the public school system, Jones discovered that the world was no longer colorblind. Stepping onto a public bus, or walking into a classroom, the rules were truly black and white. Lines were drawn. His "black buddies" disappeared.

"The thing that bothers me sitting here today is why I didn't ask more questions back then," Jones says. "Why did you see the black customers? Why were they always there when you went home? But I didn't see them in the schools! Why weren't they there on the junior high football team with me? Why didn't I see them on the other teams we played? Looking back on it, it makes me feel bad that I didn't at least ask, 'What is going on here?'"

EACH DAY, THE CITY BUS WITH THE PACKED REAR SECTION WOULD head west down East Broadway, dropping most of the students at street corners within walking distance of the all-black schools. The other four or five passengers rode to the end of the line at Fourth Street Junior High, an airy four-story red brick building with tall rows of brightly painted windows.

Fourth Street was a citywide melting pot for white kids. From the blue-collar neighborhoods of Baring Cross and Rose City came the ones in blue jeans and work shirts. Their parents worked mostly for the rail companies. From Lakewood came the upper-middle class, which, in those days, meant they had a few dollars in their pockets. During the 1950s, the average family income in Arkansas just happened to be the lowest in America. At Fourth Street Junior High, the poor kids tried to keep up with the not-so-poor kids.

"The Rose City kids had to fight to keep what they had," remembers junior high school football coach Gene Blenden. "They didn't have a whole lot. But what they had, they were proud of. They didn't come to school in brand-new clothes. They came to school in blue jeans, but gosh, they were clean. They just about all wore blue work shirts."

The five-block walk from the school to the football practice field led the squad past the Silver Eagle Lounge, where the late afternoon customers listened to country-and-western music on the jukebox as they pulled heavily from cans of Pabst Blue Ribbon. From the back porch, they waved at the Fourth Street Bulldogs, who raised a loud racket as their steel-tipped cleats scraped the asphalt street.

Set in a hollow next to the Missouri-Pacific tracks, the practice field appeared, on the surface, to be like any other, with white chalk lines and green grass that would fade to brown in late October. A goal post stood at one end, with a couple of blocking dummies and a blocking sled at the other.

Hidden below the surface of the field, though, were black lumps of coal that had been accumulating for decades. As the trains rumbled through town, black chunks of coal that had been burning red-hot in the fire boxes would be discharged through the large stacks of the steam engines. Nearing the roundhouse, an engineer would often blow open the stacks, sending black soot flying in all directions.

As the Bulldogs collided and grunted on the practice field below, the tracks thundered with 7000 series steam engines that pulled more than one hundred cars. Ten minutes into a practice, even before the Bulldogs had finished a round of side-straddle hops, their white nylon pants would be coal-black. With every stride, their shoes raised coal soot that would eventually mushroom into a low-hanging cloud.

Practices rarely ended before dark, meaning that the buses along East Broadway were long gone by the time Jones had showered the black soot off his sweaty frame. Sitting on a rock wall outside the Elks Club on Broadway, the young quarterback waited for a car to stop at the red light.

"I would just literally run out there in the street and ask for a ride," he says. "I would tell them I was headed for 3902 East Broadway and it was rare that anybody turned me down."

By the eighth grade, Jerry Jones's weight was all the way up to 120 pounds. He was a hard rail of a kid, playing quarterback in the single-wing formation, and a safety on defense. Blenden knew him as a smart and gritty player who had few reservations about ramming opponents with the crown of his helmet or hurling his body into the biggest player on the field. He played with reckless intensity.

"Mostly, what I remember about Jerry when he was a kid were those eyes," Blenden says. "Jerry still has those eyes that look into you and then down through you. Sometimes it seems that he's looking right into your soul."

Blenden, however, sensed that Jones had lost his courage when he ran into a 215-pound fullback named Nicky Avance in a game against Forest Heights. Just as he had done all season, the fullback bowled over the Bulldogs. Smaller kids, with an average weight of eighty pounds, were overmatched against the big fullback. Blenden sensed that even his tough little safety was being intimidated.

"Jerry came in to tackle big Nicky and just kind of slid down him," Blenden remembers. "He really didn't put all he had into it. He looked like he was a little timid. So I pulled Jerry out of the game. I got him on the sideline and said, 'Jerry, you will never play for me again.' That almost killed him. He yelled back at me, 'What! Why, coach?' And he said it with those intense eyes. He said, 'Coach, put me back in there and I swear you will never have to worry about me again.' "

The psych job worked.

"I put Jerry back into that game and he made tackles all over the field," Blenden says. "Every time that Nicky Avance moved, Jerry Jones was there. He was there and hitting him. And he was putting him down. It was just a matter of heart over matter. As a 120-pound human being, Jerry Jones found that day that he could do things that he didn't know he could do."

Jones was never pulled from another game. In fact, he talked both the coach and his father into letting him play his ninth-grade season with a hairline fracture of his upper right arm, an injury that limited his passing.

For a skinny 120-pound kid who played on grit, eating became an obsession. Jones would start the evening with a plate of chicken-fried steak, mashed potatoes with gravy, fried okra, navy beans, and cobbler. He'd wait fifteen minutes and order another round of carbohydrates. Dessert was wheat germ stirred in a glass of milk. Wheat germ is the hardened circle at the bottom of a grain of wheat that's filled with vitamins and protein and overloaded with calories. As for taste, it's comparable to eating sawdust.

"You're going to make yourself sick eating that God-durn stuff," Pat Jones would say. "I know those football coaches want you to get bigger. But god-durn, Jerry, you're going to get sloppy fat. I'll tell you what's going to happen. They're going to end up putting your butt in the offensive line."

Hung from an huge air-conditioning tower next to the store was a tread-worn tire that became the next target of obsession for Jones. For hours, the young quarterback practiced his throws, aiming for the center of the tire, hoping to hear the ball smack the wooden casing after sailing through the center of the ring. The hard work paid off. With Jones as the ninth grade starting quarterback, the Bulldogs went undefeated and won what was considered a state championship.

By 1956, and the start of high-school two-a-day workouts, Jones's weight had crept up to 150 pounds. The wheat germ and the carbohydrates were working their magic. Although weight-lifting was neither popular or part of the program at North Little Rock High in those days, Jerry Jones and his best friend Jerry Sisk pumped iron for hours.

At the same time, a more aggressive, even mean streak started to show. Out in the barren lot next to Pat's Supermarket, the two Jerrys were transformed into afternoon warriors.

"We would get out there and just knock the shit out of each other without any pads on," Jones says. "I'd get down in my stance and fire off and pop into him. Then he'd fire off and pop into me. We'd do it all afternoon. That's what football is really about, just knocking the shit out of each other."

The high school team's two-a-day workouts were held just off the highway on a parched practice field tracked with crusty mud ruts. Between sessions, most players dragged their tired bodies and cramped legs home, where they'd drink tall glasses of iced tea and lie beneath window air conditioners that rattled and hummed, straining against the August furnace.

Jerry, however, stocked and swept the store until it was time for the afternoon workout. Under a blazing afternoon sun that often drove the thermometer over the 100-degree mark, the bony kid from Rose City never showed fatigue, even when coaches refused water to the dehydrated players. To avoid "cotton mouth," he stuck lemons in the top of his Riddell helmet, sucking the tart moisture during breaks. He was a madman at "bull in the ring," a drill that subjects one player to a series of attacks from twenty others arranged in a ring around him. He fended them off with flying elbows called forearm shivers.

It wasn't really speed or size that triggered the change in Jones's position from quarterback to fullback in eleventh grade, and his ascent into the starting lineup, and finally to team captain. It wasn't athletic ability that led University of Arkansas chief recruiter Wilson Matthews to come down from Fayetteville to North Little Rock to check out "the Jones kid."

"Jerry didn't have a lot of speed," remembers North Little Rock head coach Jimmy Albright. "In fact, he didn't have a whole lot of anything as an athlete. But when he started something, he didn't quit. Even at that early age, we were starting to see that work ethic that would carry him to his great success. It was already starting to show. This kid just worked his ass off night and day."

Another advantage that a slow, white fullback had was that North Little Rock High had gone on blithely segregated. The federal desegregation order only included Little Rock Central. Jones was part of the last generation that didn't have to compete with black athletes. Through his final season in 1959, although he played games throughout the state, Jones never encountered a black player.

On defense, Jones was the starting "monster man," a cross between a linebacker and a safety. The monster lined up wherever he figured the action was headed, and was free to hurl his body at anything that moved. Jones was a true Godzilla.

"He would run through a brick wall," says Jim Bohanon, who doubled as assistant coach and trainer. "He would run through it again if you didn't stop him. He would run over you and laugh at you. He was the fiercest competitor we had—no, he was the fiercest competitor we *ever* had."

It was traditional for North Little Rock players to touch the Wildcat head mounted over the dressing room door as they left for the field. Jones and Sisk took the tradition a step further during pre-game warm-ups. They would carry the Wildcat head to mid-field, where they would do a kind of Indian rain dance around it. Their antics whipped the home crowd into a frenzy.

Not since 1951 had the Wildcats beaten Little Rock Central High. But in Jones' senior year (1959), he caught a touchdown pass late in the game as the Wildcats beat the perennial state champions. Only a tie with El Dorado High kept the Wildcats from a state championship.

There was also a painfully low point to the season, when North Little Rock lost to Conway, a school from a lower division. Jones felt so bad about the loss that he rounded up the entire team and brought them to the First Baptist Church at Sixteenth and Maple streets—where Albright attended services every Sunday.

"I was coming out of Sunday school, heading for church, and here comes Jerry Jones and Jerry Sisk leading the entire team," Albright says. "They had come to apologize for losing the game. Well, I didn't feel so bad about it. I just stood them all up and introduced them during church."

To this day, Jerry Jones is still at a loss to explain how he fell in love with football. The game wasn't in the family's blood—Pat and Arminta had never been to a game until Jerry came along. He claims that his first love was baseball.

"I liked baseball a lot better. Going out and playing baseball, on some of those lush fields around Little Rock, it just made you feel like you were at Yankee Stadium. I could have played baseball forever."

"Football was another story," he says. "It hurt to play football and, believe me, I eventually got tired of the pain. But I felt like I had to play football. There was just something inside me that told me that I had to play football. I guess it might have been one of those macho things that boys are supposed to do."

Until the late fifties, few folks around Little Rock really gave a hoot about football. High school football must have seemed like small potatoes—only seven schools played in division 4A, the largest classification, and there were no post-season playoffs. And until coach Frank Broyles came along in the mid-fifties, the Arkansas Razorbacks were a forgotten team up in the mountains.

But when Broyles and his chief recruiter, Wilson Matthews, started to round up a new level of talent, a certain North Little Rock fullback who doubled as the monster man on defense caught their eyes. And after leaving Dogtown for Fayetteville, nothing about football would ever seem small-time to Jerry Jones again.

CHAPTER 3

Jonesie

A COLD, MISTY RAIN FELL ON DALLAS AS THE ARKANSAS RAZORBACKS began dressing in the damp locker room beneath the south end zone of the Cotton Bowl. For weeks, the starting right guard had avoided the locker room scales. It was the first day of 1965 and this would be the final game of his career. After having his ankles taped, he walked barefoot across the cold concrete floor and stepped onto the steel scales. One hundred and eighty-two pounds. The coaches would shudder, he thought. He had weighed more in high school.

Jerry Jones—or Jonesie, as he was called by his teammates—sat down bare-assed on the wooden bench in front of his locker and pondered this last assignment in football. He would be mixing it up with a Nebraska defensive line that averaged more than 230 pounds per man. It was the biggest front five in the country.

The Razorbacks had ripped through the final five weeks of the regular season, beating opponents by the combined score of

116-0. They were ranked second in the country. But today they would play Nebraska, and the game would be on national television.

★ ★ ★

JONES, LIKE MOST OF HIS TEAMMATES, WAS LUCKY TO BE A COLLEGE athlete in the early 1960s. Big-time college football in the South was still a closed society. Jon Richardson was five years away from becoming the first black player to suit up for Arkansas. At the stadiums in Little Rock and Fayetteville, where Arkansas's home games were played, fans still berated opposing black players. "Give the ball to Leeee Roy," they would yell. Southern college football was still all white, and that gave some of the smaller white boys an opportunity they wouldn't have just a few years down the road.

Barry Switzer, an assistant coach for the 1964 Razorbacks and co-captain of the '59 team that beat Georgia Tech in the Gator Bowl, remembers, "Jerry was typical of the players of that age. Most of us made the team with hustle and try-hard. All of us white boys weren't exactly separated by our athletic skills. But we were smart enough to bust our butts. That's how we made the football team. But you wouldn't exactly call us a bunch of big-time athletes."

In large part, due to the recruitment of quality black players, teams in later years would become bigger and faster and far more athletic. Only a handful of Razorbacks from the '64 team would play professional football, and most of those careers were short-lived. Freddie Marshall, the starting quarterback, got a tryout in the Canadian Football League. He was sent home almost as quickly as an overnight letter. Defensive end Lloyd Phillips would win the Outland Trophy, but his career with the Chicago Bears ended after three seasons. Wingback Jim Lindsey had the longest pro tenure—seven years with the Minnesota Vikings.

The mid-sixties also marked the end of one-platoon football, where players would participate on both offense and defense (only the quarterback and center didn't play defense). In the late fifties, LSU had found some loopholes in the rules and figured out a way to expand their substitutions. The rules were changed after the 1961 season to allow unlimited substitution. But when Jerry Jones arrived in Fayetteville in 1960, nine men on the field still played both ways.

★ ★ ★

WHEN JERRY JONES FIRST SHOWED UP AT THE UNIVERSITY OF Arkansas, there were only two stoplights in town. The local airport could handle only light aircraft. Nestled in the Ozark Mountains in the northwest corner of the state, Fayetteville was a quiet little town of 10,000 that exploded into a sea of red and white with the start of the football season every September. When the 42,000 frenzied fans at Razorback Stadium roared their school cheer of "woo-pig-sooie," it sounded like a bizarre fight song from another planet. Opposing teams found it nearly impossible to win there.

Coach Frank Broyles had essentially created Arkansas football—turning a sleepy backwater program into a national powerhouse. After years of campaigning for the Arkansas job, he had finally received an offer in 1958—even though he had been a college football head coach for only one year, at Missouri in 1957. Contacted by Arkansas athletic director John Barnhill, Broyles accepted the job in a matter of seconds over the telephone. According to the *St. Louis Post Dispatch*, Broyles "fled in the night" across the state line into Arkansas.

Playing quarterback in the 1946 Orange Bowl for Georgia Tech, Broyles had passed for 279 yards, a record that lasted for twenty-five years. He began to develop his coaching philosophy and style while serving as an assistant coach under Georgia Tech's Bobby Dodd from 1951 through 1956. Dodd was a pioneering coach who stressed the importance of the kicking game.

At Arkansas, where the football program had been up and down for the past decade, Broyles searched for an edge. His early teams were small, quick, and technically sound. Broyles liked to recruit small but scrappy players who would out-hustle their larger opponents. Using a blueprint that would be laughed at today, he converted running backs into linemen. His lines usually averaged less than 200 pounds a man. Instead of overpowering the opposition, his undersized Hogs would win with finesse, versatility, and superior conditioning. They also won with numbers—there were about 200 players in the football program when Jerry Jones arrived.

Like many in his field, Broyles was quick to copy the successful formulas of others. But after just a few seasons at Arkansas, other coaches were copying his. Before long, Dan Jenkins wrote, "God love Frank Broyles, but don't cash his personal check. Frame it."

It was a game early in the 1960 season that showed that the Hogs were for real—a 24-23 win over Texas. Mickey Cissell's 29-yard field goal had wobbled like a dying bird just inches over the crossbar with twenty seconds left. It was the biggest win in the history of Arkansas football.

Hours after the game, as the team plane touched down at the Fort Smith Airport, Razorback fans broke through the barricades. They were running like wild boars toward the chartered flight that carried the Arkansas team back from Austin.

Noting that the propellers were still rotating, Broyles shouted for the pilot to shut down the engines. "Some of our students were so excited that they were going to run right up under the plane," Broyles remembers. "It was like a mob coming at us. For a second or two there, it was pretty darn scary. Some of those people were about to get chopped up."

Broyles was on his way to becoming a cult hero. After the 1960 season, thanks to the running and receiving of a baby-faced Lance Alworth, who was also the national leader in punt returns, the Razorbacks played in the Cotton Bowl for only the second time since 1947. Though they lost to Duke 7-6 on a missed extra point, they had proved that Broyles and the Arkansas program were among the best in the country.

The party was on in the Arkansas hills. With the Razorbacks coming of age, Arkansans finally had something to shout about. No longer were they the shoeless hillbilly folks from the backwoods. They had a reason to walk tall. They had a winner.

In a cover story for *Sports Illustrated*, Dan Jenkins wrote, "There is a special kind of hysteria in Arkansas now. It is the kind that comes with a winning college football team. It dabs small, rosy blotches of pride on the cheeks of everyone. And it spreads like measles. It happened in Oklahoma with Bud Wilkinson, in Iowa with Forest Evashevski, in Mississippi with Johnny Vaught, in Texas with Darrell Royal and in Alabama with Bear Bryant."

Texas defensive coordinator Mike Campbell once said that playing a game in Fayetteville was like "parachuting into Russia." Before a game against Texas, pastor Andy Hall posted a sign meant for the Longhorns' coach outside his First Baptist Church: DARRELL ROYAL—DO NOT CAST YOUR STEERS BEFORE SWINE. Years later Hall posted another message: FOOTBALL IS ONLY A GAME, GOD IS ETERNAL. NEVERTHELESS, BEAT TEXAS.

SPORTING A FLATTOP AND SOME NEW MUSCLE, JONES FELT LIKE AN insignificant part of Coach Broyles's huge machine. There were days when he felt lost in the system. At six feet and 190 pounds, he was larger than most of the backs. But Broyles was determined to convert him into a guard.

First, though, he had to survive the grueling boot camp tests. Jones entered with a class of sixty freshman players. Only eleven would be around by his senior year.

The tests began with the Gore Drill. With face masks added to the helmets in the 1950s, many coaches were teaching the technique of spearing with the headgear. In the Gore Drill, the defensive players were encouraged to ram their helmets into the ball carrier, even as he lay on the ground. Playing the role of the ball carrier one afternoon, Jones was speared in the thigh. A deep bruise would send him to the sideline for several weeks of his freshman season.

"It was an absolutely vicious drill," says Jones. "That drill ended more Arkansas college football careers than any other drill there was. It really did separate the people who wanted to play. I saw better players leave than I saw stay."

Says Switzer, who was Jones's freshman coach, "It was an absolutely senseless drill. Even Frank finally admitted that and he outlawed it himself. That drill never really had a place on the practice field, or on a football team. Coaches wouldn't even think of doing it today."

To the Razorback players, Broyles was a taskmaster. He drilled his teams in the same manner that Darrell Royal whipped his Longhorns into shape down in Austin. Perhaps the only difference between Arkansas and Texas was that Royal's brutal tactics were documented—by ex-Longhorn Gary Shaw in a book entitled *Meat on the Hoof.*

"Our philosophy was to find out who could push themselves," Broyles says. "We had to push and push our players hard because we wanted to dominate in the fourth quarter. We wanted to push them when they couldn't think as well. I had to train them to think as well when they were tired. If you started out slow during practice then your players were not tired during practice. We did it in reverse. We worked them hard from the moment they walked onto the practice field. It was a radical departure from what everyone else was doing. Except Darrell."

Broyles would tell his players, "Do not come to practice in a good mood. Football is not supposed to be played in a good mood."

"When bowl-time practice rolled around, it was like a live war," says Jones. "When I was a freshman or a redshirt sophomore, they knew I wasn't going to play in the bowl. So they just put guys like me through a living hell. For seven, eight, or nine days in a row, you felt like your life was on the line. They didn't mind if you got hurt. They knew that they could get you well before spring practice rolled around."

Almost daily during that first year, Jones fought the temptation to clean out his locker. Because there were virtually no scholarship limits, Broyles kept close to two hundred players around. Many scholarships in the early 1960s were for only one year. Players were here today and gone tomorrow. Since he was scheduled to be redshirted as a sophomore, Jones knew that three years might pass before he got into a game. So he finally stopped checking the depth charts and tried to stop worrying about where he stood. Still, in the back of his mind, he knew he was running seventh or eighth string in the offensive line.

"To complicate the whole thing, I got very homesick," he admits. "When I was in high school, I never even wanted to spend the night over at somebody's house. I wanted them to come over to my house. I moaned a little bit about it with my mother and my father on the telephone. Given the least bit of encouragement, I was going to quit. But they were going to make sure that I didn't do that. They knew psychologically they had to straighten me up."

ANYONE WHO HAS ENCOUNTERED JONES IN THE BUSINESS WORLD during the last three decades would be shocked to learn he once had a gullible side. His first two years in Fayetteville marked the end of that naiveté, but his coaches and teammates had fun with him while they could.

During his freshman year, Jones became friends with an upper-class defensive end named Jim Grizzle. One afternoon a homesick Jones was sitting around Wilson Sharpe House, an athletic dorm high on a hill above Razorback Stadium, bemoaning his seventh-string status, when Grizzle invited him down to his room.

"Jim looked at me and said, 'Jerry, I know that you're homesick,'" Jones remembers. "He took me down to his room and there was a box as big as the box that a man's suit came in back then. It was full of cookies—chocolate chip and oatmeal. He said, 'Now, Jerry, don't mention these cookies to anyone. Before long, everybody in this dorm will be down here if you do.'"

They met for several straight days in Grizzle's room until the cookie supply began to dwindle. One afternoon, Jones found a note in the bottom of the box. It read: "Dear Jerry: Your sister Jacque and I miss you very much. Hope you enjoy the cookies. We can't wait to see you over Christmas. Love, Mom."

Remembering that day, Jones throws back his head and laughs. "Here I was going down to Jim Grizzle's room to eat my own cookies!"

Jones made a number of lasting friendships as a Razorback. Billy Moore, a cocky quarterback from Little Rock Central, was the most celebrated athlete ever recruited from the state and one of the best roll-out quarterbacks of his time. Like Jones, Moore walked around smiling as if he had just polished off a canary.

One afternoon during Jones's freshman year, he heard a knock on his dormitory door. Moore, who was two years older, was breathing heavily as if he had just run up several flights of stairs. He had a female companion with him. Females were off-limits in the athletic dorm, a rule strictly enforced by Broyles. Moore had little time to spare. He pushed Jones under his own bed and proceeded to have sex with the coed.

"That was one of the damnedest things that ever happened to me in my life," Jones says with a smile. "Billy Moore became a friend of mine for the rest of my life. He was my hero."

Jones and Moore remain close friends today. Moore, now working for an investment company in Little Rock, was among the two planeloads of friends that Jones flew to Atlanta for Super Bowl XXVII.

More than thirty years later, Moore says, "Jerry Jones is one of the best guys you will ever meet in your life. And there is something else about him. He will party with you. I found that out right away."

Amid the rigors of Arkansas football, the players still found time to have fun. Late one night, Switzer rushed into the dorm and announced that several grass fires were burning out of control in nearby Springdale. The fires were threatening the chicken houses belonging to Don Tyson, who was just beginning to build his poultry empire.

Recalls Switzer, "I walked in and said, 'Did ya'll hear about the grass fires up in Springdale? They're burning down all of the chicken farms. Tyson is paying $5 an hour for help.' Those guys bailed out of that Wilson Sharpe House like they were headed for a panty raid."

Five carloads of Arkansas players headed off into the hills. They drove on virtually every dirt road and stopped at practically every farmhouse between Fayetteville and the Missouri state line. They were unable to locate even a wisp of smoke.

Around 2:30 that morning, one player turned to another said, "Have you thought about what day it is?"

"Yeah," the player responded. "It's April the first."

The cars turned around and headed south to Fayetteville. Back at the dorm, they began pounding on Switzer's door. All they found was a picture of Smokey the Bear with a caption that read "Smokey Bear Lives Here." Switzer, however, was sound asleep in a room on another floor. The dormitory prankster had struck again.

A few nights later, Jones borrowed the keys to a teammate's car for a date. He walked outside and got into the car. As he depressed the clutch and shifted into neutral, the turquoise-blue Ford Fairlane began rolling down the steep hill behind the Wilson Sharpe House. When he couldn't work the key into the ignition, Jones stepped out to take a look at the car. He realized it was the wrong car, but he'd forgotten to set the emergency brake. The car began gaining momentum down the hill, and crashed nose-first into a tree about fifty feet away. If not for that tree, it might have rolled all the way to Razorback Stadium.

It wasn't until almost twenty-five years later that Jones finally broke the news to Switzer, the owner of the turquoise-blue Ford Fairlane. "Actually, one of our college buddies finally prodded Jerry until he told me the truth," says Switzer. "We laughed all night about that old car."

Jones and Switzer clicked as friends almost from the day they met. Switzer was a hard-edged country boy from south Arkansas who had played linebacker and center for Broyles in the late fifties. Although he was a prankster and a free spirit, he was a student of the game and had decided to make it his life. Both he and Jones had a taste for night life, cold beer, and Arkansas coeds. But they were also bonded by their passion for football. Young boys growing up in Arkansas dream about being Razorbacks from the time they hear "woo-pig-sooie" for the first time.

Switzer on Jones: "I knew that he was different from the first day that I met him. He just jumped out at me. Jerry has always been a total extrovert. A salesman. A promoter. He always had that tremendous energy level. Jerry had a drive and an authority even then that made him so well-liked."

Jones's romantic life was also in high gear. On his first weekend in Fayetteville, Jones had met Eugenia "Gene" Chambers. It was love at first sight. She had won the statewide Poultry Princess title. Her beauty-pageant good looks hit Jones like a blitzing linebacker. They went to a nearby county fair on their first date and were virtually inseparable from then on.

"We went out there with two or three other couples," Jones says. "It seemed like everybody else was winning those little teddy bears for their girlfriends except me. Finally, I went off down the midway by myself and came back with a teddy bear. I told her, 'Look what I won for you.' I didn't tell her that I had just walked down the midway and bought the damn teddy bear for her. It was the only way I was going to get one."

Gene Chambers was a petite, brown-haired banker's daughter from the tiny Arkansas town of Danville. She smiled a lot. But she rarely spoke around Jerry. She quickly learned that a conversation with Jerry, who was always full of energy, was usually a one-way affair.

To the despair of her father, John Ed Chambers, Gene soon decided to date no one else but Jerry, the boy from the fruit stand. Chambers placed a call to Little Rock banking executive Ed Penick to find out about the young man's background. Penick told him, "Jerry is a very smart boy. Look at it this way, John Ed. He's smart enough to want to marry the banker's daughter, isn't he?"

By the end of their sophomore year they were married. Both were twenty years old. "It wasn't a shotgun wedding, but the closest thing to it," said Jones. He moved out of the Wilson Sharpe House and into a spacious off-campus apartment with his new bride.

Jones played sporadically on the freshman team in 1960. The next year, he was redshirted, leaving him in limbo for the entire 1961 season. The Hogs went 8–2, then lost to Alabama 10–3 in the Sugar Bowl. During the 1962 season, he was listed far down the depth chart. The Razorbacks lost only one game, then were defeated again in the Sugar Bowl, this time by Mississippi 17–13.

Jones finally started to see some action during the 1963 season. He was moved briefly to the offensive backfield where he started the first two games of the season. But after a 7–6 loss to Missouri, he was moved back to the offensive line where, ironically, he was listed behind a stocky lineman named Jimmy Johnson on the depth chart at left guard. Heartbroken, Jones again considered quitting the team until assistant coach Wilson Matthews informed him that Broyles had plans for him for the following season. The Razorbacks finished 5–5 and watched the bowl games at home.

The seniors on the 1964 team swore it wouldn't happen again. Johnson was moved to defense for the season, paving the way for Jones to move into the starting lineup as a senior.

Everything came together for the Razorbacks during the 1964 season. Because his team lacked great athleticism, Broyles preached playing mistake-free games. The defense didn't allow a single point in the second half of the season. Meanwhile, the offense plugged along behind its "little-bitty" line, with Marshall occasionally turning the big play, usually a deep sideline toss to receiver Bobby Crockett.

"What stood out at the time is that they were superbly conditioned and extremely quick and very smart," says sportswriter Orville Henry, who began covering the team in 1945 and still writes about the Razorbacks for the *Arkansas Democrat-Gazette*. "They were like Alabama at the time. They had just been so well coached. And so many from that team would go on to coach." Among the coaches and players, seven would become Division I head coaches. Johnson, of course, would win two Super Bowls with the Cowboys.

Offensive line coach Dixie White had taught his players to scramble block—going after the defender's knees. It was considered an outdated concept, but it worked for the smaller Hogs. It was especially effective since Razorback players did little or no weight training. "From the waist up, we looked like we had been on a death march," Lindsey says. "But Coach Broyles ran our butts off during practice. So our legs and hips were always well developed."

Jones ran constantly. During the summer, he ran the dirt roads around Springfield, Missouri, where his parents had moved from Rose City and where he spent his summers with teammates Jerry Lamb and Jim Grizzle. A month before the start of his senior season, he found a bull grazing in a field. He wrapped a rope around the bull's neck and decided to go for a ride. The bull proceeded to buck him several feet into the air. When Jones's leg got entangled in the rope, the bull took Jones for a long ride over hill and dale, raking his body over the dry, rugged terrain. When it finally stopped, Jones was battered, bruised, and bloody. But it added another layer of toughness to his already hard outer shell.

The season featured an seemingly endless series of pep talks. The senior co-captains met every Thursday to discuss locker-room psychology. Broyles had lit the fire. And now he had an orator on the team who could deliver the message.

"Jonesie had this unique way of verbalizing in a very few sentences his very innermost feelings and convictions," remembers Lindsey. "He might not have been the best guard on the team. But he won the starting job with blood, sweat, and tears. In the process of energizing himself, he was able to energize everyone around him. I played four years of college football and seven more in the pros. But I was never around a more inspirational leader. Even Jimmy Johnson was a laughing and joking kind of guy. He couldn't compare to Jonesie."

Studying Jones's play on film clearly reveals his strength and speed. He was always the first Arkansas lineman off the ball. Defensive linemen were often still in their stance when Jones delivered the first blow. His hands were extremely quick.

By the end of the 1964 season, with his weight plummeting from 215 to 182 pounds, Jones might have been the fastest player on the team. It was he who ran down an opposing linebacker during the Baylor game, not one of the receivers or running backs.

Although pro scouts never gave Jones a passing thought, he was a co-captain on the 1964 team. But so were all of the ten seniors, including Jimmy Johnson, his road roommate.

Of Jones's contributions, Henry says, "He was the least important man on the team from my standpoint. He was just a little-bitty guard. But it wasn't unusual in those days that the little-bitty boys could play. It really wasn't until around the mid-1960s that the fat boys started coming into the line."

WITH HIS SLEEVES ROLLED UP AND ARMS PUMPING, BROYLES WAS A KIND of Elmer Gantry around the locker room, sermonizing about the necessity of "character." Speaking with a deep Georgia drawl, he pronounced the word "carektuh." He often said, "There will come a time in a game when you will have to show your carektuh. Carektuh is the single most important aspect of football. Just remember. On game day, you will have to reach down and show your carektuh."

The Razorbacks opened the season with a 14-10 win against a Walt Garrison-led Oklahoma State team, then beat Tulsa and Texas Christian. Playing Baylor in Little Rock, the Razorbacks offense opened the game with a 70-yard drive that fizzled with a missed field goal. On the sideline, Broyles gathered the offensive team for one more speech on "carektuh."

On the next offensive possession, the Razorbacks ripped through the Bear defense, moving the ball eighty yards to the 1-yard line. But a swing pass was intercepted at the goal line by Baylor linebacker Bobby Maples, who took off down the field. Eighty yards later, Jones ran him down from behind. Maples fumbled and the ball rolled to the 4-yard line, where it was recovered by Arkansas offensive tackle Glen Ray Hines. In the Arkansas offensive huddle, players were gasping for air. Looking around the huddle, Jones drew a long breath and said, with as straight a face as he could muster, "Men, if we can just take it in from here, we've got carektuh."

Remembers Lindsey, "We laughed so hard that we could barely get our breath back. We all had just run eighty yards as fast as we could and now we were laughing so hard we couldn't run the next play." They won 17–6.

Given his size and overall strength, Jones was not supposed to be the starting right guard that year. And the Razorbacks were not supposed to fly into Austin midway through the season with a respectable chance of beating the Texas Longhorns, the previous year's undefeated national champions and the top-ranked team in the country.

But somehow both happened. Arkansas parlayed an 81-yard punt return by Ken Hatfield and a 34-yard touchdown pass from Marshall to Crockett into a 14–7 lead. But the Longhorns rallied, just as they had in 1962 when they scored the winning touchdown against Arkansas with twenty seconds to play. This time, Ernie Koy made it 14–13 on a 1-yard run with under a minute to play. Royal didn't even think about kicking the extra point and going for the tie. Texas was number one. They would go for the two-point conversion and play to win, as a number-one team should.

In a situation reminiscent of 1962, Royal waited until the last second to put halfback Hix Green into the game. Green was better suited to be a receiver than a ball carrier. So Arkansas's hastily-arranged defense was designed to pressure quarterback Marv Kristynik. It worked. With defensive end Jim Finch in his face, Kristynik threw the ball into the ground.

"If it hadn't worked, I would have jumped off the top of their stadium," Broyles said more than thirty years later. "It was just that big to me. They had fooled us with their alignment in 1962. They didn't fool us in 1964."

Arkansas climbed in the polls from eighth to fourth after the victory over Texas. And they kept on winning—propelled not so much by their talent as by their collective will. Or was it "carektuh"? They finished the season with wins against Wichita State, Texas A&M, Rice, Southern Methodist, and Texas Tech (in which the defense didn't allow a single point).

What happened to the Razorbacks in 1964 seems as improbable as a Rockefeller getting elected governor of Arkansas. Of course, that happened, too, when Winthrop Rockefeller defeated the Democratic incumbent Orval E. Faubus in 1966.

"All year long it was the culmination of fantasy and dream becoming reality," Lindsey says. "No one thought we could do it other than the coaches and us. And sometimes, even we didn't think it could happen. It started happening and it just kept happening. We just felt that destiny was ours. It was not any different than when North Carolina State won the NCAA championship under Jim Valvano (in 1983). It was a form of destiny that you can't stop."

EVEN ON THIS VERY SPECIAL TEAM, JONES STOOD OUT AS UNIQUE. HE was spending less and less time around Fayetteville. A fifth-year senior, he already had graduated and was finishing up his master's degree in business by taking six hours's worth of classes. At night after practice, he traveled through Arkansas and Missouri, recruiting salesmen for Modern Security Life and speaking at seminars. Stephen Jones had been born to Jerry and Gene the previous June.

"I'd be out on the road at night, speaking at some banquet or something, and I'd run into Jerry," Broyles remembers. "I'd say, 'Jerry, what are you doing out there?' Then I'd realize that Jerry was virtually out of school, that he had a wife and a child and that he was just out there making money. Shoot, he was wearing new clothes, driving a new Cadillac Eldorado and carrying around a briefcase. None of my other players were doing that."

On Halloween night in 1964, Arkansas players were loading onto the bus outside of the locker room in College Station, Texas. Arkansas had just beaten Texas A&M 17–0, running their record to 7–0. As Broyles stepped onto the bus, one of the Aggie locker room attendants ran up to the coach, waving a large diamond ring.

Broyles remembers the youngster yelling, "Coach, coach, you forgot your ring." Laughing, Broyles told him, "This isn't my ring. This ring must belong to Jerry Jones." Indeed, it did.

Remembers Henry, "It was obvious right from the start that this guy was going to be very successful. He was already wheeling and dealing when most of those guys were worrying about going to class."

Now, with his master's degree under his belt, the Cotton Bowl was the final stop on this stage of Jones's journey. On a cold and damp morning in Dallas, Jones was about to bask in the cries of "woo-pig-sooie" for one last time. The first thing he noticed walking down the long end zone tunnel was the sea of flaming red inside the Cotton Bowl. He figured the entire state of Arkansas had made the trip to Dallas. Then he remembered that Nebraska wore red, too.

The game was a defensive struggle most of the way. In the fourth quarter, with Nebraska leading 7-3, the physical grind began taking its toll on the smaller Hogs. Cornhusker halfback Harry Wilson ran 45 yards to the Arkansas 35. Nebraska seemed poised to blow the Razorbacks through the back of the stadium. Then, nose tackle Jimmy Johnson made three straight plays that will not soon be forgotten in Arkansas football lore. He stuffed two runs at the line of scrimmage, then sacked quarterback Bob Churchich on third down. Johnson had a way of driving opposing teams crazy. Just before the ball was snapped, he would stand up and point in the direction he thought the play was going. He may have been the among the first breed of "trash-talkers."

Nebraska punted, and Marshall put together the drive of his career. As fate would have it, Lindsey made the key play in the 80-yard march, catching a throwback pass and rambling 27 yards down the sideline to the Nebraska five. Bobby Burnett scored the winning touchdown from the 3-yard line. Final score: Arkansas 10, Nebraska 7.

That year, for the first time ever, the Orange Bowl was played at night. It was also the first college football game ever to be televised in color. That night, from the Holiday Inn on the Central Expressway where the post-game celebration was held, Jones and his teammates watched as the Texas Longhorns did the Razorbacks a great favor by beating number-one Alabama 17–13. Playing on sore knees, Alabama quarterback Joe Namath couldn't handle the quick Longhorn defense. Alabama's loss left Arkansas as America's only unbeaten team.

Unfortunately, for the last time ever, the final wire service polls had come out right after the regular season. (Beginning the following season, the final polls appeared after the bowls.) Both Alabama and Arkansas ended the regular season with identical 10–0 records, so Arkansas was left without an "official" national championship. But a special six-man committee of the Football Writers of America voted one-sidedly to award the Grantland Rice trophy, representing the national championship, to Arkansas. To this day, any Razorback loyalist will tell you that the Grantland Rice trophy is all that matters. The 1964 Hogs were clearly the number-one team in the land.

Throughout his senior year in college, Jerry Jones had more balls to juggle than most student athletes could ever imagine. Now finished with college, he was revving his engines to fly off into the clouds of high finance. Those who had known him in Fayetteville knew that Jerry Jones was going places. They just couldn't imagine the altitude—or the speed—at which he would soon travel.

CHAPTER 4

The Oil Patch

ALL KINDS OF OIL MEN HAD WALKED THROUGH MIKE McCOY'S OFFICE door. Cowboys and corporate vice-presidents. Men with money in their pockets, others who were flat broke. Dreamers. Schemers. Old wildcatters with nothing to offer but a wrinkled map in their jeans pocket. Men with a hungry look in their eye. Their plan? To hit the mother lode where others had turned up only dust.

McCoy's life had reached a crossroads. As a petroleum geologist, he felt like he was living out on the edge of the world. He was operating the regional office of Texas Oil and Gas in the small town of Fort Smith, Arkansas, close to the northwest corner of the state and just south of the Ozarks. Out his window he could see the plains of Oklahoma. Below him stretched the Arkoma Basin, the largest natural gas region in the world. A world of riches seemed to be at his beck and call. In 1980, though, he still needed a partner with enough capital to shoot for the underground gold.

"In walked Jerry Jones—somebody I'd never seen in my life," remembers McCoy, a medium-sized man with thick dark hair who looks ten years younger than his forty-five years. "Somebody had just told Jerry that I was the guy he needed to meet. I'd heard about him. But I'd never met him." Before they were through with the Arkoma Basin almost a decade later, Jones and McCoy would accumulate spectacular wealth.

FOR MORE THAN FIFTEEN YEARS, JONES HAD MOVED LIKE A HUMAN meteor. Few people could out-work or out-hustle the young salesman. Since leaving the University of Arkansas in 1964, he had helped his father, J. W. "Pat" Jones, turn his new business, a moderate-sized insurance company, into a booming success in Springfield, Missouri. He had invested in real estate, pizza, and chickens, and he had almost bought a football team. All this occurred while he and his wife, Gene, were raising a family of three children in Springfield, where they had built a house. Stephen Jones, their first child, had been born in June of 1964, two months before the start of Jones's senior football season at Arkansas. Charlotte was born in 1966, followed by Jerry, Jr., in 1969.

From the start, Jones showed the world that he feared nothing. He borrowed $50,000 from John Ed Chambers, his father-in-law, who owned a small bank in tiny Danville, Arkansas. Jones had originally asked for $15,000. But Chambers trusted his new son-in-law enough to co-sign the loan himself.

Jones had chances to invest in both McDonald's and Kentucky Fried Chicken franchises. Instead, he decided to buy the Missouri rights to a pizza chain called Shakey's. But the company lived up to its name, and lasted only a few years before going out of business. Among his few solid early investments was one in Tyson Foods, soon to become the chicken empire, in nearby Springdale, Arkansas.

"Believe me, there were times when I failed," Jones says now. "There were times when I was down on one knee, so to speak.

But I was able to draw upon those times. One of the hardest things, I would learn, would be keeping my head together during those tough times. You just have to buck up and go on to the next decision. If you don't move with enthusiasm to the next deal, you lose."

By his mid-twenties, Jones was overextended in the real estate business near Springfield and almost went broke. A combination of bad breaks and poor decisions had sent his finances into a tailspin. Trying to rent a car one day at Dallas's Love Field, he passed his charge card across the counter. The rental car company employee, discovering that Jones was far behind on his bill, began cutting the card into pieces with a pair of scissors.

"You need to pay your bills, young man," the employee scolded.

Embarrassed by the incident, Jones says it was a lesson he will never forget. "When people tell me that I haven't been down on the bottom, I tell them about that one," he says. "People say that I haven't been down before. Well, I have."

By the late 1960s, though, Jones's financial problems had become so complex and so intense that his hands would shake when he tried to hold a glass of water. His biggest financial burden was a $500,000 investment he had made on some land near Springfield. He planned to eventually build a Wal-Mart on the property. Friends advised Jones to sell off the land. Jones stubbornly stuck by his investment.

Thanks to an array of failed investments, banks started calling in his loans. "One of the hardest things you'll ever do is sit across the desk from a banker who is calling in a $50,000 loan, then turn around and ask him for another $50,000," Jones says.

One afternoon, he went to visit an elderly lady who lived in one of his rental houses. She was more than three months behind on payments. When she told Jones that she still didn't have the money to make a payment, he just turned and walked away. As he drove off, he whispered to himself, "How can I be so desperate?" Then he began to cry.

Some time later, the banker who had made the half-million-dollar real estate loan learned of Jones's generosity to the old lady. He persuaded the bank to give Jones an extension on his payments. Thirty years later, Jones still owns the property, which has long been paid off. The Wal-Mart he planned stands next to a new interstate highway. The land is now valued at $20 million.

Despite his early setbacks, Jones chased another dream that dated back to his football days at Arkansas. Only two years out of college, he considered trying to buy the San Diego Chargers of the old American Football League. At that point, the Chargers carried a price tag of $5.8 million. For advice, he went to see Kansas City Chiefs owner Lamar Hunt, a man from Dallas who also happened to be the son of an oil-rich father. "You are a very young man to be so wealthy," Hunt told Jones.

The truth was that by the age of twenty-three, Jones was paying $120,000 in annual interest on his loans. Still, he had financial backers ready to help him purchase the team. But he was talked out of buying the Chargers by his father, who was convinced that a football franchise was not worth that kind of financial risk. Six months later, the Chargers sold for $11 million. Again, young Jerry had lost out on a profitable investment—and a chance at realizing one of his dreams.

In 1970, after Pat Jones decided to sell Modern Security Life, Jerry moved his family to Little Rock, where he began planning his plunge into the oil business. All over the country, people were bailing out of the business, but Jones decided to buck the trend.

When Jones put out the word that he was ready to enter the oil business, a relative in New Orleans introduced him to Oklahoma oilman Bill Sparks. At the time, Sparks was down on his luck. And like so many others, he had a map that he believed in. All he needed was an investor who believed in him.

Like most of his breed, Sparks had ridden the crests and valleys of the oil business, all the while struggling to stay afloat financially. The business chewed up oilmen almost as quickly as they could put their bits in the ground. But Sparks planned to snap his long losing streak by drilling in the Red Fork Sand.

Before he met Jones, Sparks had worked for Monsanto, a chemical company in Oklahoma City. One of his duties was introducing potential investors to an oil-drilling site in western

Oklahoma—the Red Fork Sand. One day, while touring the region, he told a group of investors that a river channel of oil existed more than seven thousand feet below the earth's surface. The next day, the company fired him.

"Let's just say that the company I was working for thought I was completely out of my mind," says Sparks, a reserved, taciturn man. "They just couldn't believe there was oil seven thousand feet below the ground in Red Fork Sand. They thought I was making up the whole thing. That's why they fired me."

The Red Fork Sand is located eighty miles northwest of Oklahoma City, and seventy-five miles east of the Texas Panhandle. The Cimarron River runs to the north, and the Canadian River to the south. The closest town is Fairview. It is a desolate area, where the blue northers cut down from Colorado like a keen blade. There are times in the heart of winter when it seems that icicles hang off the cattle's noses. Most of the trees and plants in the area are dead or dying. A drilling bit, even when it doesn't strike oil, often causes salt water to belch to the surface, killing what little vegetation remains.

The oil Sparks was looking for was in a meandering oil river that trended from the northeast to the southwest far beneath the ground. Oil and natural gas move like a river. River channels of oil or natural gas form in underground rock that has been tilted and compressed over millions of years. In the Red Fork Sand, the channel runs one to three miles deep. Those who had drilled there said they couldn't find any pattern to the channel, which, after following a straight line, could turn ninety degrees in an instant. For years, oilmen had been drilling into blind zones and coming up empty.

McCoy says, "The Red Fork Sand wasn't a very agreeable place and a lot of people gave up for good reasons. It attracted a lot of rough people. What you basically had was a bunch of portable toilets and a bunch of hard-working gamblers out there. A lot of people didn't mess with the Red Fork Sand because it was a lot easier to miss than to hit. Bill Sparks had worked for years to find this elusive target. But really, back in the early 1970s nobody believed that you could find much out there."

What the other oil men didn't realize is that they were barely missing the big hit.

"It wasn't that they had completely failed," Sparks says. "They just weren't looking for what we were looking for, or, at least, looking in the same places. Most of the oil was just a lot deeper than what they were accustomed to."

Sparks had a plan for drilling in the Red Fork Sand that hadn't been tried before. Unlike most of the other oil men at work in the field, he had tracked similar channels in both Louisiana and western Mississippi. He recognized that the underground rivers of the Red Fork Sand contained bar sand—a specific type of sand that appears only in certain geological formations. His experience in Louisiana and Mississippi told him that rivers with bar sand do not stop abruptly. They might continue for one mile or ten miles on a winding and snaking path. One river they had located was actually fifty miles long.

"Some of the channels were one thousand feet wide," Sparks says. "I knew that you could move the bit five hundred feet and still hit oil. The hard part was that you could go between them without hitting anything because the thing snaked back and forth so much. But once you were inside the channel, you were there. We were drilling anywhere from four- to eleven-thousand feet. And we were hitting."

"At the time, Jerry wouldn't have known the Red Fork if it had bit him on the nose," McCoy says. "Probably one of Jerry's worst traits is his inability to say 'no' to risky ventures. He does love high-risk, high-return ventures. So he loved this Bill Sparks idea. Bill managed to sell it to Jerry when he couldn't sell it to anybody else."

Jones and Jim Dooley, one of Jones' friends and business associates from Little Rock, were selling mobile homes when they got word of Sparks's scheme. Jones loved the idea the moment he heard it. He and Dooley teamed up with Sparks and Ran Ricks, who operated Ricks Exploration out of Oklahoma City.

By then, Jones had experienced enough troubles with the banks. Instead of seeking another loan for drilling, he scraped together most of the necessary $200,000 on his own. With his maps in hand, Sparks's job was to locate the drilling sites. Ricks would then work the well site, which was his specialty. He would drill and then complete the well.

Their plan was to drill between the dry holes. It's hardly surprising that other oil men thought they were crazy. In this case, though, Jones's faith in Bill Sparks paid off. The group hit their first well, which was worth more than $4 million.

"Hitting that first one meant that we could go to the bank and borrow money and keep drilling," Sparks says. "It meant everything in the world to us."

Their method couldn't have been more simple. After drilling and locating a river, they would use the ruler to draw a line from ground level to that particular channel. They didn't care that they were drilling between dry holes. Since Sparks knew that the rivers continued, they would trace a line on the same angle with the ruler. They were able to follow the meandering river as it snaked its way through different depths of the rock. They were, in effect, merely connecting the dots. Each dot signified yet another pocket of oil where the river continued to run.

The group hit their next well, and the next one, and the next. In all, they hit oil in the first fifteen wells they drilled.

"It was basically the most simple thing you've ever seen in your life," Mike McCoy says. "I remember another oil man saying, 'Boys, don't give up. Get your rulers and connect those dots.' What they were doing was drilling between crap and crap and finding the good." McCoy soon found himself in on the action. "I was working for a rival company at the time, and we'd heard about their success. In fact, back then, everybody was running to northwest Oklahoma to get a piece of the action. We said, 'Hell, we've got rulers, too. We can figure this thing out.'"

When Jones and company first started drilling on the dusty land, others had laughed at their high-risk efforts. It had been proven over and over that it was far easier to turn up dust at the Red Fork Sand than it was to find a trickle of oil. But Jones had faith. He believed that rolling the dice in the dusty Oklahoma oil fields was his straight shot to wealth.

"Right off the bat, Jerry believed in me," says Sparks gratefully. "Why, I don't completely know, other than the fact that he was hungry to get rich. He was just like everybody else getting into the business for the first time. He wanted to strike it rich. But there was one other thing. All he could talk about was that he wanted to make enough money to buy a football team."

After the first successful wells came in, the partying began. Jones and his three partners rented the entire Sports Page Club at the Hilton Inn West in Oklahoma City. More than 500 people showed up. There was a band, food, an open bar, and many of the young, available women who congregate around free-flowing oil money. Among the guests were Oklahoma head coach Barry Switzer and defensive coordinator Larry Lacewell. Switzer had been Jones's freshman football coach at Oklahoma. Jones and Lacewell were also destined to become great friends.

"Those were some of the damnedest parties I'd ever been to," Lacewell remembers. "They would rent out every room in the hotel. And the party would go all night."

Says one of the celebrants, "It was one of those parties where just about everybody got drunk, naked, and jumped in the pool."

Remembers Sparks, "I don't know if I could still survive one of those parties. We stayed up all night and drank all you could handle."

In the lingo of the oil business, Jones had become an independent, searching for oil without the powerful financial support of companies like Shell or Exxon. He operated without a team of engineers and without their sophisticated computers and tracking devices.

Independents are like the old-time wildcatters of the 1920s and 1930s. Larger-than-life characters like H. L. Hunt, Sid Richardson, and Hugh Roy Cullen made their fortunes in the oil fields during those fabled boom times. This first wildcatter era ended around the time of World War II.

Today's independent is always willing to leave the beaten path with hopes of striking the mother lode on land that is not known to be oil-bearing. He doesn't mind drilling where others have failed. He doesn't necessarily believe in scientific methods or computer technology. And he isn't afraid to gamble. An independent travels most of the time, eats when he can, and tries to outsmart the lease-hounds, the weather, the geologists, and the computers.

Before becoming a corporate raider, T. Boone Pickens learned the oil business as an independent. In his autobiography, *Boone*, he wrote, "Independents have always found more oil and gas in the United States than the major oil companies. And many of those independents have been every bit as flamboyant as the first wildcatters."

Through luck, perseverance, and a maniacal drive to get rich, Jones had somehow hit on the right formula. Pickens, who has been Jones's friend since 1989 and is now the chief executive officer of Mesa, Inc., in Dallas says, "Jerry knew that he'd drill some dry holes just like the rest of us. If you're gonna drill a lot of holes, you're gonna have some dry holes. If you get into a lot of business ventures, you're going to miss on a few. I will say this about Jerry. He knows how to assess risks very well. He's not gonna shoot the dice on one deal. So I don't think you're gonna find him with his dress over his head in a bad situation."

DURING THAT HEADY TIME, JONES WAS ALSO MANAGING A DIFFICULT balancing act between his professional and family life, commuting by private jet from his home in Little Rock to the drilling site in northwest Oklahoma. He was also coaching his son Stephen's Little League football team. While waiting for his dad to show up, young Stephen, already dressed in his football uniform, would pace back and forth in the house.

"Don't worry," Gene Jones would say, trying to reassure her son. "Your dad always makes it on time." Minutes later, Jones would dash into the house, pecking Gene on the lips and then rushing off to the game with Stephen. "I never missed a game," Jones says proudly. "It was too important." One of the teams that Jones coached finished with an undefeated record. Although he spent much of his time on the road, he did all he could to be more than an absentee father as his children grew up in the '70s. But Jones had to depend on his wife to be the steady parental influence around the house.

WHEN JONES WALKED INTO MCCOY'S OFFICE IN 1980, HE WAS coming off one of the greatest financial and emotional highs of his life. He'd learned that he could take huge risks and make them pay off. Jones had sold one of his oil production companies in 1976 and walked away from the Red Fork Sand a year later with a profit of more than $50 million.

"Jerry has never met a high-risk deal that he didn't like," McCoy says. "I could tell that right from the start. He's a risk taker. And the riskier the better. You have to be a gambler to play in this business. If you get disappointed over failure, you shouldn't be in this business. At the same time, if you get too high over success, you will bust yourself. Believe me, the excitement in the oil and gas business is unmatched by any other business."

Despite his enormous success, Jones was now ready to move on. He figured it was time to walk away from the high-risk oil game still in progress back in Kingfisher County, Oklahoma. It was the first sign that Jones knew when to leave the table. He was proving himself a survivor.

"With the exception of Jerry, most of the oil guys over in Oklahoma stayed at that dice table too long," McCoy says. "That dice table got turned upside down and burned."

The domestic oil industry would take off in 1981 following the fall of the Shah of Iran and government decontrol of the industry. By December of that year, oil prices had topped out at $40 per barrel. Some experts were predicting that prices were going to rise to $50, $60, or possibly even $100 per barrel. They were dead wrong. Five years later, prices would bottom out at $10 per barrel. Jones's gut instincts were proven right. It had been exactly the right time to move out of the oil fields and into the gas drilling business.

"Actually, the bottom was about to fall out of the gas industry, too; we just didn't know it," McCoy says. "We actually picked the right time to do the wrong thing. But somehow it worked out."

Within an hour after meeting McCoy that afternoon in 1980, Jones made a point-blank proposal that they become partners. Jones felt the same way about McCoy that he had about Sparks.

Here was a man he could trust, and one who could further his riches.

Conservative by nature, McCoy was at first shocked that Jones would move so quickly. But McCoy would soon learn that Jones wastes little time when the feeling is right. Many of his actions appear to be impulsive, which is contrary to how McCoy operates.

"In a lot of ways, Jerry and I tended to balance each other out," McCoy says. "I move slowly, and maybe Jerry speeds me up. Since I move slow, maybe I tend to slow him down."

However, it was actually McCoy who got the duo started on the road to riches in the gas business. In 1980, with gas prices holding strong at $10 per thousand cubic feet, McCoy proposed that they take a shot at a well in the San Joaquin Valley near San Francisco. McCoy had been keeping an eye on the project for several years.

"Jerry told me he didn't know how to find gas," he says. "I told him we would find the biggest gas well in northern California and draw a big circle around it. We found some land about 2,000 feet away from a big well. We started to drill. Actually that well had been there for years. But I told Jerry that if we missed this one, we probably should get out and try something else."

The two bought the lease on an asparagus farm for about $250,000. "Starting off, we had to buy a lot of asparagus," McCoy says.

In the meantime, they decided to try their hand at another natural gas well in Lattimer County in southeastern Oklahoma, just east of McAllister. Almost immediately, the project met with disaster when a trusted employee made a half-million-dollar mistake. After drilling the customary eight-inch diameter hole, he tried to pour cement into the casing to add support to the well. Instead, he mistakenly dumped the cement into the well itself, ruining it.

"We had spent almost a half-million on that well and I had almost no money left in the bank," McCoy says. "On top of that, I had to call Jerry and tell him that one of my best friends, and my most trusted employee, had ruined the entire well. To make it even worse, Jerry and I had just started our partnership."

To McCoy's surprise, Jones took the bad news in stride. The employee kept his job, and the partners invested another $500,000. They moved the drill bit one hundred feet. The next day, they learned they had hit a natural gas well worth $40 million. Their business was off and running. "As it turned out, the biggest mistake that Jerry and I would ever make turned out to be our biggest hit," McCoy says with a sense of relief.

Meanwhile, the first reports from the well near San Francisco were not as positive.

"My friend out there called and said he thought we had turned up nothing," McCoy says. "Then he called back eight hours later and told me that we were rich."

The well in the San Joaquin Valley would produce $40 million worth of gas over a two-year period. In effect, Jones and McCoy had made $80 million—in a matter of days—on their first two natural gas wells. But the biggest profits were yet to come. Jones was still a gambler—and not yet a player. Over the next few years, he would find himself playing for higher stakes in a much bigger game.

CHAPTER 5

Easy Money

JERRY JONES'S IMAGE IN HIS NATIVE ARKANSAS IS A COMPLEX ONE, EVEN today. He is revered for purchasing the Cowboys (the state's closest and favorite NFL team) and for converting the worst team in football in 1989 into back-to-back Super Bowl champions. Frank Broyles, the University of Arkansas athletic director and Jones's former coach, says, "When Jerry bought the Cowboys, he put Arkansas back on the map. Back then, people didn't have much to cheer about around here."

At the same time, Jones has been reviled in Arkansas as a flim-flam man who made hundreds of millions of dollars, much of it at the expense of the state's utility rate-payers. Although Jones and his partners deny any impropriety, the drilling deal he cut in 1982 with Arkansas-Louisiana Gas, Inc. (ArkLa), the state-regulated public utility, seems destined to go down in history as one of the greatest sweetheart arrangements of all time.

In Arkansas, the ArkLa-Arkoma deal has been in the headlines for nearly a decade. According to information revealed in two separate Arkansas Public Service Commission investigations, testimony in several lawsuits, and intense media coverage, Jones capitalized on his friendship with Sheffield Nelson, the president of ArkLa, to make an easy fortune in the fertile gas-drilling fields of western Arkansas. By the time Jones had finished drilling the rich Arkoma Basin, he had made a monstrous fortune, and Sheffield Nelson had become a wealthy man. And there is no doubt that the profits from the deal added critical muscle to Jones's negotiations for the Dallas Cowboys, which began in the latter part of 1988.

When syndicated columnist and public television commentator Mark Shields went to Little Rock in 1990 to write about the gas-drilling mega-deal that made Jerry Jones a Texas-sized fortune, and its role in Arkansas politics, he slammed his notebook shut during one interview and exclaimed, "My God, this is not a column—it's a novel." The ArkLa scandal certainly contains the makings of a great novel—a labyrinthine plot, circular loyalties, rotating friendships, and enough money to put a good-sized Third World country back on its feet.

SHEFFIELD NELSON IS ONE OF THE MOST POWERFUL MEN IN ARKANSAS— as well as one of Jerry Jones's best friends. Like Jones, Nelson came from humble beginnings. He was raised in real poverty in the rice country of East Arkansas. His father was an alcoholic. His childhood was spent in the backwoods, without electricity or running water.

Like Jones, Nelson worked his way from childhood rags to present-day riches. His improbable journey upward from his impoverished East Arkansas roots got a major boost when he married Mary Lynn McCastlain, the daughter of state representative Doris McCastlain. Doris McCastlain was a friend of one of the most powerful and perhaps the richest man in the state, Witt Stephens. The investment firm that Stephens started would become the largest brokerage outside of Wall Street. In the early 1950s, Stephens bought the company that eventually became ArkLa Gas.

McCastlain introduced her son-in-law to Stephens, who immediately found a soft spot in his heart for the young go-getter. Thanks to their relationship, Nelson landed a job with ArkLa when he graduated from college.

Witt Stephens later turned his brokerage firm over to his brother Jack. When Witt stepped down from his post as president of ArkLa in 1972, he designated Nelson, then only thirty-three years old, as his successor. Folks around Little Rock were shocked that Nelson had been handed so much power at such a young age. But Nelson had won the faith and the trust of the Stephens brothers, who virtually ran Little Rock. Nelson may not have been born with a silver spoon in his mouth, but he had certainly inherited one from the Stephenses.

It wasn't long, though, before a feud of Shakespearean dimensions set in between Nelson and the Stephens family. Jack and Witt Stephens wanted to continue to influence the direction of ArkLa Gas. One of their goals was opening a gas pipeline from the Arkoma Basin to buyers from outside the state. Nelson, however, was determined not to be treated as merely a surrogate for the brothers. To the Stephenses' shock and dismay, Nelson blocked their plans for the pipeline. Stephens took his case directly to the state legislature. But Nelson, even though he was a decided underdog against the powerful Little Rock family, won the battle. And it wasn't long before Nelson began moving ArkLa in his own direction—a direction that would prove immensely profitable to his best friend, Jerry Jones.

JONES AND NELSON'S FRIENDSHIP BEGAN IN 1970, WHEN JONES MOVED his family back to Arkansas from Springfield, Missouri. Besides sharing modest backgrounds, both were determined men who, in spite of the odds against them, quickly made their way to financial success. They ran in some of the same Little Rock social circles—and it wasn't long before they became close friends.

Jones and Nelson would collaborate on a series of political campaigns and business arrangements. Together, they owned a television station, a race horse, a farm, and a condominium. They even helped manage a prizefighter. During the 1980s they became partners with Jim McDougal of Whitewater fame. Unlike Bill and

Hillary Clinton, Jones and Nelson made a sizable profit on McDougal's business brainstorms—and didn't have to face a special prosecutor's inquisition.

Nelson and Jones invested with McDougal in land on Campobello Island, located between Nova Scotia and New Brunswick. Jones and Nelson put in $225,000 apiece and bought 3,400 acres. Ironically, it was the Campobello development, not Whitewater, that eventually drove McDougal's Madison Guaranty Savings and Loan Association under.

In 1989, just as Jones was buying the Cowboys, Madison Guaranty was placed under the control of the Resolution Trust Corporation, which found itself the owner of the Campobello property. Fortunately for Jones and Nelson, Tommy Trantham, a former bank regulator, University of Arkansas football star, and friend of Jones, had taken over Madison Guaranty as part of his supervision of the Federal Home Loan Bank in Dallas. At Trantham's request, the bankrupt thrift bought Jones and Nelson out for $725,000.

The deal had its critics. When L. William Seidman, former head of the Resolution Trust Corporation and the Federal Deposit Insurance Corporation, learned of the arrangement, he told the *Fort Worth Star-Telegram*, "I can't believe it. It's an extraordinary event. It wouldn't have happened when I was in charge." Both Trantham and Jones vigorously denied that they had discussed the deal or that there had been any special treatment. Amazingly, Jones and Nelson walked away from the Madison mess smelling like roses, and with a profit of $137,500 apiece.

★ ★ ★

BACK IN THE 1970S, JONES AND HIS FRIEND AND BUSINESS PARTNER Bill Sparks had made millions of dollars playing their high-risk oil-drilling game at the Red Fork Sand in the Oklahoma oilfields. At the time, Jones told Sparks that his goal was to make enough money from the petroleum business to buy a NFL team. By the end of the decade, Jones was ready to move on to bigger deals with bigger payoffs—and with targets that would be easier to hit.

By comparison to Jones's Red Fork Sand enterprises, drilling for gas inside the Cecil and Aetna Fields of the gas-rich Arkoma Basin in western Arkansas was about as risky as throwing darts at the ground. The basin extends 250 miles east to west from McAlester, Oklahoma to Russellville, Arkansas. The north-to-south depth is about twenty miles. The heart of the basin is considered to be in Fort Smith, Arkansas, on the Oklahoma border.

By the time Jerry Jones got interested in the area, it was no secret that the fields were rich in gas. ArkLa and its predecessors had drilled fifty-nine times in the Aetna Field without hitting a dry hole, and seventy-four times in the Cecil Field, hitting seventy-one. That translates to a success ratio of nearly 98.4 percent.

Leases in the field already had produced half a trillion cubic feet of gas, and Norman F. Williams, the state geologist, estimated that there were at least a half a trillion cubic feet of reserves still to be discovered.

Leonard Jordan, an ArkLa exploration expert in western Arkansas, analyzed the potential of the Cecil Field in a memo to ArkLa vice president Bill Harrell. The memo, which would be referred to as a "smoking gun" during the ensuing investigation, stated, "It appears that ArkLa will be able to drill this field (Cecil Field) for years to come ... and increase our company owned gas reserves."

The memo also noted that ArkLa could force drillers—including the Stephens brothers' production company, which had a major interest in the fields—to continue their work under the terms of their current agreements. Under these long-term agreements, signed many years earlier, ArkLa had a financial hammer lock on producers in the Arkoma Basin. ArkLa was paying only 55 cents per cubic per thousand cubic feet in the Cecil Field, and 16 cents per thousand cubic feet in the Aetna Field. The going market rate at the time was $3 per thousand cubic feet. Under the contracts, the production companies could even be fined if they refused to continue drilling. ArkLa had its producers over a barrel. Jordan strongly urged the company to stay the course with its current agreements, and develop the gas-rich territory on its own.

★ ★ ★

Jones knew that there was gas in the Arkoma basin, and he knew that if he could figure out how to get ArkLa to pay more for it, he could make the money he needed to buy his way into the exclusive club known as the National Football League.

As usual, he wasted little time in putting his plans into action. In January 1981, two days after forming a new gas drilling company, Arkoma Production, Jones and partner Mike McCoy found themselves competing head-to-head with ArkLa Gas for leases on the old Fort Chaffee reservation in western Arkansas. They managed to outbid ArkLa on 20 of 22 leases, sometimes by the tiniest of margins. During the course of the PSC hearings, Arkoma's bidding on the Fort Chaffee leases came under careful scrutiny. Bill Harrell, a close friend of Jones identified by the media as one possible source of the bidding information, told the *Arkansas Gazette* the charges of bid-rigging were "100 percent pure politics."

Jones also began to show his hand in the Aetna and Cecil Fields. Arkoma began to buy the royalty rights from landowners in the area, paying about $300 an acre in exchange for rights to future royalties. The gas-drilling duo seemed to know that something was about to happen inside the Arkoma Basin. Three years later, in 1984, during a deposition over a stockholder lawsuit, Jones admitted that he had sat in on meetings with ArkLa executives when they discussed information about its reserves.

The stage was set for Jones's entry into the Arkoma basin. In late 1982, Sheffield Nelson arranged a deal that ceded ArkLa's half-interest in natural gas leases on some 28,500 acres in the Cecil and Aetna Fields to Arkoma Production. Despite the utility's own track record in drilling in the basin, and the below-market-rate contracts already in place, Nelson convinced the board that cutting a deal with Jones would help the utility spread the cost, and the risk, of developing the field's reserves.

According to testimony before the Public Service Commission, the deal included a number of unusual features.

Jones and McCoy had to pay ArkLa $15 million to launch the deal. But ArkLa financed $11.25 million of that amount at the charitable rate of 10 percent, which was about 3.5 percent below the rate banks were then charging their best corporate customers. In return, Arkoma Production committed to provide all the gas it could find to the Arkansas utility.

One attractive aspect of the deal was Arkoma's agreement to dedicate 100,000 acres of prime gas-producing acres in Arkansas, Oklahoma and other states to ArkLa. In a memo sent to the board two days before it approved the deal, Nelson said that Jones and McCoy would dedicate "in excess of 100,000 prime acres in eastern and southern Oklahoma," one of the richest gas regions in the country. Unfortunately, the land Arkoma eventually turned over was in East Arkansas and Mississippi, a gas-poor producing region. ArkLa never received a foot of gas out of the land.

From a financial point of view, the contracts for purchasing gas that accompanied the deal were far more lucrative than any of ArkLa's previous arrangements. It allowed Jones to sell gas to ArkLa at a price far higher than what the utility was paying others in the field. Arkoma Production would receive $4.50 per thousand cubic feet, more than nine times what the previous producers had been receiving. Furthermore, ArkLa couldn't renegotiate those prices even if the market value for natural gas fell through the floor. If, on the other hand, gas prices skyrocketed, Jones could renegotiate the price with ArkLa any time he pleased.

ArkLa also agreed to make the deal a take-or-pay arrangement. This meant that even if the utility company didn't need any more gas, they would have to pay for whatever quantity Arkoma Production delivered.

The ArkLa Gas board of directors ratified the agreement on New Year's Eve 1982. A short announcement appeared in the business section of the Little Rock papers a few days later. The deal went virtually unnoticed by the public. No one questioned a possible conflict of interest between Nelson and Jones, even though it was no secret around Little Rock that the two had been fast friends since the 1970s. Somehow, their relationship had escaped the attention of the ArkLa board.

And no one questioned—publicly, at least—why ArkLa would turn its back on its existing strategy of depending on long-time producers in the region. Years later, when confronted with Jordan's memo to Harrell, Nelson would only say that the document reflected internal discussions at the company—implying that it wasn't the final word on the field's potential. As it turns out, Harrell was another of Jones's close friends. Harrell's son-in-law was Jones's partner in the Louisiana Bayou Oil Company. Again, Jones's extensive personal and business relationships with a key decision-maker hadn't been revealed to the ArkLa directors.

ArkLa, its board of directors, and all of the ratepayers in the state would soon come to regret the take-or-pay and non-renegotiable aspects of the agreement. In 1985, the natural gas industry was deregulated, and the price of gas dropped dramatically. Unfortunately, under the terms of their agreement with Arkoma, the utility was committed to buying as much gas as Jones could produce at the maximum legal price.

Not surprisingly, Jones and McCoy quickly went to work securing all of the acreage they could find in western Arkansas. Their plan was to drill as much as they could, as quickly as possible. They also made deals with other gas producers to turn their leases over to Arkoma Production. McCoy and Jones pointed out to landowners and potential lessors that they could receive a much higher return on their gas by working out deals with Arkoma—instead of continuing their low-paying contracts with ArkLa. Jones made this kind of arrangement with Jack Stephens, who was one of the major producers in the fields, and one of the smartest men in the history of Arkansas oil and gas. Stephens, along with others working the fields, wound up making far more money than he would have under his existing contracts.

The deal also brought Jones into direct conflict with one of Stephens's operations. Thanks to a mix-up with ArkLa, Stephens and Jones ended up drilling side-by-side on the same lease in western Arkansas. When the two men couldn't resolve their differences, Jones told Stephens he would leave the area on one condition.

"We really had a right to drill right next to Stephens," Jones says. "But he got pissed off. So we said, 'Okay, Jack, we'll trade you this well for another well that you have at another location. You make the call.' They said, 'Okay, we'll make that trade.'"

Jones's string of luck held true to form. Stephens's company stayed on the site and hit a dry hole. As Jones remembers, "We moved our equipment over to the spot that we traded for and we hit Godzilla." The well that Stephens traded to Jones turned out to be one of the biggest hits in Jones's seven years of drilling in the region.

IN 1984, SHEFFIELD NELSON RESIGNED AS PRESIDENT AND CEO OF THE ArkLa board of directors. Jones, thanks to Nelson's clout, was by then one of the ArkLa directors. He made the motion that Nelson receive a fat bonus. Nelson exercised stock options worth $3.6 million. He was now a wealthy man.

In the meantime, Jones and McCoy were punching holes in the gas-rich sands of the Arkoma Basin as quickly as they could move their equipment. They were bringing in new gas wells as quickly as they could drill them. By 1986, ArkLa had all of the gas it could use—and much more. But Arkoma Production was producing a virtual tidal wave of natural gas. And Jones expected to be paid for it.

The man who succeeded Nelson as president and CEO of ArkLa, Mack McLarty, realized that he had big trouble on his hands. In 1992, McLarty would leave ArkLa to become President Bill Clinton's chief of staff at the White House. But back in 1986, he had to figure out what to do about the Arkoma deal he had inherited from Nelson. ArkLa was paying Arkoma Production $40 million a year for gas it didn't need. The deal was shaking the financial foundations of the utility.

Faced with mounting bills from the take-or-pay arrangement, and with obligations running into the hundreds of millions of dollars in the years ahead, McLarty tried to negotiate a way out. First, he asked Jones to resign from the board, raising, according to the PSC complaint, the issue of Jones's potential conflict of interest. On January 2, 1987, ArkLa announced it had bought Arkoma Production for $49 million. ArkLa said it was paying Jones and McCoy $14 million for Arkoma's stock and $35 million for its assets, including its mineral leases. It seemed like a lot of money. But at least ArkLa would be unshackled from the take-or-pay contracts.

At the time, the ArkLa deal looked like a good solution to the problem. In fact, it looked like McLarty had ridden in on a white horse and saved the company. Once again, the information that reached the public was incomplete.

The facts about the deal would finally begin spilling out during the 1990 governor's race. ArkLa had actually bought Arkoma Production, which had been started from scratch in 1981, for $174.8 million, almost four times the price that had been announced back in 1987. Also unbeknownst to the public, Jones and McCoy had been allowed to drill for two years after McLarty's 1987 arrangement started. Granted, they were drilling at a much lower rate—$1.20 to $1.38 per thousand cubic feet rather than $4.50—but they still opened sixty-five new wells during that two-year period.

By 1989, Arkoma Production had walked away with more than $300 million. Jones and McCoy had drilled more than two hundred wells. And they had come up empty on exactly one dry hole. Jones had all of the money—and more—that he needed to buy the Dallas Cowboys.

Jones had many close relationships during his days in Little Rock, but none was closer than his friendship with former Congressman Tommy Robinson. Robinson and Jones had been close friends for more than forty years, dating back to their days in the first grade in Rose City Elementary School. For two years during Bill Clinton's tenure as governor, Robinson was the state director of public safety, overseeing the state police and the Arkansas National Guard.

Even though Robinson was in the public spotlight, Jones had the more dominant personality. He also had more money, thanks to his success in the oil and gas fields. He loaned Robinson hundreds of thousands of dollars, backed his political campaigns, and even paid him to help run his two duck lodges down in Stuttgart while Robinson was still sheriff of Pulaski County. When Jones's daughter, Charlotte, invited the senior class from Central High to her house for a party in the early eighties, Robinson's sheriff's deputies supervised the grounds and the parking. Some of the deputies even provided cab service. Robinson later hired Charlotte, fresh out of Stanford, to work in his Washington, D.C. office as an administrative aide. At a salary of $60,000 per year, she was the highest-paid member of his staff. Her salary was the subject of hot controversy in the Little Rock media.

In 1984, Jones worked vigorously to get Robinson elected to his first term in the U.S. House of Representatives, where he would become the freshman whip for the Democrats. Robinson would serve three two-year terms. He switched to the Republican party in 1989 in a ceremony at the White House.

One day in 1989, after Jones had bought the Cowboys, Robinson and Charlotte flew to Dallas to see Jones and to seek his advice. Robinson was getting itchy to come back to Arkansas. He was considering running against Bill Clinton for governor in 1990. Robinson wanted to know what Jones thought about his plans.

"Jerry told me point-blank, `You go ahead and run against Clinton,'" Robinson says. "He said, `Tommy, I want you to run because Sheffield (Nelson) can't beat him. I'm going to tell Sheffield that he shouldn't run.'" Robinson decided to run, believing that he had Jones's support.

Months later, to Robinson's surprise, Nelson announced his candidacy on the Republican ticket. He would be running against Robinson in the Republican primary. Robinson couldn't believe what he was hearing—that Nelson now had Jones's full financial support.

Furious, Robinson called Jones in Dallas and said, "Now, I know about you, Jerry Jones. Shit, you stole the money in that

ArkLa deal. You're backing Sheffield because he helped you steal the money. Go to hell, Jerry.'" As far as Robinson was concerned, Jones's decision to back Nelson ended their friendship. "I was blinded by Jones," Robinson says now. "I would have walked to the end of the plank with him. But once you stop and smell the roses, you realize that Jerry Jones is full of shit."

★ ★ ★

ROBINSON'S FEELINGS OF BETRAYAL MARKED THE BEGINNING OF A political firestorm in Little Rock. The real story of the ArkLa fiasco, previously hidden on the financial pages of the Little Rock newspapers, turned explosive as Robinson dragged it out into his primary battle.

Running against Nelson in the Republican primary, Robinson turned almost overnight from being Jones's best friend to being one of his worst enemies. Robinson announced that he would have a team of investigators get to the bottom of the ArkLa-Arkoma deal. There was even talk of criminal investigations. Attorney General Steve Clark sided with Robinson, saying he was horrified at the amount of money that Arkansas ratepayers had ended up turning over to Jones. Then-governor Bill Clinton finally asked the Public Service Commission to conduct a full investigation.

Thousands of pages of testimony, pleadings, motions, and exhibits seemed to reveal just how many millions Jones and McCoy had made on the deal—and how little risk Arkoma Production had taken. Nelson, Harrell, and other ArkLa officials continued to defend the deal. Nelson, in the political battle of his life, told the *Arkansas Gazette* that the PSC hearings were a "kangaroo court" designed to promote Governor Clinton's political agenda. After the nastiest Republican primary in the state's history, Robinson lost—barely—to Nelson. The revelations from the hearings had come too late to save Robinson's candidacy.

But between the primary and the general election, Nelson found himself constantly on the defensive—trying to explain away the ugly testimony about the deal with Jones and McCoy.

Accountants hired by the attorney behind the ratepayers' complaint to the PSC said ArkLa had disguised many of its purchases of high-priced gas from Jones. "Never in my twenty-eight years of experience in reviewing utilities and pipelines' gas costs have I encountered this situation," testified Herbert J. Vander Veen, partner in the accounting firm of Ernst and Young of Washington, D.C. According to Vander Veen's testimony, ArkLa had filed reports with the state Public Service Commission that recorded gas bought from Jones under the name of other gas producers. This was clearly a violation of state law, although ArkLa's representatives claimed the improper records were the result of a simple accounting oversight.

This misattribution of gas purchases made it impossible to know completely just how much Jones and McCoy had profited from the deal. J.T. Mitchell of Dallas, who owned a petroleum industry consulting firm, estimated that because of the agreement with Jones and McCoy, ArkLa spent between $59.5 million to $97 million too much for gas between 1983 and 1989.

The special commission held off until after the election to render its judgment. In December, six weeks after the election, it decided that the deal had been imprudent and ordered ArkLa to refund $21.4 million to the ratepayers.

It hardly mattered in the general election. The word had gotten out through the media that Nelson had collaborated with Jones to make the Cowboys' owner a fortune—at the expense of Arkansas ratepayers. Clinton defeated Nelson handily, receiving 57 percent of the vote.

THE RELATIONSHIP BETWEEN JONES AND ROBINSON CONTINUED TO deteriorate after the election. Years earlier, Jones and Robinson had bought a 1,921-acre farm in East Arkansas worth $1.2 million. Robinson borrowed from Jones to buy a 50 percent share of the farm. Robinson said he soon learned that even though ownership of the farm was supposed to be split 50-50, Jones held the voting stock on the farm. Robinson eventually bought out Jones's interest in the farm. But negotiations on the deal turned extremely ugly.

"He tried to bankrupt me," Robinson says. "He also threatened me. He said, 'If you keep pursuing this, I will cause you some great pain.' But my conscience wouldn't let me back down."

Today, Jones bristles when Robinson's name is brought up. "He is one of the most irresponsible mouths who has ever spoken to the media," he says. "That he would be critical of me, after all of the things that I did for him, speaks volumes of the man. I bought him clothes for his children, paid his hospital bills, played Santa for them for several years. When he ran for office, it was acknowledged that I was the one who fundamentally helped him."

Robinson's personal and political debts to Jones grew by leaps and bounds during the 1970s and 1980s. Jones bankrolled each of Robinson's early political campaigns. Federal Election Commission records show that in 1989 Robinson owed Jones between $250,000 and $500,000. Robinson said those loans have been completely paid back.

"I've paid him back every penny," Robinson says. "But if he came back to Arkansas, I wouldn't cross the street to greet him."

Robinson still owns and works the farm near Brinkley, Arkansas, which is now a profitable family operation producing rye, wheat, and soybeans. It has now been expanded to almost 7,000 acres. He says he has no thoughts of reentering politics.

ROBINSON, ALONG WITH OTHERS IN ARKANSAS, CLAIMS THAT JONES couldn't have made his deal for the Cowboys without the profits from the ArkLa deal. Jones has been hearing these accusations for years.

"Ridiculous, absolutely ridiculous," he says. "The financial statements would reflect that long before Arkoma, long before 1983, I had the financial qualifications to buy the team."

That may be true. Before the ArkLa scandal, Jones had struck it rich in the oil and gas-drilling business. He had made about

$50 million in the Oklahoma oilfields back in the 1970s. Then, he and McCoy had hit back-to-back $40 million gas wells—Godzillas, if you will—within days of each other in Oklahoma and California. Jones certainly had substantial financial clout, even before ArkLa.

But Jones's claim that he made only enough money from the ArkLa deal to pay off quarterback Troy Aikman's first contract—worth about $11 million—seems like a gross understatement. In 1986, Jones and partner Mike McCoy sold their company, Arkoma Production, to ArkLa Gas for $174.8 million. (At the time of their partnership in the 1980s, Jones held 85 percent of Arkoma and McCoy 15 percent.) According to the most conservative estimates of financial experts in Little Rock, they made another $100 million selling gas to ArkLa. All told, Jones and McCoy probably made $300 million on the deal, and possibly more.

The drive down I-30 from Little Rock to Dallas is 320 miles. In 1989, Jones could have lined that highway with $100 bills. The ArkLa scandal helped him put Little Rock in his rearview mirror. Now, he was setting his sights on the bright lights of Dallas.

CHAPTER 6

Jethro

FROM HIS HOTEL SUITE AT THE MANSION ON TURTLE CREEK, JERRY Jones watched the lights of downtown Dallas. The glistening glass towers made him think of Oz. On the western edge of downtown, he could see the Hyatt Regency tower, shining like a giant golf ball perched on a tee. It was February 24, 1989, and the oil wildcatter from Arkansas was just twenty-four hours away from joining the Dallas elite. The thought was intoxicating. The bright lights of the big city were calling, and Jones knew he should close the drapes and ignore them.

The next morning, he would sign the papers giving him control of the Dallas Cowboys—and make football history by firing Tom Landry.

Landry had been, as everyone in America knew, The Only Man To Ever Coach The Dallas Cowboys. As a young man Landry had played at the University of Texas with the great Bobby Layne, and then with the New York Giants. Since then he had achieved legendary status while compiling the secondwinningest record in the history of the NFL—behind Chicago's George Halas. Perhaps even more impressive than his 270 career wins were the Cowboys' twenty straight winning seasons from 1966–85, eighteen playoff appearances, and five trips to the Super Bowl. His rigid and stoical sideline demeanor, along with his trademark snap-brim hat, made Landry one of the most familiar figures in sports. In Texas, where football is religion, Landry was God.

Now Jones faced a major headache. No one had gotten around to telling Landry that he wouldn't be coaching the Cowboys in 1989. Landry had been working long hours at the team's Valley Ranch facility, designing a strategy to bring them back from their dismal 3–13 season. Ten days earlier, he had announced that he planned to coach into the 1990s. Little did he know that within the week Jimmy Johnson would be sitting behind his desk, occupying his chair, coaching his team.

From behind Jones came a voice. "I want to go out to dinner," said Linda Kay Johnson, Jimmy Johnson's wife.

"I do too," said Jones's wife, Gene.

"Wait a minute," Jimmy Johnson said. "Jerry, do you know what the deal is here?"

The business was still supposed to be top secret. Jones was dodging the media, even though Channel 5, KXAS-TV, had reported the previous night that he was in town with millions in hand to buy America's Team. Johnson had been summoned to Dallas to assure a minority owner that he would indeed leave Miami to coach the Cowboys. Kay and Jimmy Johnson's flight from Miami to Dallas had been as clandestine as a CIA operation, and they had checked into The Mansion under aliases.

In spite of the supposed secrecy, Jones felt trapped in the hotel suite. The next owner of the Dallas Cowboys could contain himself no longer. Like the sirens of Greek mythology, the city was calling. As they say in Arkansas, Jones was "ready to get out among 'em." He was going to be a big man in this town, he thought. Why not start tonight?

Jones turned to face Johnson and the two women, and ignored his question. "I got this little place I know about," he said, rubbing his hands together. "And, boy, am I hungry for some Mexican. There won't be nobody there tonight. We'll just kinda slide in and slide out of there. Let's go."

Lost in the fast-food neon of Lemmon Avenue was Mia's, known in Dallas as a Tex-Mex joint. Although it has since moved down the street to larger quarters, in 1989 it stood at the end of a nondescript strip shopping center and was barely noticeable from the street. Mia's appeared to be just another hole-in-the-wall where a man in the public eye could get lost. But looks can be deceiving.

Only a few steps inside the front door, the foursome was spotted by *Dallas Morning News* college football writer Ivan Maisel. Maisel had spent the better part of the afternoon staking out The Mansion's lobby on the strength of a rumor, hoping to catch Johnson off guard. He had questions about unconfirmed reports that Johnson would replace Landry. After several hours, Maisel and his fiancee, Meg Murray, had decided to give up and dine out. Of all places, they chose Mia's.

Contrary to Jones's prediction, the restaurant was packed wall-to-wall with people. His party squeezed into a small opening next to the register and ordered a round of beers. Soon, Maisel walked up behind Johnson and tapped him on the shoulder. Johnson turned, then said, "Oh, shit. What are you doing here?"

"I live a block from here," Maisel said dryly. "What are you doing here?"

After the two parties were seated, Maisel began his search for a telephone. Trying not to alert either Jones or Johnson, he avoided their table by exiting through the kitchen. He then jogged down a back alley to a nearby Chinese restaurant, where he found a phone. He called assistant sports editor Chris Worthington, who dispatched a photographer to the restaurant. "My face was white and my stomach was churning," Maisel said later. "Because this was a story that every reporter in town was trying to get."

Less than fifteen minutes later, the photographer stood in front of the table, preparing to shoot. Johnson protested. "No, no, no, we don't need this! Jerry, dammit, tell him we don't need this!" Jones, grinning from ear to ear, said, "Aw, go ahead and shoot. This is a done deal."

As she left the restaurant, Meg Murray asked the cashier if she knew where Jimmy and Jerry had heard about Mia's. "Oh, maybe Coach Landry told them about us," the cashier said. Mia's just happened to be Tom and Alicia Landry's favorite Tex-Mex place. But Tom Landry telling Jones and Johnson about Mia's was as likely as President Bill Clinton inviting Rush Limbaugh to the White House for dinner.

OWNING AN NFL TEAM HAD BEEN JERRY JONES'S DREAM SINCE HE played for the Arkansas Razorbacks in the early 1960s. In the oil fields in the 1970s, Jones told anybody who'd listen that someday he would be a power broker in pro sports. As early as 1982, he had started sharing his blueprint with his old college roommate Jimmy Johnson, who was then head coach at Oklahoma State. Jones did quite a bit of gas drilling in Oklahoma and had stayed in touch with Johnson. One afternoon at a bar in Oklahoma City, Jones told him, "You just keep doing what you do best—coaching—and I'll just keep doing what I do best—making money. And one of these days we'll get together in the NFL."

Until Saturday morning, Jones and the Cowboys' current owner, H. R. "Bum" Bright, had only a handshake agreement. But Jones had known since Thursday morning that nothing could derail the deal.

One factor in Jones's favor as he maneuvered to land the Cowboys was that his first order of business would be to fire the coach. Bright hated Landry and had ordered Cowboys general manager Tex Schramm to fire him several times. Bright felt that Landry was too old to coach at age sixty-four, and that his offensive and defensive systems had gone stale. Bright once said he was "horrified" by Landry's play-calling.

But there was a much larger burr under Bright's saddle. He felt shunned and ignored by Landry, who barely acknowledged him during the team's annual Christmas parties, or anywhere else. "In the five years I owned the team, I talked to Tom Landry for a total of fifteen minutes," Bright says now. None of the other prospective buyers had even discussed firing Landry.

Bright is a stump of a man with a short, thick neck. He wears black horn-rimmed glasses and a crewcut that dates to his days as a member of the Texas A&M Aggie Corps. He speaks in a nasal foghorn voice. In his heyday, Bright was an ornery, no-nonsense Dallas businessman who found wealth in trucking, oil, real estate, and banking. In the early 1980s his oil business was making $8 million a month, but by 1989 his financial empire was crumbling. His bank was in utter disarray, having suffered catastrophic real estate losses. On the day he sold the team to Jones, Bright Banc was being run by federal regulators as part of the government-supported bailout of the beleaguered savings and loan industry. His net worth had plummeted from $600 million to $300 million.

Bright was motivated to sell for the same reason that forced original Cowboys' owner Clint Murchison Jr. out in 1984. He was in financial free fall and the ground was coming up fast.

"He had turned completely sour against the Cowboys," says one acquaintance. "He wanted nothing to do with them. That is the biggest reason that he kept Tex (Schramm) and Landry in the dark. He hated the way that Schramm had spent money. But he hated Landry the most."

Schramm was the most powerful general manager in the NFL. He ran the Cowboys like an owner and even held the team's voting power at league meetings. Cowboys' executives were known for having enormous expense accounts and regularly entertaining friends and members of the media. Personnel director Gil Brandt had the largest annual scouting budget in the NFL, more than $3 million. Brandt spent hundreds of thousands of dollars on miscellaneous expenses, and even rented a suite at the NCAA Final Four basketball tournament just to entertain college coaches. The Cowboys spent more than $1 million a year to train every summer in Thousand Oaks, California.

With Murchison ready to sell in 1983, Schramm had hand-picked Bright to buy the Cowboys. When Bright initially scoffed at the notion, saying he had attended only two Cowboys games in his life, Schramm said, "Clint wants *you* to buy the Cowboys." Bright relented when he was persuaded that there was enough depreciation in the team to be used as a tax write-off for his booming oil business. He put together a partnership, and before long, he began buying out some of the smaller investors until he held 41 percent of the team.

He soon learned that the Cowboys were a much more expensive proposition than he had expected. In 1988, the last year he was the principal owner, the team lost $9 million. More than ninety of the luxury crown suites that Bright had constructed above the rim of the stadium were sitting empty. Attendance had dropped almost 25 percent from 1984 through 1988. Only one home game had sold out in 1988.

Most of the team's financial problems were due to their failure to win consistently in the late eighties. Bright clearly had an ax to grind with Schramm regarding the way he ran the team. To get even, Bright pursued his negotiations with Jones without telling Schramm. Bright had even told Jones he didn't want him spotted around town. Schramm had written off Jones as a viable candidate, believing he didn't have enough up-front capital to meet Bright's asking price, even though a potential deal had been reported two months earlier in the *Dallas Times Herald*.

When Channel 5 sportscaster Scott Murray aired the story that Jones was about to buy the team on Thursday night, forty-eight hours before the deal was final, Schramm was both shocked and confused. He received a phone call at home from Channel 8, WFAA-TV sportscaster Dale Hansen. Schramm told Hansen, "Your little friend over in Fort Worth (Murray) just made the biggest mistake of his entire professional life." A member of the Cowboys' public relations staff was also telling reporters, "Channel 5 just stepped in it."

For weeks, Schramm had been trying to organize an ownership group to buy the Cowboys, hoping to save the team's management structure. He had encouraged former Cowboys' quarterback Roger Staubach, who owns one of Dallas's most successful real estate companies, to organize a group of potential investors.

Staubach made some phone calls, but soon dropped the project when he found little interest.

It wasn't until Friday morning that Schramm finally got the definite word on the Jones deal. And it came all the way from Miami. Just the day before, Johnson had called Miami Dolphins coach Don Shula to say he was putting together a coaching staff for the Cowboys. He wanted to hire two of his assistants, linebackers coach Dave Wannstedt, along with Shula's son, David, the quarterbacks coach. Don Shula happens to be Schramm's best friend. So Shula placed a call to the Cowboys' general manager at Valley Ranch to let him know the deal was almost done.

The future was now scrambled. "We'd better get ready for some big changes around here," Schramm told public relations director Doug Todd.

THE NEXT MORNING, AS LANDRY WAS EATING A LARGE BOWL OF oatmeal, his wife Alicia handed him the Saturday edition of the *Dallas Morning News*. From the front page, Johnson and Jones seemed to be thumbing their noses at the legendary coach. Jones smiled like a cat locked in canary heaven.

Landry shook his head. He said to his wife, "How in the world could they have found out about Mia's? I didn't think anyone went there but us." Landry had known for more than a year that the Cowboys were for sale. But two prospective buyers, movie magnate Marvin Davis and Bob Tisch, the CEO of the Loews Corporation, had backed out. Word in business circles was that Bright's asking price of $180 million was too high. Bright had talked to more than seventy-five prospective buyers and seemed to be getting nowhere fast. Landry had never heard of Jerry Jones until the Channel 5 story.

After a five-minute drive to the Daljet facility at Love Field, Tom, Alicia, and Tom Landry Jr. began loading golf clubs and luggage into the family's airplane. After getting clearance from the tower, Landry aimed his Cessna 210 down the Love Field runway and into the blue Texas sky. Cowboys' president Tex Schramm had called that morning and asked him to "stay close, just in case something happens." But Landry had decided to fly the family to their getaway home near Austin in Lakeway Hills. He still couldn't figure out how an obscure, fast-talking wheeler-dealer from Arkansas could wind up owning the Dallas Cowboys. And how could he possibly fire the head coach with the second-highest number of wins in the history of the National Football League?

With his focus locked on the gauges of the instrument panel, Landry tried not to think about the Cowboys. The flat plains stretched for almost two hundred miles before meeting the Hill Country just north of Austin. Less than two hours later, Landry put the plane down safely. Now, on the ground at Lakeway, their plan was to play golf that afternoon at the Hidden Hills course and to forget the storm brewing back in Dallas.

At approximately the same time that Landry's Cessna had banked away from Love Field and headed south toward Austin, the Cowboys deal had been going down a few hundred feet below at the Bright Banc on Stemmons Freeway. Jones and Johnson had arrived at the executive offices—just five miles west of Love Field—at six that morning. By the time the Landrys flew over, the final details had been negotiated and Jones was signing the papers. The Cowboys' blueprint of the past twenty-nine years was now in ashes.

After the deal was done and the lawyers and secretaries had left the office, Jones looked across the desk at Bright and said, "Let me ask you. If I had kept negotiating, is there anything you would have given in on?"

Bright looked at him, then said, "Oh, about $300,000."

"Let's flip for it," Jones said.

Bright pulled out a coin, called heads, and tossed it in the air. The coin landed in an ashtray, heads up.

Meanwhile, Schramm had arrived at the executive offices. He took one look at Johnson and said, "You need to get your ass out of town. You people have embarrassed Tom Landry enough already."

That afternoon, with reporters milling around the downstairs lobby, Jones and Schramm followed a fire exit into the back parking lot. Ten minutes later, they took off in Jones's private Lear Jet to find Landry. Schramm had called ahead to tell Landry that he and Jones were flying down to discuss the Cowboys' future. After landing at the Austin airport, they rented a car and headed for Hidden Hills. The drive took more than an hour.

It was nearly dark when the car pulled up to the putting green. The Hidden Hills golf course was virtually abandoned except for Tom Landry and Tom Landry Jr. Two other men were still practicing their putting. The Landrys had arranged to have the meeting in a sales office about 250 feet from the practice green.

Landry and Jones sat face to face. Tom Jr. and Schramm stood. "This is with absolutely no disrespect to you," Jones said. "But I'm here and so is Jimmy."

Landry tried to remain calm, but couldn't. "You could have saved your plane trip down here," he said heatedly. "As a matter of fact, you could have handled this whole thing a lot better. This whole thing is just a bunch of grandstand tactics. You had no obligation to do this. You could have saved your gas." He and Jones stood up. Schramm and Landry shook hands, and both men began to cry.

In *God's Coach*, Skip Bayless's 1990 book about Landry, Jones is quoted as saying he was worried about a large crowd that had gathered outside the sales office. He compared the crowd, which he said included Landry's wife, Alicia, and daughter, Lisa, to a lynch mob. Both Alicia and Lisa were sobbing, says Jones. He says, "Walking back to the car past all of those people outside was the longest walk of my life."

But according to both Schramm and Landry, there was no such crowd. Schramm says that no one was in the area when he and Jones began walking back to the rental car. "I don't know why Jerry would want to make up a story like that," he says. "But he has a tendency to do that."

Recently, when asked for his recollections of the events, Jones said, "It all happened pretty fast and I don't remember much." It does appear that he was so flustered that he tried unsuccessfully for several minutes to jiggle a key into the door of the wrong car. At any rate, he had just become known as The Man Who Fired Tom Landry.

Back at the Cowboys' complex in Valley Ranch, the press was getting itchy. Jones used Schramm's private lavatory to shave. Schramm then called in public relations director Doug Todd to brief Jones on what to expect from the media mob. Jones was now wearing a freshly starched shirt. He knotted his tie in the reflection of the ten-foot office glass window. "You'll enter the room and there will be a dais on the right," Todd began. "And over here will be a row of chairs …"

"Hold on," Jones said brusquely. "I can handle it. I can handle it."

Todd remembered later, "It was like he was saying, 'Go away, little boy, go away.'"

That night, Jones faced the largest media contingent in the history of the Cowboys. It would become known as the Saturday Night Massacre. All three local network TV affiliates broke away from regular programming to carry the news conference live. What Jones said that night still haunts him. He opened with a rambling seven-minute address that didn't mention Tom Landry or his firing once. When Jones said, "I feel like it's Christmas," he didn't realize the sale of the team was second-page news compared to the Landry dismissal.

He also raised a few eyebrows when he talked about his college relationship with Jimmy Johnson. "We have known each other for twenty-five years," he said. "In fact, we'd be laying in bed in college together—and I told him then that I always wanted to be in the football business." He also said, "The facts are that I wouldn't have been an owner if Jim Johnson wasn't the head coach." Clearly, he had not considered keeping Landry on as his coach for a second.

A reference to "socks and jocks" would become his legacy. "I intend to have an understanding of the player situation," he said. "I intend to have an understanding of socks and jocks …" For years, he would be known as "Socks and Jocks Jones." Jones had bloodshot eyes, and looked tired. Fatigue may have contributed to his awkward and disjointed statements—like this one, about

Johnson: "He doesn't fish much, and he doesn't play golf much. He footballs." And this one: "Coaching is so fortunate to have him. Doctoring, the medical profession, could have a Jimmy Johnson, a surgeon or an engineer." On overlooking Landry in his opening address, Jones said, "Boy, there is a very important person missing in this question session about Tom—and that's Tom." Asked if Landry had been offered a job in the organization, Jones said, "We haven't gone beyond the very awkward, just basically trying to say something basically that you just can't say, that I'm here and so is Jimmy."

Following his introduction of Jones, Schramm had turned to find his chair behind the dais. But it had been taken by minority owner Ed A. Smith, who showed up at the last minute. (Smith had once asked Landry if he could give the team a pre-game pep talk. Landry flatly refused.) Schramm was left to sit awkwardly in the corner on a file cabinet. Asked where Schramm now stood with the organization, Jones pointed over his right shoulder and said oddly, "He's standing a little behind me tonight."

Around midnight, after the newspaper stories had been filed, Schramm held a party in his executive office with about fifteen writers. The scotch and beer flowed. But the mood was more like a wake. Schramm sat in the middle of the office, head bowed, looking like a man who had gone fifteen rounds with Muhammad Ali.

"I have a lot of work to do with this son-of-a-bitch," he said, referring to Jones. "Goddammit, I just can't believe he would say those things."

Bernie Miklasz, the *Dallas Morning News* beat writer, said, "You know, Tex, he kind of reminds me of a young Bob Irsay." Irsay is the volatile owner of the Indianapolis Colts, who, without warning, moved his team out of Baltimore to Indianapolis in the middle of a snowy January night in 1984. He once barged into the team's coaching booth in the press box to call plays.

Far down the hallway, some of Jones's family and friends were watching a replay of the ten o'clock news. They cheered wildly with every mention of Jones, just as they had done hours earlier at the news conference. However, as they heard the skeptical remarks about Jones from reporters and anchors, the mood turned somber. "Oh, my God," one said. "Let's get out of here." They moved quickly through the front door and into the darkness of early morning.

★ ★ ★

ON SUNDAY MORNING, THE LANDRYS FLEW BACK TO DALLAS FROM Austin. The Cowboys' ex-coach headed straight for the Cowboys' complex. That afternoon, he began packing twenty-nine years of memories into boxes. The blinds to the office windows had been closed, and the office lights were dim. Walls that had been lined with framed pictures and other memorabilia were bare.

This Landry was a dramatically different one than the man America was used to seeing standing erect and resolute on the Cowboys sideline. He was casually dressed, slump-shouldered, and looked like a man in shock.

"It hurts," Landry said, his eyes misting over. "But I don't feel bitterness right now. I try not to feel bad when things happen that I have no control over. I always accept things as they are, so I don't worry. Besides, Jones and Johnson were buddies and this was going to happen." As he continued to pack, a noisy group passed in the hall, unaware that Landry was just inside the door. Some were laughing loudly. It was several of Jones's family members and friends, who were touring the building.

The following morning, Cowboys players trudged into the auditorium where Jones had held his infamous news conference two nights earlier. They waited for their coach without speaking.

"I put on a big hooded sweatshirt and sat in the corner," linebacker Jeff Rohrer says. "I knew that I was going to cry. I don't think there was a dry eye in the room when he finished. There were some guys who felt that it was time for Landry to get his. He had been giving guys shit for years in team meetings. But years later, the guys who wanted to see him go finally realized they were idiots. Tom Landry was an incredible guy."

This morning Landry was more composed, and had dressed in a coat and tie. He spoke to his players for more than fifteen minutes. He told the team that he'd looked forward to bringing them back from the 3-13 season. As he finished, tears welled in his eyes. "I thought the hardest thing I'd ever do was tell ya'll guys good-bye," he said. "You're a great bunch of football players. This is a pretty tough moment for me." As Landry wiped his eyes, the more than fifty players, many of them in tears, gave him a standing ovation.

He spent the next hour saying individual farewells to the players in the locker room and weight training area. Eventually there was some laughing and joking.

For the next two hours, Landry sat in the office with bare walls and shelves and traded hugs and handshakes with well-wishers. Friends and Cowboys' employees cried openly in the hallways. Then, for more than thirty minutes, he did live TV interview after interview in the misting rain outside. At one o'clock, with dozens of TV cameras rolling, he emerged again from his office. This would be his final exit. Atop his head was the familiar snap-brim hat. The media horde followed him through the front door. As he backed his car from the parking space marked LANDRY and pulled away, he rolled down the window. Some who listened closely expected a philosophical farewell. But he just smiled and said to his son, who was about to leave in his own car, "T. L., I guess I'll see you later." With that, a Cowboys era ended.

MEANWHILE, JONES'S PUBLIC RELATIONS HELL WAS JUST BEGINNING. NFL commissioner Pete Rozelle said of the Landry firing, "This is like Lombardi's death." An editorial in the *Dallas Morning News* began, "Shock. Disbelief. Anger." Columnist Frank Luksa wrote in the *Dallas Times Herald*, "Landry brought more than victory and glory and fame to the Cowboys. Of all his human qualities, I think now of dignity and thoughtfulness. I think of those traits because of the undignified, thoughtless manner he was fired Saturday." In the *Philadelphia Inquirer*, columnist Bill Lyon wrote, "Tom Landry is a certified coaching legend. There will come a day when the new owner of the Dallas Cowboys will sorely regret his impetuosity." Linebacker Jeff Rohrer said, "You could take two people with IQs of three, put them in a room together and let them brainstorm for ten minutes, and they could have found a better way to fire Tom Landry." According to *Morning News* columnist Dave Casstevens, Jones was "dumber than a box of rocks, public relations-wise."

Doug Todd was sitting in the Cowboys p.r. office on the morning after the Saturday Night Massacre, chain-smoking and sorting through the rubble, when Jack Dixon walked in. One of Jones's trusted friends from Arkansas, Dixon would soon be named the club's treasurer.

"Sure had a lot of people there Saturday night," Dixon said. "I can't believe we got that much publicity."

"Yeah," Todd grunted.

"You know," Dixon continued, "Since the iron's so hot, Jerry wants to take advantage of the situation. He'd like to go on all of the talk shows, do whatever the media wants."

That did it. "Wait a minute," Todd snapped. "Did you happen to read the newspapers this morning? Do you know what they're saying about this guy all over the Dallas, all over the country." Todd took a breath, then said, "I'll have to talk to Tex."

"No," Dixon said. "There is no longer any reason to talk to Tex." He turned and walked out the door.

Two days after the Saturday Night Massacre, Jones traveled back to Little Rock to address the Arkansas legislature. He mentioned during the speech that he'd already received two death threats in Dallas. "They were an emotional reaction to Coach Landry," he said.

Jones's actions were getting a thumbs-down across Dallas. Psychologist Franklin Lewis, who had worked in the city for seventeen years, said, "Virtually every patient I see, male and female, eventually gets around to mentioning Jerry Jones in a less than endearing way."

One of the first to arrive in Dallas with Jones was Mike McCoy, his partner in the oil and gas-drilling business since 1980. McCoy remembered seeing the pain on Jones's face away from the public eye. "He certainly suffered more than he let on in public," McCoys says. "No one wants to be portrayed as an idiot, especially from coast to coast. And that is what Jerry was portrayed as for several months—an idiot. I think that other than his family and friends, no one really knew how bad he was hurting. I could see it. Not that Jerry would sit down and say, 'Boy, I'm having a hard day.' But it was there."

JEFFREY CHARLES ROHRER WAS A HARD-HITTING COWBOYS OUTSIDE linebacker. At heart, though, he was a beachboy from Manhattan Beach, California. Growing up just a few blocks from the Pacific, he loved to surf. His father was a lifeguard. To further complicate this personality portfolio, Rohrer had received a degree from Yale in administrative sciences.

Of his six seasons with the Cowboys, Rohrer now says, "I was the bad boy. I was the crazy kid. I was the smartass."

Two days after Jones bought the team, Rohrer was pumping iron in the Cowboys' weight room when a TV crew from Channel 8 approached. Never shy, Rohrer began singing a song that had been on his mind the last couple of days. With the camera rolling, he began:

> *The first thing you know ol' Jer's a millionaire.*
> *The kinfolks said, Jer, move away from here!*
> *They said, Dallas, Texas, is the place you wanna be!*
> *So he hopped in his Lear and bought America's team.*

It was a takeoff on the theme song of *The Beverly Hillbillies*, the hugely popular sixties sitcom about a poor family from Tennessee that struck it rich and moved to Beverly Hills when (appropriately enough) oil was discovered on their land. The patriarch of the family was Jedd Clampett. But the name that would be attached to Jerry Jones was "Jethro"—as in Jethro Bodine, the hay-seed nephew played by Max Baer Jr. In the sitcom, Jethro was a kind of Lil' Abner thrust into the Beverly Hills jetset.

After Channel 8 aired their story that night, Jerry Jones became known as "Jethro" everywhere in Dallas. Some called him "The Eighth Blunder of the World." Two popular bumper stickers around Dallas read "Money Can't Buy Class, Mr. Jones" and "The Dallas Cowboys ... From One Bum to Another."

Six months later, during training camp in Thousand Oaks, California, Rohrer was cut by the Cowboys.

"It cost me my job," Rohrer claims. "I had a lot of bad things going. Number one, I was coming off an injury. Number two, I was making a lot of money. And number three, I had a big mouth. I heard from the inside that I was gone regardless of how I performed during training camp. Jimmy and Jerry had a thing going. They didn't want any smartasses around."

Years later, though, during a visit to Dallas from Los Angeles, where he is an independent television producer, Rohrer approached Jones at a bar close to Texas Stadium.

"I told him that I probably shouldn't have said the things I said and that I shouldn't have sung that song back in 1989," Rohrer says. "And he said those first couple of days in Dallas didn't come off as well as he'd hoped. We're on speaking terms now."

NOW IN HIS EARLY SEVENTIES, TOM LANDRY MAINTAINS A GRUELING pace, zigzagging across America and making speeches for just about anyone who asks. He is still immensely popular. During a three-month stretch early in 1995, Landry was scheduled to spend no more than twelve days at home. He speaks on behalf of several organizations, including the Fellowship of Christian Athletes. He is chairman of the Dallas International Sports Commission and runs the Landry Investment Group. And on nearly every Sunday he shares his testimony—in one of the scores of churches he speaks in all over America.

Landry continues to do most of his own flying in a four-seat Cessna 210. Returning from Austin with his family on March 3, 1995, the plane's lone engine conked out.

Fortunately, Landry was able to draw upon his World War II flying experience. As a twenty-year-old pilot, he had successfully crash-landed a B-17 bomber in France. Flying through heavy flak, he spotted an opening in the trees and set the plane down. The plane's belly plowed the ground for more than one hundred feet, and both wings were sheared off by trees. When the nose of the plane came to rest at the base of a tree, everyone in the plane began to shout. The entire crew was safe.

Fifty years later, he was trying to find tiny Ennis Airport, just south of Dallas, for an emergency landing. But as the plane broke through the low clouds, Landry realized he was more than five miles south of the airport. Just as he had fifty years ago, he found an opening in the trees and put the plane down—on the Ennis High football practice field, of all places. The landing went so smoothly that his young granddaughter, age four, riding in the backseat, didn't wake up. Landry even avoided the muddy part of the football field. The same could not be said for the Dallas TV news trucks, which started arriving thirty minutes later and had to be towed out of the mess.

As Frank Luksa said, "Landry continues to fly with angels."

Other than agreeing to enter the team's Ring of Honor in 1993, Landry has closed the door on Jerry Jones and the Cowboys. Since being fired in 1989, he has made only two trips to Texas Stadium, once for his own induction, and again the following year for the induction of ex-Cowboys Randy White and Tony Dorsett.

For more than three years, Landry had balked at Jones' invitation to enter the honorary ring. Publicly, Landry said he was just too busy to be inducted. In spite of former Cowboy quarterback Roger Staubach's efforts to convince him otherwise, Landry refused. Jones had asked Staubach to act as a mediator between the Cowboys and Landry.

"Every time I brought up the Ring of Honor to Alicia Landry, she would just run away from me," Staubach says. "There were some hard feelings for Jerry on the part of both of them."

Landry sent word to Jones through Staubach that he would accept the invitation if former Cowboys' president Tex Schramm and deceased owner Clint Murchison Jr. were also included. Jones flatly said no. "I thought that he should at least put Tex in," Landry said. "He was the architect of the team." Not only is Schramm still outside the ring, but Jones shows no inclination to induct him.

But eventually Landry gave in and agreed to his induction. "It's just that now the timing is right," he said afterwards, rather cryptically. But a large part of the credit must go to many of his former players, who encouraged him to accept the honor. As legendary '60s wide receiver "Bullet" Bob Hayes said, "We've been pulling on his coat a long time, telling him to get his butt off that ego, and bring him back where he belongs."

In spite of the distance he maintains from Jones and the Cowboys, Landry says he harbors no bitterness. But he also says, "Jerry and those people are just different than me. I don't know why they do some of the things they do. All the same, there is nothing that says that I have to be around them. You can't hate them for what they are. It is hard for me to hate a person. But it just seems that he took over the team and kicked a lot of people out and then he locked the doors. Of course, he is winning. So he just feels that he can do whatever he wants to do."

More than six years have passed since Jones flew into the Texas Hill Country to fire the coaching legend. Landry said he has put that painful night behind him. But he also says, "I still don't agree with it. But again, he bought the Cowboys and paid a pretty good price for them. So he had the right to do whatever he wanted to do. I still don't understand why he wanted to do it himself. He could have done it in a better way than he did. His treatment of Tex and everybody else was bad. I didn't feel so bad about myself. But I felt extremely bad about Tex. The way he handled Tex in the press conference just wasn't right. He could have done a better job with everything."

Neither Bright nor Murchison focused on the bottom line during Landry's twenty-nine years of coaching. Bright admitted he initially bought the team for a tax write-off. Murchison owned the team from 1960 to 1984 and made only one trip to the executive offices. He gave the coach a ten-year contract in 1964 when Landry's record was 13–38–1.

But it is clear that Jones has different priorities. He is obsessed with controlling the Cowboys and turning huge profits. He has used virtually every marketing and sales tool at his disposal to do so. Of this incessant drive for profit-making, Landry says, "He seems to only measure himself when it comes to money. That is not right. Of course, he is not the only person in our country who does that. But at the same time, all you hear about him is the amount of money he's trying to make."

Asked if he prays for Jones, Landry pauses. Then he says, "Yes, I pray for Jerry, and people like Jerry, because I believe that we all need a spiritual approach. Whether he has one or not, I don't know."

CHAPTER 7

A Walking Contradiction

SOME SAY THAT JERRY JONES WASN'T REALLY BORN IN LOS ANGELES and raised on the second floor of an Arkansas drive-in fruit stand. They say he invented himself. The more he saw of life, the more he wanted. And the higher he climbed, the more expansive his vision became.

From the first day he walked into the Cowboys complex, Jones has proven that he can sell, sell, sell. Of course, his selling skills and his deal-making abilities shouldn't be surprising, given his background. After all, he's been smiling and selling since the late forties, when as a nine-year-old he greeted customers at the family supermarket back in Arkansas. In college, he sold shoes from the trunk of his car. He would make up to $700 selling student tickets before his college football games. He often dashed from the locker room in full gear just fifteen minutes before kickoff to make sure his customers got through the players' gate. He has sold virtually everything under the sun, from chickens to real estate.

"I grew up with a philosophy that I still use," he says. "Have a big front door and a small back door." This philosophy has brought Jones great success—but gained him a reputation for putting money above everything else. As long-time Associated Press sports-writer Denne Freeman says, "He's slicker than stewed okra."

★ ★ ★

JONES IS AN ADRENALINE-CHARGED BLUR OF A MAN. HE CAN accomplish more on two hours of sleep than most men can on a full night. He begins the morning with several cups of coffee at home. On the way to the office, he stops at a convenience store for the biggest travel cup he can find. The caffeine-loading doesn't stop there. He is rarely without a large plastic cup of iced tea around the office. Somehow, Jones can work on five different projects at once and manage to keep track of each one—and he's never afraid to make a decision and pull the trigger. He calls these caffeine-wired frenetic times his "peak-on-peak modes." Wild-eyed, his hands moving a hundred miles an hour, his mouth in a wide, crooked smile, he moves at blinding speed.

In February of 1989, Jones hit the ground running so fast that no one was sure which way he was going. After the Landry firing, word spread like a prairie fire that he was going to clean house at the Cowboys' complex. Five days after purchasing the club, he called the Cowboys' department heads into a large conference room that had been transformed into his personal office. He was introduced around the room by then-president Tex Schramm.

Rising from his chair and folding his hands in front of him, Jones said, "The key thing is that I need you more than you need me. There will not be any more changes in this office. I really don't know how to run a football team. I need all of you."

After the meeting, Jones emerged into the hallway to meet a handful of reporters. He told them, "I need those people as much as they need me. There shouldn't be any worries around here."

Seven weeks later, six of the eleven employees who attended the meeting had been fired by Jones. Schramm read the handwriting on the wall and resigned. Vice president Joe Bailey also quit, saying, "I don't know what more I could do." Personnel director Bob Ackles lasted eighteen more months before he was fired. Administrative director Steve Orisini and counseling services director Larry Wansley eventually resigned on their own. Within three years, all eleven employees who had attended that meeting were gone.

Public relations director Doug Todd had no warning about his fate. Three weeks after attending the meeting in Jones's makeshift office, he had a one-on-one talk with the Cowboys owner. Jones told him, "Everything I've heard about your department is number one." Jones gave Todd, who had worked for the Cowboys for eighteen years, the thumbs-up sign.

On April 27, Todd received a call from Jones's secretary. "Mr. Jones would like to see you in his office," she said. The day before, treasurer Don Wilson had received his letter of dismissal. It had been written by Jack Dixon, the man who would replace him.

"This is not going to be a good meeting," Jones told Todd. Then, abruptly, he said, "You're not going to be with us."

"Huh?" Todd said. "I don't understand."

"We're making changes and you're not going to be with us," Jones said. "We're going to be lean and mean."

Not until Jones received a phone call from NFL commissioner Pete Rozelle did Todd receive his severance pay from the Cowboys. Just a few months later, in June, the NFL passed what is still called the "Jerry Jones rule," which denies prospective owners the right to make substantial changes in a franchise before ownership is approved by the league.

Jones moved aggressively but blindly in 1989. His strategy was to change everything—a philosophy radically foreign to the folks who had been running America's Team. It was as if the new owner was saying, "Even if it ain't broke, fix it anyway." He took a wrecking ball to the past. Within a year, the only things still standing in the Cowboys' rambling 80,000-square-foot-complex were the walls.

"You could tell right from the beginning that he didn't give a damn about history," former general manager Tex Schramm says. "You can tell this man has absolutely no feeling for the past. You almost expected him to take the stars off the helmets."

In setting about his new job, Jones did little research on how the Cowboys had been run before, or how other successful franchises had operated. He was worried that studying the past might cloud his judgment and paralyze his thought processes. He was going to run the Cowboys just as he had wildcatted back in the dusty Oklahoma oilfields. He would put the bit in the ground and drill until he hit something—whether it was dry rock or black gold. The oil-field gambler rolled up his sleeves and went to work. By busting his butt, trusting his gut instincts, and out-working the competition, Jones figured the gushers would come.

Dallas sports psychologist Don Beck is fascinated by Jones. "He really has the oil patch mentality," says Beck. "He's a raw, rugged entrepreneur. From the oil patch, you learn to make the fast deal and the quick buck."

"I made the decision to run this football team without NFL football experience," Jones says. "I didn't know that some of the things we would try couldn't be done. No one sat down with me and told me, 'There's no way you can have this organization put together the way you want it if you don't get some longtime NFL experience.' I thought the way we were doing it was the only way we could do it."

Respected front-office executives like Schramm, who knew the ropes about operating a franchise, were out of the building within weeks after Jones bought the team. Between Schramm and Bailey alone, the Cowboys lost more than fifty years of combined experience in managing a professional football team.

"When I came in here, there was absolutely no handbook on how to run a NFL team," Jones says. "If you had tried to do things in a traditional way, you could make a case that it just wouldn't have worked out. I came in here with the purpose of rolling the dice. And to be honest, I really don't care how people around the league feel about that. That is just my way of doing business. I didn't see any other way of doing business and making money."

Back in 1989, he didn't care that he had no road map or compass to guide him. He didn't want Schramm around to tell him how to run the Cowboys. Getting lost was the least of his worries. (Although it did happen. While walking the labyrinthine hallways of the Cowboys complex a few weeks after buying the team, Jones got lost in the maze. He picked up the nearest phone and called his secretary. "I'm at extension 43," he said. "Come find me.")

Jones further alienated himself from the football establishment by flaunting his new and radical methods. He didn't care how things had been done before. He was duty-bound and hell-bent to make changes. It didn't matter how many doors he was going to knock down, or how many fights he would start.

Suddenly, Jones was a stranger in a strange land. Many Texans had a hard time accepting the fact that an upstart from Arkansas had grabbed the reins of one of their state treasures. ABC's Sam Donaldson described Jones as "an invader from Arkansas." Even though Texas and Arkansas abut at a small cross-roads town called Texarkana, the two states could not be more different. Dallas has a flat terrain and earnestly cultivates a cosmopolitan image. Little Rock has rolling hills and a small-town quaintness. Texans think of Arkansans as backwards people from a backwater state. So it wasn't surprising that Jones got the cold shoulder wherever he turned.

Naturally, many of his moves were roundly criticized. The Dallas media pounced on each mistake like wild dogs on a bone. Jones even received several death threats during his first few weeks on the job. When he was out to dinner one night in Dallas, a little old lady walked up and kicked him in the shin. She was upset with his handling of the Landry firing. Jones laughed, but felt more like crying.

Although he walked the streets of Dallas with a broad smile back in 1989, there was fear in his heart. "It was hard on me," he admits now. "But I knew that I would be a failure for the rest of my life if I ever had to back off from owning the Dallas Cowboys, running the Cowboys, and making them work. The fear factor really came into play much more so than anything that had ever happened to me. What if I'd had to go home to Arkansas to tell people that I'd failed? Would my spirit have been broken? I thought about it every day. But I was going to do it my way because I don't think it would have worked any other way."

From the start, Jones' biggest challenge was to turn the Cowboys around—and turn them around fast. The first step would be to return the Cowboys team he and Johnson had inherited from Landry and Schramm to its former greatness. Jones knew that all of his marketing gambits depended on putting a top-notch competitive team out on the field. And he knew he was embarking on a major-league gamble—that he and his staff would need to evaluate football talent and desire as well as he, Mike McCoy, and Bill Sparks had read drilling maps. It would take all of his oil-patch instincts, deal-making savvy, and plenty of quick bucks to make his enormous investment in the Cowboys pay off.

Leigh Steinberg knew he had an Arkansas Razorback by the tail. He had been introduced to Jerry Jones just that afternoon, but Steinberg felt like he had already made a valuable connection. Now the conversation was flying non-stop across a tiny table inside a hotel bar at the Dallas-Fort Worth International Airport. Midnight was approaching, but no one mentioned the time. Coach Jimmy Johnson was also at the table. Dinner had been written off hours ago, and now the three were munching on potato chips and popcorn, and chugging cold beers almost as fast as they could be served. Judging from the scattered empty bottles and cellophane wrappers on the table, they could have been a threesome in a late-night bowling league rehashing their missed splits. Instead, it was a sports economic summit focusing on a mega-million dollar deal. At stake was the Cowboys' ability to sign Troy Aikman, one of the best college quarterbacks to hit the league in several years, and the Cowboys' most likely first pick in the upcoming April 1989 NFL draft.

Steinberg, an affable, laid-back West Coast sports agent, is far more comfortable in blue jeans than suits, but sports executives have learned not to be fooled by his casual dress. He is a tough negotiator who also understands that deal-making is not always cut and dried. Steinberg is the master of the creative deal. His success can be measured by the large number of NFL quarterbacks in his stable, including Aikman and San Francisco's Steve Young, both Super Bowl MVPs. In the last seven NFL drafts, Steinberg has represented six of the seven top picks, including Penn State running back Ki-Jana Carter in 1995.

Six years after that all-night meeting in 1989, Steinberg has nothing but praise for Jones and the way he does business. "I have a keen ability to stay up all night and to outlast general managers and owners," he says. "But here was somebody who was right there with me. He was sharp. Here was one extraordinary individual. He didn't seem to waver as we moved right on into the night. Even from the start, it was exhilarating just to talk to Jerry Jones."

The conversation had begun late in the afternoon back at Jones's executive office at the Cowboys' complex at Valley Ranch. Jones had just returned that day from Washington, D.C., where he'd met President George Bush. A staunch Republican, Jones swaggered into the meeting with Steinberg and began spinning stories about his trip to the White House.

"I just told ol' George," Jones began, "That the best measure of a man is when he's on one knee." Jones knelt on his right knee and grinned at his audience. "I told him that any successful man can find an easy way to live. But the man who's got to get up from one knee, well, that's the true measure of a man. You know, I think ol' George agreed with me." Jones then pumped both arms into the air, stood up, and strode to his chair.

"The impression I had of the guy before meeting him was, 'Here's another Jed Clampett,'" Steinberg says. "Here was a guy who had just besmirched the icon of Tom Landry. I thought he would be all down and depressed about things. But he was running at top speed, like nothing had ever happened."

From the Cowboys' offices, they had driven to the Amfac Hotel where the threesome found a bar to continue their discussion of Aikman. Sure enough, the two o'clock closing time came way too early. They had much more to talk about. At Jones's suggestion, they moved to another table inside the hotel lobby. Jones and Steinberg continued their frenetic conversation, often straying off onto related subjects, both waving their arms to make points. They talked about the need for new blood, more enthusiasm, and a willingness to take risks in the National Football League. It was still 1989, but they were already talking the language of the '90s—how sports franchises could be vertically integrated into other businesses, for instance. They also got around to talking about Aikman's contract.

Out in the lobby, Johnson fell asleep and began to snore. His chin jerked forward like a man bobbing for apples. But Steinberg and Jones barely noticed. Around four o'clock, a hotel employee began to work a noisy vacuum cleaner near their table. Leaping to his feet, Jones bellowed, "Why don't you take your goddamned vacuum cleaner and go vacuum somewhere else! Can't you see we're talking here? If you don't get that goddamned vacuum cleaner out of here, I'm going to calling the fuckin' manager." Even though the vacuum wasn't loud enough to wake Johnson, the man quickly moved his work to another part of the hotel.

"Jones just had this incredible force of energy," Steinberg says admiringly. "Here was a guy who was very charismatic. We'd been drinking for hours and hours and hours. The next thing I knew it was seven-thirty in the morning. Jimmy was still sitting there sleeping. And Jerry and I should have been drunk. But we're still just talking away. It seemed like very little time had passed. We were immersed in the conversation. We talked about everything, including how his chicken and oil business could be helped by the Dallas Cowboys. I didn't think we would ever stop talking."

As negotiations continued in the weeks to come, Steinberg would learn another thing about Jones—that money talk can transform him into a raging Godzilla. Paul Hayward of the *London Times* once described Jones as "an iron man with a vicar's smile."

During a break from the contract negotiations, Jones told the *Dallas Morning News* that Aikman should play for half the money he might expect as the first player drafted. Why? Because, Jones said, Aikman grew up as a Cowboys fan just across the Red River in Oklahoma. Early in April, when negotiations seemed at a stalemate, Jones became so frustrated with Steinberg that he slammed his fist onto his desk one day and declared, "Go ahead, keep it up, goddamn it, and we'll draft Tony Mandarich!" Jones may have been bluffing. It was difficult to tell. Drafting Mandarich, the highly touted offensive tackle from Michigan State would have been disastrous. He was drafted by the Green Bay Packers, never played much, and is now out of football.

Then Jones made an abrupt about-face that shocked Steinberg. He agreed to the deal Aikman and his agent had wanted all along. The Cowboys' owner couldn't wait to tell the media—gleefully—that he'd just signed Aikman to the biggest rookie contract in the history of the National Football League—a deal worth $11 million.

"We were at the news conference and he just sort of blurted it out," Steinberg says. "He instantly understood that his franchise was down. So he had to change. He didn't feel abashed at all that he'd paid Troy so much money. He took a potential negative point and turned it into a positive. The guy just amazes me."

IN THE NEXT CENTURY, NFL HISTORIANS WILL REVIEW JONES'S blueprint for reconstructing the Cowboys and shake their heads. His plan was a total departure from all of the formulas NFL teams had tried in the past. Granted, teams had tried to improve themselves through trades throughout the seventy-odd years of the league's history. But Jones and Johnson went at the trading process like kids in a candy store. The NFL had never seen anything like it.

"You have to understand," says Giants' owner Wellington Mara, who has been in the league since the early 1930s. "We never really had been around anything like those two guys from Dallas. They pretty well turned the league on its ear."

In the first year alone, the Cowboys made twelve trades. Johnson stripped the roster to its bare bones and watched the

Cowboys go 1–15. Many experts believed Dallas could have gone 8–8 by keeping virtually the same roster of players around, along with Landry. But that wasn't the Jones way.

The Cowboys made thirteen trades in 1990 and eight more in 1991. In their first four years on the job, Jones and Johnson completed an unheard-of forty-five trades. But nothing in team history can compare to the blockbuster deal they made in October 1989—one that still has NFL experts shaking their heads. Some have called it the largest and most significant trade in league history.

In 1989 Herschel Walker was considered one of the NFL's true superstars. He was still a darling of the media and fans, having combined for 2,000 rushing and receiving yards the previous season. Walker had come to the Cowboys after the USFL folded in 1986. He signed the biggest NFL contract of his time—$5 million for five years—and was one of the few Cowboys worth watching in the late eighties. In a game against Philadelphia that first season, he had both rushing and receiving touchdowns of 84 yards. Dallas still lost the game.

Early in the 1989 season, Johnson told personnel director Bob Ackles that the Cowboys needed to make a blockbuster deal. Johnson knew the Cowboys were going nowhere fast with their current roster. But their only tradable commodity was Walker. "Jimmy told me that he'd trade Herschel in a New York minute," Ackles says. "Jimmy just wasn't shot in the ass with Herschel. But we didn't know what we could get."

Although Johnson didn't care for Walker or his stiff, upright running style, there were plenty of NFL coaches who coveted him. Late in September, the Cleveland Browns lost running back Kevin Mack for the remainder of the season to a knee injury. Browns' owner Art Modell, believing his team was a Super Bowl contender, called the Cowboys to see if they would be interested in trading Walker. That in turn triggered Johnson's curiosity concerning Walker's trade value around the league. The Cowboys told Modell they would get back to him. Then Ackles and Johnson started perusing the rosters of other teams. Figuring that Minnesota might be looking for a big running back, Ackles called Vikings' general manager Mike Lynn.

"When I got Mike Lynn on the phone and told him we were thinking about trading Herschel, I could almost hear him having an orgasm," Ackles says. "So I told Mike that we needed to do something fast because Cleveland had a great offer on the table. About four hours later, he sent us a fax with the deal we just couldn't believe. We were just absolutely dumbfounded when that offer came into the office."

Lynn's offer seemed too good to be true. "I knew that Mike Lynn was a used car salesman at heart and that he couldn't be trusted," Ackles says. "I knew there had to be a trick there somewhere." Ackles stops to laugh, then continues. "But we were so darn greedy that we actually tried to get more out of Lynn. We tried to take the guy for everything we could."

By now, Jones, Johnson, and Ackles were dancing in the hallways at the Cowboys complex. They had completely forgotten about the Cleveland offer. They privately wondered if Lynn had somehow erred in his faxed proposal.

"I really think that if Mike Lynn had consulted with his coach (Jerry Burns) or his personnel man, Frank Gilliam, he wouldn't have made us that offer," Ackles says. "But he just went off on his own."

The deal went down on October 12th. For Walker, the Cowboys received seven draft choices—three first-rounders, three second-rounders, and a third-round pick from Minnesota. Dallas also got five players. But the eye-popping part of the trade was the seven draft choices. They would be largely responsible for turning the Cowboys around so quickly and winning a Super Bowl within three years. The deals the Cowboys were able to make with those picks eventually brought superstar players like defensive tackle Russell Maryland and Emmitt Smith to Dallas.

"At the time, I knew that some kind of deal was going down on Herschel," says Giants' general manager George Young. "Right before I went to bed that night, I heard about the deal that Minnesota had given Dallas. I didn't sleep at all that night. I knew the Dallas Cowboys weren't going to be down on the bottom very long." Meanwhile, Lynn was predicting that the deal would put the Vikings back into the Super Bowl.

As part of the deal, the Cowboys agreed that for every one of the five ex-Minnesota players they kept past February 1, 1990, they would return one of their seven draft choices to the Vikings. The players were linebacker Jesse Solomon, defensive tackle Alex Stewart, running back Darrin Nelson, linebacker David Howard, and cornerback Isaac Holt. "Lynn thought we would fall in love with the players, keep them all, and give them back the draft choices," cackles Ackles.

Months later, with the February 1 deadline approaching, and the NFL owners meeting in New Orleans, Jones called for a meeting with Lynn. Ackles had prepared a letter to NFL commissioner Paul Tagliabue stating that the Cowboys were going to release all of the players acquired in the trade.

"Mike Lynn always had this nice suntan," Ackles says. "But when Jerry had me hand over that letter to him, the guy turned absolutely pale. He knew he had just made the biggest screw-up in the history of the NFL." Lynn became so frustrated that he told the Cowboys to keep both the players (at the time, only three remained on the roster) and the draft picks. The Cowboys managed to do more than that. Six months earlier, they had traded Nelson to San Diego for a sixth-round draft choice. They would trade linebacker Jesse Solomon to New England for another sixth-rounder.

In all, the Cowboys ended up with nine draft choices and Holt, who would play for almost four more seasons. "In the end," Ackles says proudly, "It was the biggest theft in the history of the National Football League."

But there was more to making the trade work than just exploiting Lynn's weakness for Walker. The Cowboys had to make the trade appealing to Walker, who could have scotched it. Herschel and his wife Cindy were happy living in Dallas. Walker was making over a million dollars in local endorsements. To convince Walker to leave, Jones had to pay the running back $1.2 million and give him a car, a rent-free house in Minneapolis, and twenty round-trip airline tickets from Minnesota to Dallas.

"That in itself should have told you the commitment I had to putting a winner in Dallas," Jones points out. "Who else would have paid a player $1.2 million to leave town?"

Johnson and Jones would later battle over who should get credit for the Herschel Walker deal. However, without Art Modell, the trade might never have happened. So who should get credit for the blockbuster trade? "Art Modell for getting it all started," Ackles says. "Jimmy for pursuing Minnesota. And Jerry for writing the check to get Herschel out of town. But the truth of the matter is this. If not for Mike Lynn making us that dumbfounding offer, it never would have gotten done." The Vikings lost to San Francisco in the first round of the playoffs that season, 41–13. Walker had almost no affect on his new team, and never seemed to fit in with the Minnesota offense during his 2 1/2-year stint there. After three solid but unspectacular seasons with Philadelphia, he signed with the New York Giants in the spring of 1995.

SIGNING AIKMAN AND TRADING WALKER WERE BIG PARTS OF REBUILDING the Cowboys, but Jones, Ackles, and Johnson didn't miss a trick in putting together the team they wanted. Many NFL executives laughed at the Cowboys when they dove head-first into the Plan B free-agent pool in 1990. The Plan B pool offered down-and-out teams a way to get rich quick. Teams were allowed to "freeze" just thirty-seven of the players on their roster—their other players could be signed by any team that could put together a good enough offer. Inexplicably, the Cardinals left tight end Jay Novacek exposed after the '89 season. The Cowboys snapped him up. In the last five seasons, no NFL tight end has caught more passes than Novacek's 277. Also scooped up from the Plan B market were linebackers Vinson Smith, Ray Horton, and James Washington. All three started for the Cowboys before moving on to other teams.

Also in 1990, the Cowboys made a first-round trade on draft day that allowed them to bag running back Emmitt Smith out of Florida. Again, luck was on their side. They traded their 21st pick in the first round, along with a third-round pick to Pittsburgh for the Steelers' 17th pick. The Steelers had already etched their draft plans in stone. They intended to draft obscure tight end Eric

Green out of Liberty, and knew he would still be available in the 21st slot. Again, the Cowboys had played their cards perfectly.

Call it luck or simply great planning, but the 1991 draft will go down as one of the best in club history. The day started with the Cowboys picking future starters in tackle Russell Maryland, wide receiver Alvin Harper, and linebacker Dixon Edwards in the first two rounds. Then they picked up future All-Pro offensive tackle Erik Williams in the third round, and future All-Pro defensive tackle Leon Lett in the seventh. Future starting cornerback Larry Brown was taken in the twelfth and final round.

In 1992, another trade provided what many considered to be the final piece to the Cowboys' Super Bowl puzzle. The Cowboys acquired defensive end Charles Haley from the San Francisco 49ers for second- and third-round draft choices. Even though Haley would produce only 22-1/2 sacks over the next three years, his dominating presence caused defenses to change their blocking schemes, which, in turn, allowed the Cowboys to exert more pressure on the quarterback.

After the Haley trade, another tug-of-war for credit began between Johnson and Jones. But scouting director Larry Lacewell says the deal almost never got off the ground. "I had a message to return a call from John McVay," Lacewell says. "I didn't return it for two days because I didn't know who the hell John McVay was." Lacewell had been on the job for only a few months.

McVay, the 49ers' vice president, was calling to offer Haley to the Cowboys. Two days later, Lacewell finally returned the call. The deal was finalized the next day.

Of course, the real turnaround had started all the way back in 1989, when Jones and Steinberg negotiated a pre-draft contract for Aikman. In spite of the 1–15 season that year, the Aikman deal set the wheels in motion

"I still think we were lucky," says Ackles, now the personnel director of the Philadelphia Eagles. "I think some great moves were made. But at the same time, luck had to fall our way to make all of those things happen."

★ ★ ★

JONES WAS BOUNCING OFF THE OFFICE WALLS ONE AFTERNOON IN December of 1994. He was trying to negotiate Michael Irvin's new contract with agent Steve Endicott. The Cowboys had one regular-season game against the Giants remaining. A question arose about the $75,000 bonus Irvin could earn under his current contract if he finished the year with eighty receptions. At that point, Irvin had seventy-six catches, and his chances of playing that Sunday with a deeply bruised thigh were no better than fifty-fifty. The game meant nothing in the standings or to the Cowboys' post-season positioning, and coach Barry Switzer didn't want to risk further injuries with the playoffs just around the corner.

Without warning, or telling Endicott where he was going, Jones lurched from his chair, charged through his office door and ran down the long hallway of the Cowboys' complex. Head down and arms and knees pumping high like an old fullback, he passed the men's rest room, then took a right turn through the double doors of the coaches' wing. Following this shortcut through the narrow halls, he half-jogged past a cluster of tiny offices. A left and then another right took him into the locker area, where a quick left sent him barging into the middle of a team meeting.

"Don't worry about me," Jones said as several startled players turned to see what outsider had crashed their meeting. Drawing a deep breath, he said, "Michael, come with me. I need to talk to you."

Out in the hallway, a surprised Irvin said, "Jerry, slow down, man. What's going on here? Jerry, you all right?"

"Look, Michael," Jones said, his eyes shining intently. "You got the $75,000 bonus. I'm gonna give it to you. You don't even have to play Sunday. You don't need another catch. Just consider the $75,000 yours."

"Great," Irvin said. "But the next time, Jerry, all you gotta do is call me to your office. And, by the way—thanks."

★ ★ ★

CALLING AHEAD TO SET UP A MEETING JUST WOULDN'T HAVE BEEN Jones's style. He's obsessed with speed—with making decisions and acting on them as quickly as possible. He doesn't fear flying into a crisis, or into a meeting room full of Cowboys receivers. Jones runs the Cowboys like an oil wildcatter playing his hunches. He'd learned to take his risks in bunches in the Oklahoma oil fields. His reasoning: Some of your risks are bound to be busts. The more risks you take, the better the chance of one of them hitting.

But Jones's reckless pace, his compulsive actions, and his hard-driving intensity often raise the eyebrows of even his closest friends. Don Tyson, who built the Tyson poultry empire in Arkansas and has been Jones's friend for more than twenty years, says, "Jerry called me about the Cowboys deal when he first started negotiating. And I said, 'Jerry, I wouldn't make a good partner. You're too intense for me. You need the whole thing. It's your baby, 110 percent.' I know a lot of intense people. But nobody like Jerry Jones. He's going to win, and he's going to win his way. Hell, Jerry's always been this way. You know, Jerry can be a little crazy."

Agent Leigh Steinberg has negotiated many contracts with Jones, including multi-million-dollar deals for quarterback Troy Aikman and defensive tackle Russell Maryland, who were the first players selected in the NFL drafts of 1989 and 1991, respectively. Steinberg respects and admires Jones. But he says the Cowboys' owner can change moods without blinking. "Jerry clearly has two sides to him, two personalities," Steinberg says. "On one side, you have P. T. Barnum, the raconteur and the great philosopher on life. But on the other side is this tough businessman from Arkansas. There are times when he'll flip on you without warning. He can go from that charming mode to a very tough man. One minute, you'll be talking to Jerry and he'll be quite animated. He'll get close, put his arm around you. He'll use his body language to make a point. But when that change comes and he goes into that steely business mode, it can happen in an instant. Psychologically, the person dealing with him can get caught off guard. Here you are having this warm and cordial discussion. And then, all of a sudden, the atmosphere turns cold."

Few people who have met Jones really know how to read him at first. His complexities can be disarming. His ability to switch gears suddenly can make him difficult to understand.

Long-time business partner and close friend Mike McCoy says, "He's not simple. First appearances with him may be deceiving."

Jones often becomes consumed by his own work ethic and manic negotiating style. It is a game that must be played until the final gun. Only in this game, the rules are vague and there are no boundaries.

"He runs into any project believing that he can beat any man at anything," says McCoy, "because he believes he is putting 500 percent on the line compared to another man's 100 percent. Sometimes that's good. Sometimes that's bad."

Says ESPN's Roy Firestone, who has done several interviews with the Cowboys' owner, "Life is not about smelling the roses with Jerry. Life is hard work. He just doesn't have any time for things like philosophy or poetry. You also get the feeling that if you cross him, you will never cross him again. You get the feeling that he will break your balls if you cross him."

"Sometimes Jerry will negotiate right down to the final dime with somebody," McCoy says. "It's the point of proving that he can win. Then he'll turn right around when the bargaining is over and he'll give something back that you've been negotiating over for days. Sometimes it's just like a game to him."

Running back Emmitt Smith, who was involved in a protracted and nasty contract negotiation with Jones back in 1993, knows all about Jones's ploys. "Jerry, he just blows so much smoke," he says. "It's hard to cut through it all. You have to be on guard with him all of the time."

Barry Switzer has known Jones since 1960, when they were part of the Arkansas football program. Switzer leans back in his office chair and laughs loudly when asked about Jones the deal maker. He says, "One minute, he might be a tough negotiator. And the next minute he might turn right around and give the entire ranch away. You never know. Deep inside, he has a great heart and he's a compassionate and caring person." Then he pauses, and says, "I see in him a lot of me."

★ ★ ★

FROM DAY ONE, IT WAS CLEAR THAT JONES WAS CONSUMED WITH making huge profits from the Cowboys. He was determined to convert a club in financial free fall into a lean, mean money machine. The Cowboys had lost $8 million the year before he bought them. There was nothing he wouldn't try, no risk he wouldn't take to return the team to profitability. He is committed to squeezing every possible revenue dollar out of every available square inch of Texas Stadium. Clearly, Jones sees it as a potential gusher.

A few months after buying the team back in 1989, Jones was relaxing with the coaching staff when someone predicted the Cowboys would be back in the Super Bowl within two years. A somber Jones said, "I'm not as worried about the Super Bowl as I am about getting the damn luxury boxes sold." The luxury suites are worth between $400,000 and $1.5 million apiece. Selling a suite offers an additional bonus: According to rules established more than two decades ago, revenues from the boxes aren't shared with other NFL owners the way most ticket revenues are.

When Jones bought the team, only six of the 188 luxury suites situated around the rim of the stadium had been sold. As the team started winning again, Jones and his sales staff were able to either lease or sell most of the rest. The suites are now between 95 and 98 percent occupied. Profits from the suites alone have topped $50 million since Jones bought the team.

Before the 1992 season, he sold the best location inside the Stadium—the press box. At the time, the Cowboys' press box, situated between the lower and upper decks, was considered the best in the NFL. The seats assigned to writers from the Dallas and Fort Worth newspapers were squarely on the 50-yard line. But Jones moved reporters to the other side of the stadium, above the upper deck. Remarkably, there were no complaints from the media, even though, when asked about it in 1989, Jones had denied he would sell the space.

Not long after Jones bought the team, he began recalling thousands of season tickets that had belonged to former players, former employees, and friends of the club. These tickets would eventually be resold to new season ticket buyers through ProSeat, a new company Jones had started. There was one catch. To obtain these tickets, the new purchasers also had to put money down for "seat options." The options alone cost from $1,500 to $15,000 per seat, depending on their location, even though they don't include the actual price of the tickets—they just give the option-holder the right to buy the tickets for that seat.

While evaluating the stadium's potential for generating revenue, Jones kept asking himself, "Where did the previous owners go wrong? Why did they lose so much money?" So he began adding rows of seats where no one had dared to build them before. He built a row of seats behind almost every portal, the entrances leading from the concourses into the seating areas. Because they were new seats, they could be sold as season tickets—again, with the cost of a ProSeat option tacked on. Between the 30-yard line and the 50-yard line, the Cowboys now charge their fans $15,000 just for the right to buy tickets for those seats. A family of four might have to prepay $60,000 just to get options on seats in that area. Seat options between the 30-yard line and the end zone cost $10,000. In the corners of the end zone, they go for $5,000. Some buyers are paying up to $3000 for an option on an end-zone seat. Again, the Cowboys' cash register goes "cha-ching."

Jones, of course, often talks about his regard for Cowboys' fans. But season ticket-holders had filed dozens of lawsuits against the Cowboys by the spring of 1995. In most cases, Jones is being challenged for moving season ticket-holders into seats in less attractive locations to make room for his new ProSeat customers.

By manipulating the rules on season tickets, Jones managed to open up between 4,000 and 5,000 premium seats between the 30-yard lines. In some cases, season ticket-holders were moved out of their seats without warning. Those seats were, in turn, resold to ProSeat customers in order to collect the lucrative seat option revenue.

Some ticket-holders who were used to paying for their season tickets on an installment plan were notified that they'd now have to make one-time annual payments. Fans who couldn't meet the new stringent payment plan lost their tickets.

The ProSeat plan has turned Texas Stadium into a veritable gold mine. On ticket premiums alone, the Cowboys made between $700,000 and $1 million per month for three consecutive years between 1991 and 1994.

★ ★ ★

AT TIMES, JONES'S MONEY-MAKING SCHEMES SEEM ENDLESS. HE broke from Cowboys' tradition when he began selling signage inside Texas Stadium—something that had never been done before. Suddenly, advertisements for beer companies, car companies, and banks began popping up on the stadium walls. Jones even put the logo of a supermarket chain and a bank on the field during a summer exhibition season game.

Next, the Cowboys' owner set out to convince the Irving City Council to grant the stadium a license to sell beer and wine. Like a good politician, Jones began wining and dining members of the council. He gave them free seats in the luxury suites. He brought some of them into the locker room after games. When the Cowboys reached the Super Bowl in 1993, five council members flew to Pasadena free on one of Jones's chartered jets—and received free tickets to the game.

Before Jones could get his liquor license approved, though, he had to address a moral issue. Irving, Texas, sits squarely in the middle of the Bible Belt. Even though social mores have changed in the region over the last decade, Jones still had to convince the good people of Irving that he wouldn't be sending a legion of drunken drivers out onto the city's streets and highways after the games.

Jones came up with a brilliant strategy. Oddly enough, fans had been allowed to bring cans of beer into Texas Stadium for years. The only restrictions had been that bottles were prohibited, and coolers had to be small enough to fit under the seats. It wasn't unusual to find beer cans strewn all over the stadium after games. So Jones had his stadium attendants count the empties left in the stands after a home game. The final count came to 70,000 cans—more than one per customer at a stadium that at that point seated 63,000 fans. Jones made the point that many fans were leaving the stadium drunk anyway. If he could sell beer and wine inside the stadium, and fans were prohibited from bringing in their own six-packs, his trained concessionaires could control over-consumption. Jones won his vote at the next city council meeting. The payoff has been tremendous. Revenue for beer and wine sales at Cowboys' games alone has averaged more than $1.5 million per season since 1992.

Millions and millions of dollars were now rolling in from previously untapped resources—but Jones's pursuit of the fans' money seems relentless.

When the Cowboys made the playoffs after the 1994 season, season ticket-holders were required to pay in advance for two post-season games. The Cowboys were assured of playing at least one playoff game at Texas Stadium. But the location of—not to mention the participants in—the NFC title game was up in the air. The game, as it turned out, was played January 15 at Candlestick Park in San Francisco.

But season ticket-holders didn't receive an immediate refund for the tickets they'd bought to the second game. In fact, Jones didn't get around to broaching the subject of a refund until several weeks later. He received a call from a disgruntled buyer during his weekly radio show with Norm Hitzges on KLIF in Dallas. Jones announced that according to his new plan, season ticket-holders would have to notify the Cowboys before getting their money back.

Not only does the refund policy seem unfair, it is completely out of line with those of other NFL teams. With the exception of Dallas, every other team automatically refunds ticket money for games that weren't played at home just after the end of the season.

★ ★ ★

JONES HAS ALSO DEVELOPED A REPUTATION AS A RUTHLESS COST-CUTTER. After committing the team to holding its 1990 training camp at the Cowboys' traditional summer home in Thousand Oaks, California, Jones reneged and moved the team to Austin. Not only did the change save the Cowboys $1 million per year, but it gave Jones another source of revenue. He now holds the rights to the sales of all caps, T-shirts, and merchandise involving the Cowboys around the training site.

Less than a year after buying the team, Jones threatened to walk away from the Cowboys' office complex at Valley Ranch. In response, the mortgage company holding the property cut his payments in half. Overnight, Jones had cut his debt on the property from $10 million to $5 million.

He also began to slash the organization's staff and, more important, to reorganize the workplace. He began hiring sales and promotions people while weeding out non-revenue-producing jobs. "Just take a look around this office," said a Cowboys' employee in the fall of 1994. "You won't find many people around here, with the exception of scouts, coaches, and secretaries, who are not making money for Jerry Jones."

Jones then reduced his scouting budget from $3 million to $1 million, giving the coaching staff additional responsibilities for gathering data on draft-eligible players.

"Jerry can be pretty funny about money," says college scouting director Larry Lacewell. "He might go out and spend $5,000 in a bar in one night. The next day he might get mad over a $100 expenditure in the office."

Nobody has more experience with this aspect of Jones's business strategy than current and former players and employees. When the Cowboys reached the playoffs in 1991, Jones became the first NFL owner not to spread playoff bonus money around to vital members of the staff, including scouts, equipment men, trainers, and public relations personnel. When the Cowboys won Super Bowls in 1992 and 1993, he did pay bonuses to the scouts. But he refused to pay bonuses to many other staff members who had worked long hours during the post season. Equipment manager Buck Buchanan, who had received a full playoff share of almost $10,000 when the Cowboys were going to Super Bowls in the 1970s, didn't receive a penny this time around.

NFL owners receive $1 million from the league office when they reach the Super Bowl. Ordinarily the money is used for expenses like travel, parties, Super Bowl rings, and playoff bonuses. Jones attempted to placate employees who didn't receive bonuses by awarding more Super Bowl rings than most NFL teams. But in many of the rings, the traditional diamonds were replaced by zircons. Assistant trainer Don Cochren was surprised at the appraisal given him by a Dallas jeweler of his 1993 Super Bowl ring. "He basically said it was worth less than the high school class ring that I had given to my son," Cochren says. "It was worth about $90." Jones claims that the real Super Bowl rings given to players, coaches, and upper management are worth close to $13,000.

The only major-league sports owner comparable to Jones in limiting post-season rewards to employees has been Cincinnati Reds owner Marge Schott, who also withheld playoff bonuses to key employees when her team swept the Oakland A's in the 1990 World Series. Like Jones, Schott became the first owner in her sport to do so.

Says *Dallas Morning News* columnist Randy Galloway, "Of everything that I've said bad about Jerry—and I've said a lot of bad things—the thing that makes him the maddest of all, the one thing that causes volcanic conditions, is when I call him the Marge Schott of the NFL. They are the first in the history of the United States not to give front-office employees some form of financial bonuses when their teams won championships. If I have a problem with Jerry it's that he forgot where he came from, that he grew up on the wrong side of the tracks in Arkansas, that he once was a little guy, and that he worked for a living.

"And I think for the most part that he treats his employees like shit."

★ ★ ★

JONES REVEALED A COLD-HEARTED SIDE WHEN HE RECALLED THE SEASON tickets belonging to Allie Allen, the widow of former Cowboys' assistant coach Ermal Allen, who had been with the team for twenty-one years before his death in 1983. Allie Allen had been paying for her tickets—but Jones wanted to resell them through ProSeat. When Allen learned her tickets had been recalled, she telephoned the Cowboys and tearfully asked for them back. She was denied.

Weeks later, a reporter tried to get word to Jones that Mrs. Allen was upset over losing the season tickets that she'd held since the early 1960s. A few days later, Cowboys vice president Stephen Jones approached the same reporter and said, "What's the big deal here? My dad has friends in Little Rock he can't get tickets for. He can't take care of everybody."

Jones's handling of tickets has created far more enemies than friends, especially among former players. Ed "Too Tall" Jones hasn't been to a game in two seasons, and vows not to return until Jones sells the team. Former All-Pro defensive end Harvey Martin talks loudly and flails his arms when the Cowboys owner is mentioned. "Jerry Jones doesn't give a shit about the former players," says Martin. "And you know what? The former players don't give a shit about him. But Jerry Jones should realize one thing. We are his legacy. Without us, he doesn't have America's Team. We are the reason there is an America's Team."

Former All-Pro safety Cliff Harris says, "I broke my neck for the Dallas Cowboys. And I can't even get two tickets to home games."

When the Cowboys played in Super Bowl XXVIII in Atlanta, Martin, along with several other former players, was unable to purchase tickets through the team. Former Cowboys' running back Tony Dorsett, now a member of the Pro Football Hall of Fame and the Cowboys Ring of Honor, said he was promised tickets, but that Jones later reneged on his promise.

Dorsett is not the only former Cowboys' player to have a ticket request granted and then revoked. Defensive end George Andrie, who played for the Cowboys from 1962–1972, called former Cowboys' fullback Robert Newhouse, who works for

Jones in sales and promotions, and asked about two tickets for Super Bowl XXVIII in Atlanta. Newhouse returned Andrie's call five days before the game and said he could pick up the tickets the following day at Texas Stadium.

When he arrived at the ticket office, Andrie was told by a teller that she had no tickets under his name.

"Let me talk to the head guy," Andrie insisted.

"There's no reason to do that," the teller said. "Ex-players aren't getting any tickets."

Andrie was directed to a small sales office next to the stadium. By the time the 6'-4", 260-pound ex-Cowboy reached the office, he was in a blind rage. He walked through the door and began kicking the walls. He knocked a plant off a secretary's desk.

"I started tearing up the place pretty good," Andrie remembers. "Some of the secretaries started running and hiding. To somebody else, it might have seemed funny. But if you had been in my shoes, it didn't seem funny at all."

Newhouse tried to calm Andrie down, but Andrie shoved him away.

"Newhouse told me that Jones had held a meeting the night before and he said that no tickets were going to ex-players," Andrie says. "He was going to use all of those tickets on his sponsors and friends. I just went into a rage when I heard that. I told Newhouse, 'I don't care who did who wrong. I just want my tickets to the Super Bowl.'"

The next day, Stephen Jones, who was in Atlanta, heard about Andrie's tirade. He telephoned Newhouse back in Irving. The Cowboys managed to come up with two tickets for Andrie. Now, though, Andrie says he will never attend another Cowboys game or function.

Harvey Martin said he was flatly turned down on his ticket request for Super Bowl XXVIII in Atlanta. "Look at it this way," Martin says. "I was the Co-Most Valuable Player in Super Bowl XII. And I couldn't even get two tickets to a Super Bowl from my own team. I think that is just pretty shitty. I'm not talking about giving me the tickets. I'm talking about me paying for the tickets."

Many ex-players complain that Jones has overlooked their requests for tickets in order to accommodate sponsors, suite-holders, and his rich and famous friends from around Dallas. Jones, in fact, chartered two airliners from Express One Airlines to ferry his personal guests to Super Bowl XXVIII. Not only did they receive free tickets to the game, but Jones even picked up their hotel tabs in Atlanta.

★ ★ ★

JONES HAS SO LITTLE REGARD FOR FORMER PLAYERS THAT HE SUED sixteen ex-Cowboys, trying to recover $1 million awarded to them under worker's compensation. He claimed the players "double-dipped" because they were paid by the Cowboys while they were injured and receiving worker's compensation. Jones's pursuit of these claims seemed particularly aggressive, especially since the sixteen players received their payments from the pre-vious owner, Bum Bright. Still, Jones continued his legal fight—to reclaim money that was never his to begin with.

"We're not even talking about money that once belonged to Jerry Jones," says former All-Pro lineman John Dutton, one of the players named in the lawsuit. "What an asshole Jerry Jones is. He's trying to steal from his former players."

Stuck squarely in the middle of these controversies is Pro Football Hall of Fame quarterback Roger Staubach. Jones has treated Staubach like a demigod from the day he stepped foot in Dallas. The former Cowboys' great has been an honorary captain for the last three NFC championship games. When Jones had no luck on his own luring Tom Landry into the Ring of Honor, he asked Staubach to act as a mediator. And when Jones had trouble selling tickets after the 1–15 season in '89, he asked Staubach to do some radio ads.

All of this has left Staubach in an awkward position with his former teammates. Cliff Harris mocked his former teammate during a Cowboys' party after the 1994 season. "Roger here can get anything he wants from Jerry Jones," Harris said to a group that included Staubach. "Hey, Rog, by the way, can you get me some tickets from Jerry?" Clearly embarrassed, Staubach tried to laugh it off. (Staubach's real estate company owns a Texas Stadium luxury suite, where he sits during home games. But he also buys ten more seats to each game for friends and clients.)

Of his relationship with Jones, Staubach says with a shrug, "I guess some people think that because of the honorary captain thing that I'm in his camp. I get along with him, but I'm just not that close to him. I'm not socially involved with him and I don't know him very well."

But in almost the same breath, Staubach, who has always been known as a straight shooter, says, "I don't think he was totally to blame for what happened to Landry." That, of course, isn't the popular opinion of the Landry firing in Dallas.

Staubach is worried about the perception by ex-players and some former teammates that he is blindly loyal to Jones. In fact, Staubach says he breathed a sigh of relief when the Cowboys lost the 1995 NFC title game to the 49ers in San Francisco. Staubach had been an honorary captain in the two previous championships. Since the Cowboys won both games, he was considered a good luck charm. When they finally lost, Staubach said, "Well, maybe I won't be the honorary captain anymore. I really don't want to do it anymore. Let my old teammates do it."

Jones's critics say he got lucky by hiring Jimmy Johnson, by having Troy Aikman fall into his lap in 1989, and by finding a sucker like Minnesota's Mike Lynn, who practically guaranteed a Cowboys' dynasty with the Herschel Walker trade. His critics also say his luck is bound to run out. They believe he is performing a high-wire juggling act without a safety net, and that he—and the team—will soon come crashing down.

But Jones is a complex man—and frequently, in the words of a Kris Kristofferson song, "a walking contradiction." He is a charming rogue who may be the world's greatest living advertisement for making one's own luck. It's not unusual for Jones to perform expansive acts of kindness and generosity one minute, and then turn miserly, mean-spirited, and cold the next. As McCoy says, meeting Jones for the first time is like walking onto the tip of a global-sized iceberg. Some of the terrain is smooth. Some of it is jagged. And a long, long journey is required to see it all.

Jones is hard to beat in both football and business. But he can be tougher to understand. He can be compassionate. At other times, his ego seems to be on steroids. There is no formula that can measure Jones. He may truly be without precedent. Only he knows where he's going, and when he's coming back.

CHAPTER 8

From Orlando
to Dallas

THE ADRENALINE SURGE WAS LIKE THE ONE HE FELT STANDING NEAR THE tunnel of the Rose Bowl on January 31, 1993, as Garth Brooks belted out the final stanza of the National Anthem and four Navy F-16s roared above the rim of the stadium.

Troy Aikman had just walked away from the blackjack tables of the Crystal Palace Hotel in Nassau. Playing $1,000 a hand, he had quarterbacked another Super Bowl-like blowout. He had won tens of thousands of dollars. Strolling into his suite, he picked up the telephone and dialed the number for Cowboys' conditioning coach Mike Woicik back in Irving, Texas. Aikman was in the Bahamas to do some gambling, drinking, and fishing. But he also needed to rehabilitate a body that had been battered through a nineteen-game season that included a second straight Super Bowl victory over Buffalo in the Georgia Dome just seven weeks earlier.

It was March 17, and Aikman was feeling damn good about life. Even for the team workaholic, it was okay to celebrate and

have a few cold ones in March. He could worry about the off-
season workout grind later.

Reaching Woicik's phone recorder, Aikman reminded the
conditioning guru that he needed a schedule for rehab work.

"Oh, by the way, Mike," Aikman said. "If you talk to Jimmy,
tell him that I'm knocking their asses dead down here in Nassau."

Early the next morning, standing beside the limousine that
would take him down to the wharf for some deep-sea fishing, he
was approached by the hotel marketing man who had set up the
trip. Philip Davis had met Aikman through Cowboys' coach
Jimmy Johnson on a trip to Nassau a year earlier. Now, he was
running toward the Cowboys' quarterback, waving his hand.

"Coach Johnson wanted me to let you know that he'll be
here this afternoon," Davis said. "Somehow, he found out you
were down here. I didn't tell him. But I guess Jimmy knows
everything."

Woicik must have told him, thought Aikman.

Spitting chewing tobacco into a Styrofoam cup, Aikman
walked into the casino late that afternoon smelling of salt water,
beer, and fish. The $50-million Cowboys' quarterback looked like
a cross between a Fort Lauderdale surfer and a rodeo cowboy
from eastern Oklahoma.

Johnson was waiting near the center of the casino, tuning up
for the night's action. The two had been close friends for over
three years now. Still, Aikman found it hard to believe they had
developed such a rapport and a camaraderie. Of course, they held
a common love for cards and for gambling action. Aikman even
kept a blackjack shoe at home. Sometimes, the games back in
Texas with Darryl "Moose" Johnston, tackle Mark Tuinei, and
others lasted all night.

"Why don't you go upstairs and get cleaned up," said
Johnson, whose hair and fingernails were always perfect. "Come
back down and I'll show you how to win some damn money."

"Wait a minute," Aikman said. "Tell me why you're here."

"Because," said Johnson, doing his trademark lip-smacking,
"I heard that you were killing 'em down here."

As he returned to the suite, Aikman thought about his first

two seasons in Dallas. He had hated Johnson at first, and the two rarely spoke. Aikman heard from a friend of a friend that Johnson had once said of him, "He [Aikman] was a loser in college and he'll never be anything but a loser in the pros."

But for the last three seasons, two of them Super Bowl years, Aikman and Johnson had been the perfect fit.

"He changed over the years," Aikman would say later. "He was a militant at first. And then he began to relax and get into the relationship with players. I think that after we won the first Super Bowl he relaxed and said to himself, 'I did what I came here to accomplish.' From that time on, he handled the team a lot differently."

"I'm real proud of the relationship that Jimmy and I ended up having. Believe me, it was very rocky right there at first. Those first two years were very tough. I think that it began to get better when we got to know each other a little better. When we both realized that we had the same goal, and that goal was to win, our relationship began to flourish.

"The thing with Jimmy is that he's so much like my father that it's scary. He really is just like my dad in his determination and his drive to achieve things, how he focuses in on things and nothing is going to get in his way. Jimmy is also just like my dad in that he wouldn't let the family stand in the way of his success. If success comes at the expense of the family, then so be it."

To discourage the casino crowds, the pit boss had roped off the corner table even before Aikman returned from his suite. Not only were they the coach and quarterback of the back-to-back Super Bowl champs, but Johnson liked to play at least $5,000 a hand. He also liked to play up to four hands at a time. This was a night when fame, power, and money might become a combustible mix for the Crystal Palace Hotel. Extra security was called in.

"You ready?" Johnson said to Troy and his friend, Doug Kline of Henryetta, Oklahoma. "This is the night when we kick some ass and take some fuckin' names."

In front of Aikman and Johnson were black and blue chips— black signifying $100 and blue, $1,000. The minimum bet at the table was $250. Neither Troy nor Jimmy would ever approach that minimum wager. However, because tens of thousands were being bet on every hand, the casino made an exception for Doug, who was a $5-a-hand player.

"Doug would hit on a card that he really shouldn't hit on," Aikman remembered later. "And it would wind up busting him. And it would wind up costing Jimmy about fifteen grand. And Jimmy never batted an eye. And Doug would feel awful. But Jimmy would say, 'Hey, you play your hand and don't worry about it. Just do what you feel is best. You are not bothering me one bit.' I thought that was a real sign of Jimmy showing some patience. Maybe I appreciated Jimmy more that night that I ever had."

Aikman won close to $15,000 and Johnson won between $75,000 and $100,000 that night. Aikman is a system player, whose formula doesn't often allow him to win big, but provides safeguards against big losses. Johnson, on the other hand, plays on hunches and instinct. This style provides almost no middle ground. He either wins big, or loses big.

"It doesn't matter if Jimmy is up fifty grand, or down fifty grand," Aikman said. "If he feels the hunch, he's going to plunge. He's just going to lay it out on the table. Jimmy plays blackjack the same way that he coaches. He just has no fear of losing. When he calls an onside kick in the first quarter and it's 3–0 us, he feels pretty good of getting it. But he isn't afraid of not getting it."

The friends played well into the night inside the massive hotel that towered above the blue Caribbean. They talked about the 1994 season and whether the Cowboys would somehow win yet another Super Bowl, becoming the first NFL team ever to three-peat. They talked about losing guard John Gesek to free agency, but how they would somehow replace him. They talked about Jimmy being a little burned out, but already bouncing back and getting ready to walk the walk, and talk the talk.

The next morning, Aikman headed back to Dallas, and two days later, Johnson took the hour-long flight to Orlando for the NFL owners' meetings. Their paths were scheduled to converge again in about a week back at Valley Ranch, where the real work for the next season would begin.

"I'm glad that Jimmy and I were able to spend that night together playing cards," Aikman said. "Because that really was the last time that I really ever saw him as head coach of the Dallas Cowboys."

★ ★ ★

ON THE EVENING OF MARCH 21, JERRY JONES WAS CRACKING WHAT HE calls a "coat-hanger-stuck-in-the-mouth smile." It was a beautiful star-filled night in Orlando. Strolling the grounds of Pleasure Island, an entertainment center connected to Disney World, he was pumping more hands than a would-be alderman at a county fair. With another Super Bowl ring on order, the Cowboys' owner found himself "literally floating" through the shoulder-to-shoulder squeaky-clean party crowd celebrating the twenty-fifth anniversary of ABC's *Monday Night Football*. The occasion was yet another drink-till-you-drop respite from the NFL's semi-serious spring meetings taking place just down the road at the Hyatt Grand Cypress.

By day, NFL owners and general managers contemplated possible rules changes and played political football with Commissioner Paul Tagliabue. By night, they were drinking from the heavily stocked free bars at the nightly theme parties.

For the second straight year, this was Jones's opportunity to walk the walk and to talk the talk, as Jimmy Johnson might have put it. Orlando was merely an extension of the post-Super Bowl celebration that had exploded into the Atlanta night of January 30, just hours after the Cowboys had clobbered the Buffalo Bills for the second straight year 30–13.

Jones had other reasons to strut, though. He had been the driving force in negotiating the NFL's recently signed record $4.4 billion television contract, which included a $1.6 billion bonanza from the Fox Network. Thanks to Jones, each owner would make $5.5 million more in 1994 than if the NFL had stuck with CBS. Still, some owners thought the only thing Jones knew about TV was that he liked to be on it.

Pivoting and then looking down at balding 5-foot-6-inch Larry Lacewell, Jones almost shouted, "You know, Lace, we're the toast of this whole damn party. No, the damn Dallas Cowboys are the toast of this whole damn National Football League. What do you think about that, Lace?"

The Cowboys' director of college scouting, Lacewell is a soft-spoken sage from Fordyce, Arkansas. During his days with Paul "Bear" Bryant, he learned to be a great listener during the cocktail hour. This habit carried him through the saloon-rush days of the 1970s at Oklahoma with Barry Switzer, and now through his dealings with Jones, one of the most powerful men in sports, and also one of the most gregarious, free-spirited, and talkative, especially when drinks are flowing. Lacewell is accustomed to having his back pounded.

Carrying large plastic cups of Scotch, the two men headed up a grassy hill, hoping to find more friendly folks to toast. Lacewell told Jones that he needed a rest room break. Returning to the party, Lacewell noticed that the Cowboys' owner was about twenty yards farther up the hill, continuing his handshake tour. So Lacewell veered left and headed toward a large table near the entrance where he had been drinking with Jimmy Johnson about ten minutes earlier.

Lacewell arrived at the backside of the table, standing behind Johnson, just as Jones walked up to the front. Noticing that the table was filled with current and former Cowboys' employees, Jones waved and then paused, hoping that Johnson would offer a chair. He didn't. Not overly surprised at the snub, Jones decided to raise his drink for yet another toast.

"Here's to the Dallas Cowboys, and here's to the people who made it possible to win two Super Bowls!" Jones cackled in delight.

An awkward silence fell over the table. It didn't take long to analyze the problem. Also at the crowded table were a couple of former employees, both fired by Jones. Furthermore, Jones sensed that the folks at the table had been talking about him.

"B-b-b-Bob," Jones stuttered, noticing former personnel man Bob Ackles, who initially had his back turned to Jones.

"B-b-b-b-Brenda, hello," Jones said, realizing that Brenda Bushell, recently fired as the club's TV coordinator, was also in the group. "Boy, howdy, have ya'll got a party going on here tonight."

Raising his glass once more, Jones stubbornly repeated the toast, glancing around the table and studying the faces.

"Jimmy is staring at Jerry like he has an asshole in the middle of his forehead," Ackles remembered later. "Basically, Jimmy is giving him the 'what the hell are you doing here' look?"

Hoping to crack some of the tension, Bushell haltingly raised her glass, only to have it yanked down by Jan Wannstedt, the wife of former Cowboys' defensive coordinator Dave Wannstedt, who had been named head coach of the Chicago Bears a year earlier.

Nobody breathed. Glasses remained on the table as the Orlando night turned deadly silent.

"A couple of people did try to toast in a half-hearted manner," remembered Ackles, now the personnel director of the Philadelphia Eagles. "But if you could have seen the look on Jimmy's face, you wouldn't have toasted either. It just caught everybody at the table off guard."

Jones stepped between Bob and Kay Ackles and slammed his plastic cup onto the table.

"You God-damn people just go on with your God-damn party." Jones pivoted and strode off into the darkness. Moments earlier, the Cowboys' owner had been floating on a cloud. Now, he was a raging bull charging toward the nearest exit.

WHEN JONES APPROACHED THE TABLE, HE WAS UNAWARE THAT Johnson was regaling his friends with yet another "Jerry story." At the table were Bob and Kay Ackles, Dave and Jan Wannstedt, Norv and Nancy Turner, Jimmy Johnson and his girlfriend Rhonda Rookmaaker, Brenda Bushell, and Roz Dalrymple, wife of public relations director Rich Dalrymple, who was in the rest room.

Noting that the closest bar was about ten feet away, Ackles remembers, "Just about everybody was well on their way to getting blitzed. The drinks were flowing, just as they are at most of those parties. Everybody was having a good time."

Drinking Heineken after Heineken, Johnson was in the midst of story of a pre-draft trade he had made with the Cleveland Browns. The deal had been made without Jones's approval. The Cowboys' owner had made it clear from day one that he was the final authority on all player transactions. When he learned that Johnson had soloed on a deal, Jones stormed into the Cowboys' offices on draft-day morning and demanded to see Jimmy.

After a long meeting, Jones reminded Johnson that ESPN cameras would be in the Cowboys' draft room that day. "Jimmy," Jones said. "Whenever we make a pick or a trade, I want you to look at me like we're talking about it." According to Jimmy's translation, this was Jerry's way of saying, "Make me look like the boss, even though we all know I'm not making the picks."

Johnson had become so enraged that he considered not even participating in the draft. He'd holed up in his office until Wannstedt, his best friend, convinced him that he was only hurting the team by not taking charge of the draft.

Jones arrived at the table just as Johnson finished his story.

"It was apparent after standing there for a moment that there was an awkwardness there," Jones remembers. "There was some irritation there, and that was coming from Jimmy. So I did the thing that I should have done and that is walk away. I didn't expect any of them to stand up there and say, 'Jerry, we were just visiting about you. We were just making fun of you. That's why we decided not to accept your toast.'"

"Hey, Lace," Johnson said in a familiar biting tone. "You better go catch up with your boss. He's pretty pissed off. You'd better go catch up with him, Lace. No tellin' what that fucker might do before the night is over. You know him as well as I do, Lace."

Feeling suddenly drained, Lacewell slumped into a chair next to Johnson, wondering what his next move should be. Clearing his throat, former Cowboy's offensive coordinator Norv Turner, who had been hired by billionaire Jack Kent Cooke a month earlier to coach the Washington Redskins, said, "Hey, Jimmy. If that had been Jack Kent Cooke, I would have gotten him a chair and a beer. What the hell is wrong with you? I guess you don't like coaching the Dallas Cowboys any more."

The table erupted into laughter. Everyone from Little Rock to Luckenbach knew that Jimmy and Jerry were on the outs. Their power struggle had dragged on for more than three years. Over the last few months, Johnson had taken public pot shots at Jones from coast to coast. During an appearance on the *Late Show* with David Letterman just two days after the Super Bowl, Johnson wondered out loud if Jones had pocketed $20,000 of the $60,000 given the Cowboys by the NFL office for a post-Super Bowl party. Johnson knew the barbs would cost him. How much more would the proud owner of the Cowboys take? He had decided to try to find out.

AN HOUR LATER, AS THE CAR DRIVEN BY TURNER ARRIVED BACK AT THE NFL headquarters hotel, Lacewell was still contemplating a plan to defuse this latest Jimmy-Jerry time bomb, and asking himself the obvious questions: Would Jerry suspect Lacewell of leading him to the slaughter at Jimmy's table? Would Jerry think that Lacewell was siding with Jimmy?

"Good night and good luck," Turner said to Lacewell as he stepped out of the car at curbside of the Hyatt Grand Cypress. "And, Lace, by the way, I hope you've still got a job in the morning."

Figuring there was one place to find Jones, Lacewell headed for the hotel lobby bar. Jones was sitting at a large table surrounded by eight NFL writers from all over the country. This was not surprising. In spite of the criticism, Jones was still a media magnet. Walking past the gathering, Lacewell overheard Jones talking about Cowboys' running back Emmitt Smith. He breathed a sigh of relief. At least Jones wasn't dwelling on the aborted toast.

★ ★ ★

Tᴀᴋɪɴɢ ᴀ ᴛᴀʙʟᴇ ʙʏ ʜɪᴍsᴇʟғ, Lᴀᴄᴇᴡᴇʟʟ sᴏᴏɴ ɴᴏᴛɪᴄᴇᴅ ᴛʜᴀᴛ Jᴏɴᴇs ᴡᴀs striding across the room, the broad, crooked smile having returned to his face. The owner slapped his old pal on the back and cackled.

"Boy, howdy, are we having fun tonight or not?" Jones said. "You know, Lace, I just don't think there could be more fun than winning the damn Super Bowl, and then coming to a party where everybody gets a chance to bust you on the damn back."

With the ABC party winding down, the action was picking up at the lobby bar. The Ackleses, the Turners, and the Wannstedts took a table in the corner, soon to be joined by *Dallas Morning News* NFL writer Rick Gosselin. Ackles noticed that Jones kept glancing at their table. Did Jones think the three couples were filling in the sports writer on the explosive night at Pleasure Island? If so, Ackles thought, Jerry would be itching to tell his side of the story.

Jones and Lacewell left the bar and then returned with Susan Skaggs, a member of the Texas Stadium marketing staff, who had made the trip from Dallas. The three continued to drink at one of the tables near the center of the room. Meanwhile, Lacewell felt a growing sense of relief. Maybe there would be no more explosions that night. At least Jones's mood had been elevated. Gazing across the lobby bar, Lacewell noticed that one by one, the writers were starting to head up to their rooms. In the old days, Lacewell thought, sports writers never gave up the saloon until last call. Now, just slightly past midnight, the new breed of writers was closing out tabs just when the real fun was starting. Thank God, Lacewell thought, for a health-conscious generation of reporters who wouldn't be bugging Jones for the rest of the night.

Watching a foursome head across the room, Lacewell waved good-night. In the group was *Tampa Bay Tribune* writer Joe Fisaro, Cincinnati writer Geoff Hobson, and Ed Werder and Gosselin from the *Dallas Morning News*. To Lacewell's horror, Jones stuck out his arm as the group tried to pass, putting his hand on Werder's leg and stopping him cold in his tracks.

"Why don't you guys sit down awhile," Jones said. "Let me buy you a drink. You sure as hell don't want to go to bed and miss the biggest story of the year."

Before the first round of drinks had arrived, Jones launched a bombshell.

"I think that it's time that I let you know that I'm thinking about firing Jimmy," Jones said. "I think that it's really time that we go ahead and do it before we run into more trouble. Now, I think, is the time to go ahead and get rid of his ass."

Through the silence, the writers looked at Jones and his glass of red wine, then at the faces of Lacewell and Skaggs. Lacewell had learned long ago to keep a poker face handy. His stomach, though, was twisting into a wretched knot.

Before Jones could speak again, Werder proposed that the entire conversation be considered "off the record," meaning the writers wouldn't report on anything said at the table that night. A general rule among sports writers is that bar talk is held in abeyance. That is, until, the parties meet again at a reasonable hour the following day and their blood-alcohol level has returned to normal.

Jones agreed that he would talk on the record the following day in "an assessment of his coach." But never that night did Jones insist that his remarks not be printed. In fact, it was the general opinion at the table that he was inviting the writers to dash for their lap-top computers to write the story for their final deadline. As the world would learn in the ensuing days, Jones had no intentions of backing down or apologizing. Already, he was envisioning "Jerry to Fire Jimmy" headlines.

Werder knew he had just walked into a blockbuster. It was no secret that Jones and Johnson were carrying some heavy hate around for each other. But filing for divorce just seven weeks after their second straight Super Bowl victory? It would seem preposterous to his readers.

Werder had three concerns: First, he suspected there had been a blowup between Johnson and Jones at the ABC party just hours earlier. Somehow, he needed to steer both Fisaro and Hobson away from the table. And third, he needed to figure out what to do with the story at this late hour.

But, for the moment, there was no stopping Jones.

"You know," Jones said. "You may laugh at me for this one.

But I could step out and hire Barry Switzer as coach of the Dallas Cowboys tomorrow and he'd do a better job than Jimmy. Hell, I probably could get Lou Holtz over here. I might just step out tomorrow and hire either one of them. You know that Barry and I have been friends for thirty years. And I think he'd do a great job in the NFL."

Less a month earlier, Jones and Holtz had held a clandestine meeting at Valley Ranch when the Notre Dame coach was considering a return to the NFL. Holtz joining the Cowboys seemed a logical move. But Switzer had been out of coaching for five years and had never led a pro team. The only offense Switzer really knew was the wishbone, a style that is already outdated in college football.

By now, Lacewell knew his boss had bought the farm. Had the red wine, the Scotch, and the beer gone to his head? Or had the awkward scene at Pleasure Island just hours earlier finally and irreconcilably destroyed the Jimmy-Jerry marriage?

"Let me just point out one thing before you go to bed tonight," Jones said. "There are five hundred coaches who would love to coach the Dallas Cowboys. I want you to think about that."

One of the writers asked, "Five hundred coaches who would love to coach the Dallas Cowboys, or five hundred who *could* coach the Dallas Cowboys?"

Without hesitation, Jones blurted, "I think there are five hundred who could have coached this team to the Super Bowl. I really believe that. Shit, *I* could have coached the hell out of this team."

Somehow, Werder steered the writers away from the conversation and eventually away from the table and into the hotel elevator before Jones could spill any more of the story. Werder and Gosselin desperately wanted the story as an exclusive for the *Dallas Morning News*. As they entered the elevator, one of the other writers said, "Boy that was some great shit from Jerry. That'll make a great story."

"Aw, don't worry about it," Werder said with a sly look on his face. "Jerry says that kind of stuff all of the time. He goes around threatening to fire Jimmy all the time."

The Dallas writers exited the elevator on the third floor and pushed the "down" button. As the writers from Tampa and Cincinnati got off on the fifth floor and headed for their rooms, Werder and Gosselin were on their way back to the lobby bar, hoping to find an inebriated Jones still rambling on about his soon-to-be-fired coach. If so, they would have the story to themselves.

"I ought to just go up to his room, drag his ass out of bed, and fire his ass right there on the spot," Jones was bellowing at Lacewell as the writers returned.

"You know," Jones said, his eyes turning even wilder, "I should have gone on and fired that little so-and-so a year ago. I can assure you of this right now. I'm going to fire that sonofabitch and I'm going to hire Barry Switzer."

Placing his hand on Jones's right arm, Lacewell said, "Jerry, this is not the time or the place to talk about this. If you want to talk to Jimmy, you should go talk to him tomorrow. But don't go threatening to fire him right in the middle of the night, with a head full of booze."

Ignoring his friend, Jones said, "You want to see me fire him right now, Lace? You want to see me go upstairs and drag his ass out of bed and fire him right now? I think that's what I'm going to do."

"No, Jerry," Lacewell said. "I just want you to calm down."

Jones didn't calm down, even with the writers taking mental notes at the table. In fact, he continued his open threats long after the bar had closed. After Skaggs departed, the foursome sat at the table until almost 5 A.M. Jones told Werder that he would meet them for lunch the next day to talk "on the record" about firing Johnson.

Before returning to their rooms, Lacewell said, "Jerry, I'm going to have a talk with Jimmy about this in the morning."

"Lace," Jones said. "Stay out of this. This is none of your God-damn business."

★ ★ ★

AFTER THE LONG NIGHT OF DRINKING IN ORLANDO, THE KNOT growing even tighter in his stomach, Lacewell returned to his room, which happened to be adjacent to Johnson's. Slipping into his pajamas, Lacewell knew he would have a sleepless night. After all, Johnson had been his friend for more than thirty years. It was Lacewell who had given Johnson his first real coaching job, pulling him out of a hick high school program in Mississippi and bringing him to Wichita State as the defensive line coach.

Lacewell waited until 7:30 to break the bad news. He wanted to get hold of Jimmy, to calm him down, before the reporters could reach him. Knocking lightly on the door, Lacewell was greeted seconds later by Rhonda Rookmaaker, Johnson's girl-friend.

"Jimmy went down to the pool about an hour ago," she said. "You know, they're taking that picture of all of the coaches."

Closing the door, Rookmaaker walked onto the balcony and spotted Johnson below, getting ready for the picture. It is a ritual at the spring meetings for all of the coaches to gather for a photo-graph. Johnson had showed up in 1990 wearing a green jacket, causing some observers to joke that "Jimmy had just won the Masters."

"Hey, Jimmy," Rookmaaker shouted, getting his attention. She then held an imaginary phone to her ear, a sign to call her immediately.

Moments later, the phone rang.

"Jerry was down at the bar last night telling Lacewell and a bunch of writers that he's going to fire your ass," she said. "Lacewell said it was pretty strong stuff and he needs to talk to you."

When he returned to the pool with a peculiar expression on his face, Johnson encountered Miami Dolphins' coach Don Shula.

"What's wrong, Jimmy?" Shula said. "You look pretty down."

"Oh, it's nothing," Johnson said. "I think that I've just been fired as the head coach of the Dallas Cowboys."

Back in the hotel lobby, Jerry Jones was wearing a freshly pressed suit and a wide grin. Werder and Gosselin were surprised to find him looking so refreshed and in such high spirits at nine

Jerry Jones—
the Razorback years.

The 1964 National Championship Razorbacks.
Jones is number 61 in lower left of photo.

Jerry Jones with former coach Tom Landry before the news
conference where Landry announces he's agreed to join
the Cowboys' Ring of Honor.

Jerry Jones
helps Landry
don the
ceremonial
jacket.

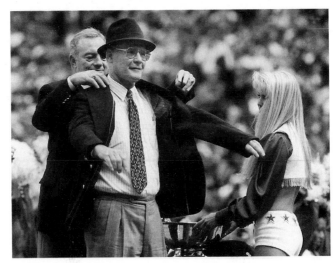

Jimmy and
Jerry—
seldom out
of the
spotlight.

Jones and new coach Barry Switzer on the day he's named
head coach of the Cowboys, March 31, 1994.

Jones and fullback Derrick Gainer celebrate during the 26-17 win over San Francisco during the 1993 regular season.

A pre-game visit with star quarterback Troy Aikman.

Hob-nobbing with Fox Network broadcasters
John Madden (left) and Pat Summerall (right).

Jones is accosted by Cowboys' fans wherever he goes.

Jones dances with an Elvis impersonator in
The Corral outside Texas Stadium.

Prince Bandar bin Sultan (on left) congratulates
Troy Aikman.

Cowboys' marketing director George Hays, vice-president
and long-time business associate Mike McCoy, Jones, and
son Stephen Jones (from left to right).

The ultimate collector's item—a Super Bowl game ball.

in the morning, just four hours after leaving the lobby bar. They were also surprised that Jones was doing an end-run on the "fire Jimmy" talk. Jones's mind had moved to league matters and the meetings of the day.

"I know that I promised you guys that I would get with you later," Jones said. "And I will. What we're going to talk about, I really don't know. But we will talk. I promise you that."

Jones strode into the elevator, toting a secret. Not even the alcohol could pry this one out of him. Inside the hotel suite, he began by dialing area code 405. Moments later, he shook Barry Switzer out of his shower in Norman, Oklahoma, and back into a world he had departed more than five years ago.

"Barry," Jones began, "I have two questions for you. The first: Do you still want to coach? The second: Would you think about coaching the Dallas Cowboys?"

"Well, yes, Jerry," Switzer said. "But what the hell is going on? Why can't you guys get along? I just want to know how ya'll two screwed up one of the greatest things in the NFL. Hell, Jerry, you just won your second Super Bowl!"

"Barry," Jones said, "You're going to be reading a lot of things the next couple of days about me and Jimmy. And your name's come up in the conversation. I just wanted you to know. Most of all, I want you to start thinking about becoming the next coach of the Dallas Cowboys."

★ ★ ★

TWO FLOORS BELOW, THE CURRENT COACH OF THE DALLAS COWBOYS was furiously packing his bags. Although Jimmy Johnson had planned to stay two more days in Orlando, he could feel the walls and Jerry Jones closing in. Reporters were already calling. Lacewell had given him the grim blow-by-blow report of the night from hell in the lobby bar. Tears welled up in Johnson's eyes as Lacewell relayed what Jones had been saying.

"Jimmy, I want you to slow down a little and think about what you're doing," Lacewell said. "You leave right now and this thing really starts looking bad. The whole thing could fall apart. You stay here and we could start working things out."

Over the last thirty years, Lacewell had seen Johnson in every state and every mood. He knew aspects of Johnson's personality that others couldn't even imagine. In spite of his brash demeanor and the swagger, Johnson could break down and cry without warning. With the team slipping through his fingers, his world was collapsing.

In Orlando, Johnson's mood had turned somber. He knew that Jones had dropped hints about firing him. But he figured that Jones couldn't face the public with a Super Bowl coach's blood on his hands. Now, though, he knew this might be his final rodeo with the Cowboys.

"Lace, you know, I haven't treated you very well lately," Johnson said. "I really haven't treated anyone very well lately. I'm sorry about that, Lace. Maybe I was getting tired or burned out or something."

At Lacewell's behest, Johnson stuck around until the next morning, when the *Dallas Morning News* story hit the streets. Johnson finished packing and went downstairs to one of the NFL meeting rooms to get the story straight from the owner's mouth.

"It was very clear that Jimmy was mad and hurt," Lacewell said. "He looked at me and said, 'Lace, what in the world have I done wrong here?' He kind of had that little-boy look on his face."

Glasses in hand, still appearing tired and hung over, Jones stepped out of the meeting room to find Johnson waiting for him and said, "Jimmy, in spite of what you've heard, you're still the coach of the Dallas Cowboys."

When there was no apology, though, Johnson realized that his days in Dallas were over.

★ ★ ★

WAS JERRY JONES DRUNK ON THE NIGHT OF MARCH 21 WHEN HE threatened to drag Jimmy Johnson from his bed at the Hyatt Grand Cypress and fire him on the spot?

"Jerry Jones, in all of my drinking periods with him—and we're talking about a lot of drinking over a long period of time—always knows and always remembers what he says," Lacewell said.

Ackles, who had observed Jones at Pleasure Island and the lobby bar, said, "Jerry knows how to handle his liquor. I was out with him many times. But think about it. He started drinking at seven o'clock at Pleasure Island. And he really didn't stop until five in the morning. Jerry was in his cups. He was annoyed and irritated enough that he wanted to get it out. You know how alcohol works. You are at a function that long and it starts to work against you. I think the fact that Jerry was drunk led to him spilling the story."

To Cowboys' fans and members of the media, the most perplexing aspect of the divorce was the timing. Jones fired Johnson just fifty-eight days after Dallas had become only the fourth NFL team to win back-to-back Super Bowls. In Las Vegas, the Cowboys were already heavy favorites to win an unprecedented third straight Super Bowl.

Where did Jimmy and Jerry take a wrong turn, and who was behind the wheel? Was the driver drunk? Did he refuse a sobriety test?

LIKE MANY MARRIAGES, JONES AND JOHNSON'S BUSINESS RELATIONSHIP had worked well at first. The two were so driven that, during their early weeks on the job, they rented adjacent hotel rooms, slept about three hours a night, then rose around 4:30 in the morning to continue their review of the tattered roster inherited from ex-coach Tom Landry.

Speaking at a $125-a-plate dinner in Little Rock before their first season, Johnson announced with conviction, "Everybody says that Jerry Jones is lucky. Well, let me tell *you* how to get lucky. Become the hardest-working son of a bitch in America, then you will get lucky, too."

Jones and Johnson were cemented at the hip throughout the first season, in spite of the team's 1–15 record. Cowboys employees often found the two huddled together in the men's rest room at the team's complex, hashing out the football business. They often bantered for long periods, ignoring others with legitimate needs for the plumbing. After practices in 1989, the two often met in Jones's office for beers.

After their embarrassing first season, the two men still cut a wide swath at the March 1990 league meetings at the Hyatt Grand Cypress in Orlando. They had designed a plan to tackle the NFL system through Plan B free agency. Throughout the week, they walked the hallways like two gunslingers—Jimmy picking the players and Jerry firing his bankroll. Six months earlier, the two had pulled off "The Great Herschel Walker Trade," picking off seven key draft choices from the dazed and confused Minnesota Vikings.

One night, while consuming enough Scotch in the lobby bar to sound the bagpipes, their testimonials to each other stretched far into the night.

"If there is one coach in the NFL who can turn around a bad football team, it's Jimmy Johnson," Jones said.

"Wait a minute," Johnson said. "If there is one man who will spend the money to put a good football team on the field, it is Jerry Jones. And this man is committed to making the Dallas Cowboys a champion again."

Ironically, almost four years later to the date, their relationship collapsed at the same lobby bar where they had traded verbal hugs. They no longer drank together, worked together, or toasted each other. Their boundless energy had turned into a deep and ugly hate. The heavy drinking that once created a spiritual bond now created an irreparable rift.

So where and when did the Jimmy-Jerry juggernaut start angling for the ditch?

"I knew as early as 1991 that I might want to make a change with Jimmy," Jones said. "My attitude at the time—and I told this to Jimmy—was 'you're doing a good job, but don't let the door hit you in the ass on the way out.' There were a couple of times during the 1992 season that he practically invited me to make the change. There were two times when I had to sit him down and tell him that this is how it's going to be or else."

Long before the divorce was filed, members of the Jones family knew the split was coming. Jones would sit at the family dining table, fiddling with his food and rambling on about how little respect he received from Johnson.

"I'm going to fire his ass," Jones would tell his family. "I can go out and find myself another coach."

Friends said the Cowboys' owner, without warning, would launch into tirades about the coach. He was clearly disturbed by Johnson's criticisms. Delivered through the media, they landed with regularity. Perhaps the most painful punches, though, were coming down the office grapevine.

Drinking heavily one night with Jones's son, Stephen Jones, soon to become a vice president, and Mike McCoy, the team executive who had made millions for Jones in the oil and gas business, Johnson started asking hard questions. Like: Why was Jones trying to meddle in the football business?

"What the hell is Jerry doing? Can you tell me this?" Johnson said, slamming a bottle of Heineken on the table. "Why in the hell won't he get out of the football business and away from my football team? He wants to coach, and nobody wants him around."

McCoy, a close friend to both men at the time, said, "Well, Jimmy, it's just Jerry's $140 million investment on the line. That's all."

Johnson slammed the beer bottle down once more. "Screw his $140 million! And screw him!"

The next day, the story got back to Jones. The owner threatened to call Johnson into his office and to "fire his ass right there on the spot." But McCoy intervened, convincing Jones to give it more time and thought. Still, Jones felt the bomb was ticking, and it was only a matter of time before it exploded.

"From the conversation that he had with Mike and Stephen, I knew right then that Jimmy didn't have the same perspective as me," Jones said. "Jimmy can't imagine what $140 million is because he hasn't gone down that road. He basically doesn't know what it is to have to bare your soul just to borrow $1,000, which I've done before. Believe me, that is no fun."

IRONICALLY, THE JONES-JOHNSON RIFT BEGAN TO DEVELOP JUST AS THE team began to enjoy its first taste of success during the 1991 season. Jones sensed that Johnson was trying to develop an "us-against-them" attitude on the practice field. Every day, Jones was feeling more like "them."

One of Jones's delights as owner was and still is attending practices. He would often bring business acquaintances or friends, or anyone interested in purchasing an expensive suite, to the closed workouts. This practice infuriated Johnson. Standing on the sideline, Jones would analyze the offense and the defense, trying to imagine the type of game plan Johnson and the coaches had devised for that weekend's game. It was on the Cowboys' practice field that Ackles realized the relationship was going to hell. Jimmy often treated Jerry as if he were a spy for the opposing team.

"Jerry would walk onto the practice field and he would make a beeline for Jimmy," Ackles said. "Then Jimmy would make a beeline away from Jerry. He would act as if he needed to talk to somebody else, and he'd just walk away from Jerry. Not only did the coaching staff notice, but the players were noticing it, too."

Ackles soon found himself stuck in the middle. He often worried about talking to Jimmy for fear that Jerry would be jealous or angry. Others could see the relationship falling apart. Ackles was approached by a trio of worried Cowboys' staff, defensive coordinator Dave Wannstedt, public relations director Rich Dalrymple, and head trainer Kevin O'Neill.

"They would all come up to me and say that somebody has got to talk to Jones," Ackles said. "It got to the point that everybody was worried, not just me. I could see the relationship derailing. So, finally I went to talk to Jerry. I frankly told him that I didn't think the dispute was good for the organization. Jerry shot back, 'Don't employers and employees normally have these things?'"

To further the anxiety, the coach and owner began to have running debates about who should get the credit for certain deals. The Cowboys had picked up seven draft choices in their blockbuster trade with the Minnesota Vikings, and used most of them wisely in rebuilding the team. During the 1990 draft, the Cowboys traded with Pittsburgh to get the seventeenth pick in the first round. By moving up four slots, they were able to draft running back Emmitt Smith. They also pulled off the Charles Haley trade during the 1992 preseason. Haley is widely credited for being the final piece in the defensive puzzle that put Dallas over the top and into two straight Super Bowls.

As early as 1991, columnist Randy Galloway said he would often be confronted by an angry Jones, who wanted more credit for the deal-making.

"I would be hanging around the locker room, and he would come up to me and say, 'Hey, Randy, can I talk to you in my office?'" Galloway said. "Any time you went into Jerry's office—even if you were in a hurry—you knew you were going to be there for at least an hour. He would say, 'Randy, you wrote that Jimmy made the Charles Haley trade. Well, that's not right. I made the Charles Haley trade.' Or he'd say, 'Randy, you gave Jimmy the credit for the Herschel Walker trade. Well, it was me who made the Herschel Walker trade.' Then he started talking this stuff that 'everything has to go through me. I am the highest power. I must approve everything. Where does Jimmy get off taking credit for all of the trades?'"

THE PROBLEMS BETWEEN JOHNSON AND JONES CAME CLOSE TO exploding as the Cowboys were preparing for the playoffs after the 1991 season. Johnson decided to start backup quarterback Steve Beuerlein over Troy Aikman in the wild card game against Chicago, and then stuck with him the following week against Detroit. Johnson explained to Aikman that he didn't want to risk further injury to his knee. More important was that Beuerlein had led the Cowboys to wins in the final four regular season games after Aikman was hurt against Washington.

Fearing that Aikman's confidence would be shattered, Jones told the *Fort Worth Star-Telegram* that Troy was, without question, the future of the team. Johnson was so incensed by Jones's intrusion into what he considered his territory that he walked around the coaches' office, holding the newspaper clipping aloft and yelling, "Maybe I'll just get out of here and take this staff with me to Tampa Bay. Who is coaching this football team anyway?"

The next morning, Johnson reasserted his position. He told the *Dallas Morning News* that Beuerlein would be the starting quarterback "as long as I am coaching this football team."

Now furious with his coach, Jones called Johnson from Texas Stadium and told him to "make a beeline to my office."

"Jimmy was basically saying that Beuerlein was no less a quarterback than Troy Aikman." Jones Said. "And I said, 'Let's get the record straight.'

"I sat Jimmy down and said that Troy is the future of this football team. And Jimmy said that is not necessarily so. And I said, 'Yes, it is so.' I told him flat that I speak for the club in these matters. Troy was our next Roger Staubach. Troy wasn't Staubach just yet. But he was going to be."

During these tense meetings, Jones said Johnson normally retreated and became very quiet.

"We would get together and I would have a harsh tone," Jones said. "I would have a condescending tone. Jimmy didn't know how to handle it. He would just sit there and pout. The things that bothered Jimmy the most were my attitude and my tone when we were together. I let him know in no uncertain terms—man to man—just how I felt. Then, the thing that bothered me the most were the things he said behind my back. He said a lot of those things behind my back."

MONEY AND POWER WERE TRULY AT THE ROOT OF THE DIVORCE IN Dallas. The money amounted to mega-millions. Jones admits he drained his bank account to secure both the cash and the bank loans to purchase the team, along with the lease at Texas Stadium. At the time, the $140 million he paid was the most ever spent for a sports franchise. The sale set into motion a series of record sports purchases, topping out with Jeff Lurie's $175 million acquisition of the Philadelphia Eagles.

The psychological effects of spending that kind of money on the Cowboys may have triggered the start of the Jimmy-Jerry demise. Jones said he was haunted by fears that he might somehow lose control of the franchise to minority owner Ed A. Smith, or possibly to former club president Tex Schramm, who still had considerable influence in the NFL when the team was sold in 1989.

He said he'd been told through sources that Schramm was seeking a legal loophole to gain control of the team. Jones admits that his fears eventually developed into near-paranoia.

"Tex just had a sweet deal with the NFL," Jones said. "There was just the thinking that Tex might be able to hold onto his vote that Pete Rozelle had given him for the team. There was the word I was getting that Tex just might contest the whole thing, and that he might try to take the team away from me. All of these thoughts were creating a nightmare for me."

Schramm had made one final desperate effort to form his own leadership group before the team was sold to Jones. He could see the writing on the wall. If the Cowboys were controlled by Jones, people like he and Landry would be sent packing. As far as trying to legally wrest control of the team after the sale, Schramm said, "That is just more Jerry bullshit. I don't know why he insists on making things like that up. Jerry just dreams a lot of stuff up. It's a pattern with him."

Jones's fears about Ed Smith also turned out to be a phantom. During his first year with the Cowboys, Smith, a Houston businessman who had tried to buy the Cowboys from Bright, held 27 percent of the team while Jones held 65 percent. Jones said that Smith made constant threats that he would try to wrest control of the team from Jones legally. In 1990, though, Jones was able to buy out Smith.

Was Jones seeing demons that didn't exist? Did the stress of overextending his resources to buy the team and then hearing the rampant criticism that was voiced throughout Dallas distort his perspective, his decision-making, and eventually his relationship with Johnson?

"These were very, very tough times," Jones said. "Here I was coming into a league that I didn't know anything about, taking on a management position that I had no experience in. And, at the same time, taking huge risks with huge amounts of money. More risks than I had ever taken in my life. Here was a person who hadn't lived a public life, and all of the sudden I was thrown in there and I was getting the public criticism. You have to understand that after I bought this football team that I had some doomsday-type thoughts. Whether it was real or imagined, I still felt that it was there."

Clearly, frustration and some mental anguish accompanied his first two years of owning the team. Because of that agony, Jones felt Johnson should have been more sympathetic.

"I can tell you that the first eighteen months to two years around here was a hellacious thing. You let all of that hit in about eighteen months and, partner, it will ball you up. It just made you wonder why Jimmy didn't have any more respect for my position.

"I bought the team and took all of the risks. And then I came in here and gave Jimmy all of the security in the world. I personally guaranteed him a 10-year contract. If he had never coached another game, if he got hit by a truck and got disabled, or if he never won another football game, he still was going to make $6 or $7 million dollars. The reason for the 10-year contract was that I wanted more of a proprietary feeling. I don't want to make the decisions in a vacuum that make me basically the sole keeper of the shop for the future around here. I want somebody else also standing right there, thinking about the future of the team. I didn't want somebody around here helping me making decisions who just had a short-term attitude. I didn't want a lame-duck coach."

The fears led to sleepless nights, and Jones admits that the lack of sleep and intense worry began to affect him. According to Jones, they also helped contribute to a cardiac arrhythmia, an irregular heartbeat. Jones claimed to have never experienced an unhealthy day in his life until he bought the Cowboys. Soon after, he started experiencing chest pains and a shortness of breath. He was sleeping between one and two hours a night.

"There is no doubt in my mind that the first two years I was here with the Dallas Cowboys gave me this condition," he said. "I would work my ass off all day. Then I would drink beer late at night and that would get me going some more. Then I would go in and sleep for an hour or two. And then I would head right back out. I never slept that much. But I sure as hell needed more than an hour or two a night.

"I would go to bed at one or two, and the moment I heard a cricket or a drip, my eyes would pop open. I couldn't sleep. All of this [pressure had] created such a challenge. I had so much that I got this condition. You can't get your breath. You hyperventilate and you pant. It comes from never honoring your body."

BY THE LATTER PART OF THE 1993 SEASON, JOHNSON WAS DEVELOPING some serious problems of his own. He had become insufferable around Valley Ranch, even to Lacewell, once his best friend. Johnson often had trouble telling people how much he cared, but never how much they disgusted him. Some thought that Johnson missed Dave Wannstedt, who had the guts to talk back to him.

With the Cowboys fighting for their playoff lives, Johnson strolled into a meeting with his coaching staff and, with a knee-jerk fury, drilled a hole in their collective psyche.

"You fuckers get it together or not a one of you will be around next year," he said. "None of your contracts are renewed yet."

An anonymous Cowboys' player told Mike Fisher of the *Fort Worth Star-Telegram*, "Jimmy would raise hell with the coordinators, then the coordinators would raise hell with the assistants. Then the assistants would raise hell with us. Then I'd go home and raise hell with my wife. And then my wife would raise hell with the kids."

Lacewell was surprised to find himself dodging Johnson in the hallways. They never drank beer together anymore. In the presence of several reporters, Johnson had "busted Lacewell's balls" for going to a New Year's Eve party with Jones at '21' in New York City, two nights before the team's regular season finale against the Giants that would decide the division title.

"Boy, Larry, that's exactly where our director of personnel should be on New Year's Eve, with the bowl games coming up the next day," Johnson said, laughing loudly at his own joke. Even though he could read the hurt in Lacewell's face, he never apologized.

Remembering Johnson's joyless struggle through the 1993 season, Lacewell said, "Jimmy had become the biggest asshole of all time. He had become very sullen. When you said something to him, it just came to the point where you didn't know what he might say back to you."

And Jones was getting tired of the bickering.

"I just got tired of the Jimmy-Jerry shit and didn't want to go through another season of it," Jones said. "I didn't want Jimmy going off telling the team that it's us against Jerry. He would have done that with my football team. And, frankly, given the hidden agenda Jimmy had of wanting to move on, I knew that it was time for Jimmy to go. I know he wanted to coach this football team one more year so he could win a third Super Bowl ring. Then he wanted to move on and take a good chunk out of this coaching staff. That just wasn't going to work. That's why I fired his ass."

Jones and Johnson had known each other since 1961. Since the day he had hired on with the Cowboys, Johnson had been testing just how far he could push Jones. His biggest mistake may have been underestimating the owner's volatile personality.

Former personnel director Bob Ackles, who had been Jones's right hand since 1989, remembers that, "Jerry could go off just like that. He could be calm one moment, and then just explode the next."

In late May of 1992, Jones had hired Lacewell, a long-time college coach, to become the club's director of college scouting. He called Ackles into his office to explain his new duties and to inform him that Stephen Jones would now handle all players' contracts.

Ackles admits that he picked the wrong time to broach a touchy subject with Jones. The Cowboys had won a wild-card game over the Chicago Bears. Months later, Jones had still not paid playoff bonus money to members of the scouting department, as most NFL clubs did.

"Jerry was going along, talking very calmly, and I mentioned the playoff money again," Ackles said. "He told me that life isn't fair and he just didn't want to hear about it any more. Then he jerked up from his chair and shouted, 'you're out of here. Get your office cleaned out by the end of the day.' He just went off and fired me out of the blue."

Jones's tirades haven't included just his employees. Johnson said he heard a knock on his door in Valley Ranch one afternoon and found a sobbing Stephen Jones standing at the door.

"He was crying because he said that Jerry had been bullying him again," said Johnson, who remains friends with Stephen. "You have to realize that Stephen Jones is a sharp guy. But Jerry was getting to him, just like he did a lot of people."

For Johnson, the bomb that had been ticking for the last three years was about to go off.

A MONTH AFTER THE COWBOYS WON THEIR SECOND STRAIGHT SUPER Bowl, Jones received a letter from Arkansas athletic director Frank Broyles, known as the Boss Hog in Fayetteville. It was Broyles who had recruited Jones and coached the 1964 national championship team. He remains an idol of the Cowboys' owner.

It was like any other congratulatory letter until the final paragraph, where Broyles tried to drive the most important point home.

"I just said right there at the end that it's too bad, that after all you have done that you just are not enjoying it," Broyles said. "At the time, I knew he wasn't enjoying it because of his relationship with Jimmy Johnson."

Jones and Broyles have remained extremely close friends. More than a decade ago, Jones called his former coach and said, "Frank, I've put you in an oil deal." Broyles profited by more than $10,000. When Broyles had to make a crucial decision regarding athletics, the first person he normally called was Jones.

Conversely, Broyles and Johnson no longer talk. There have been bitter feelings between the two men since 1983, when Broyles hired Ken Hatfield as the Arkansas head football coach over Johnson, then at Oklahoma State. Johnson accused Broyles of giving him a token interview after already offering the job to Hatfield. In his autobiography, *Turning the Thing Around,*

Johnson wrote of Broyles, "He became the first of three men I have written off in my life, all for failing to be men of their word."

Broyles's letter was not the first nor last warning that he delivered about Johnson. It became clear that Broyles was worried that Jones was losing control of the Cowboys to Johnson.

"I have told Jerry that in any organization there has to be one boss," Broyles said. "I think that CEOs all over the country could identify with Jerry when the split occurred. They saw the so-called power play of Jimmy."

What kind of impact did Broyles have on the Jerry-Jimmy divorce?

"I will say this," Jones said. "When Frank Broyles talks, I listen. His observations were very good, and also very clear."

★ ★ ★

AT 7:30 IN THE MORNING ON MARCH 28, JUST SEVEN DAYS AFTER the showdown in Orlando, Jones steered his long black Cadillac into his Valley Ranch parking space. Johnson had been told to be there bright and early for an "assessment."

As Jones swung open the door, he was met by an army of mini-cams and reporters, all wanting to know his plans. While meeting with Johnson for the next thirty-six hours, Jones appeared to be listening and trying to understand the exact nature of Johnson's complaints and intentions. The truth is, though, that Jones's mind was already made up.

"I knew what I wanted to do even before we started talking," Jones said. "I just didn't have any enthusiasm for patching things up. When Jimmy started telling me that he just wanted to coach for one more year, I knew that I had my official reason."

The mediator was Lacewell, who tried desperately to keep the two men together. He was acting as the unofficial mediator. As late at 11 A.M. on March 29, Lacewell believed the wounds could be healed, and was quietly slipping that opinion to reporters and talk-show hosts all over Dallas. The airwaves were filled with conflicting reports.

"Maybe I was dumb, but I just never thought that Jerry Jones would fire Jimmy Johnson," Lacewell said. "I just never thought it would happen."

Lacewell tried to convince Johnson to commit to more than one season, or to at least lie about it. But believing his power was slipping away, Johnson told Jones exactly what he wanted to hear—that he only could commit to the 1994 season.

"Jimmy told me that he felt like he had just lost whatever power he had," Lacewell said. "I told him that as soon he cut that first player in training camp, he would feel like he had all of his power back."

IN HIS OPENING STATEMENT AT THE NEWS CONFERENCE THE NEXT DAY, Johnson said, "We have mutually made the decision that I would no longer be the head coach of the Dallas Cowboys. We've had the most candid discussions we've ever had the last couple of days. And I will tell you this. I feel better about Jerry Jones right now for understanding me as I've ever felt."

Both men seemed close to breaking into tears during their opening remarks.

In spite of their intense dislike for each other, Jones and Johnson sat close together. They repeatedly praised each other. At the end, they stood and hugged. Jones noted that he had given Johnson a big "thank you" for his five years of service. It turned out to be a check for $2 million. *Dallas Morning News* columnist Randy Galloway might have described it best when he called the news conference a "lickfest."

Still, given several opportunities to apologize for his Orlando bombshells, Jones didn't. Before walking into the news conference, Jones telephoned Switzer in Norman and said, "Barry, get ready. If we can work out a contract, you're my coach." Even before the news conference was over, Switzer was making the three-hour drive to Dallas.

★ ★ ★

THAT AFTERNOON, JOHNSON SAT IN THE KITCHEN OF HIS VALLEY Ranch home and cried. Lacewell tried to console him. "I just can't believe that Jerry would go out and hire Barry Switzer," Johnson said. "How could anyone have the gall to hire Switzer? Not even Jerry, I don't think."

"I just can't see him going out and hiring Switzer," Lacewell agreed.

As the weeks and months passed, Jones and Johnson became less and less able to agree on what actually happened on the day of their divorce. Johnson still contends that it was a mutual decision and, that in the end, he convinced Jones to let him out of his contract. Jones's recollections of the proceedings are much different.

"The facts are that Jimmy wouldn't quit," Jones said. "I asked him to do that and he wouldn't do it. He wanted a settlement. The way I feel about it that Jimmy is just [promoting] sour grapes. The word [for what happened to him] is *fired*. Jimmy wanted to coach this team very badly for one more year. Basically, he sat there and begged me to let him do it. And here is another fact. You don't pay somebody that kind of money if you really don't want them to go away. I think what really hurt Jimmy is that I went out and hired Barry Switzer that fast. Well, fine. Feel bad, Jimmy."

Told of Jones's remarks months later, Johnson launched into a tirade.

"If that's the case, and if I was fired, then I'll just have my lawyer go by and see Jerry and we'll get millions more from him," Johnson said. "You can tell Jerry that my lawyer will be in touch."

On the afternoon of March 29, after the mini-cams and the reporters had left Valley Ranch, and before Switzer arrived, Jones quietly moved the long black Cadillac from the reserved parking space in front of the building to a grassy area in the back. The car would be parked there, next to his office window, for days. Once again, the death threats were rolling in.

CHAPTER 9

Jerry or Barry?

As the Oklahoma landscape rolls out of Oklahoma toward the Texas border, it changes rapidly from craggy hills to plains and scrub oak. The rust-colored mud of the Red River separates the two states. Folks on both sides of the Oklahoma–Texas line like their roadhouse music, their long-neck beers, and their cowboy boots. But they don't much like each other. Texans say their state will never sink into the Gulf of Mexico because Oklahoma sucks.

At the center of this animosity is the Red River War, a football game played between the universities of Texas and Oklahoma on the second Saturday of every October at the Cotton Bowl near downtown Dallas. For nearly sixteen years, Oklahoma coach Barry Switzer was one of the most hated men in Texas. He was accused by Texas coach Darrell Royal of spying on a Longhorn practice and of cheating to sign blue-chip players. Switzer returned the fire, claiming the Texas coach was getting lazy. Royal, he said, would rather stay home and "listen to guitar pickers"—a jab at

Royal's well-known friendship with Austin outlaw country singer Willie Nelson—than go on recruiting trips. Switzer was fond of reminding Texans that he was 4–0–1 against the legendary coach during Royal's final seasons in the mid-1970s.

Switzer was mired in professional burnout when he left Oklahoma University in the summer of 1989. The Oklahoma football program had been out of control for several years. There had been a shooting and a rape within eight days of each other at Bud Wilkinson House, the athletic dormitory. Quarterback Charles Thompson pleaded guilty to selling cocaine, even though he had managed to pass sixteen straight drug tests administered by the football trainer. In his autobiography, Switzer described the bizarre incidents as "shooting, raping, doping." It had all taken its toll on him.

Once he was forced out of coaching, Switzer had plenty of time to think and tackle many of his life's ongoing problems. He consulted psychologists and psychiatrists about his troubled childhood as a bootlegger's boy growing up in the rural poverty of southern Arkansas. He dealt openly with the suicide of his mother, Mary Louise Switzer, and admitted the guilt that had haunted him for more than thirty years.

Switzer had lived a chaotic childhood, bouncing around from town to town in southern Arkansas. His father, Frank Mays Switzer, held a variety of jobs—bootlegging, selling cars—and even did a stretch in the state penitentiary for his moonshining activities. Until Barry left for college, the Switzer family house near Crossett, Arkansas, had no electricity, running water, or telephone. Frank bootlegged right off the front porch. When he wasn't selling or drinking the bootleg whiskey, he was gambling, chasing women, or blowing holes in the ceiling with his .38 revolver.

Frank Switzer suffered a violent death. He was shot by a jealous girlfriend, who, feeling remorseful, helped him into the back seat of her car and drove off in a blind rush toward the hospital. Speeding down a gravel road, she drove the car into a bridge. The car exploded, and both died in the fire.

In 1959, a few weeks before the six-foot, 200-pound senior was to return to Fayetteville for his final year at the University of

Arkansas, his mother entered his room. In his moving autobiography, *Bootlegger's Boy*, Switzer describes how he said to his mother, who was loaded on prescription drugs and booze, "Mother, I would rather not ever see you again and know you are safe and well-taken care of, than to see you like this all of the time."

Mary Louise Switzer tried to kiss her son on the cheek, but he turned away. She went to a closet, took out a pistol, walked to the back porch and shot herself once in the head. She died instantly. The pain of that moment would follow Switzer for years.

UNTIL THE CALL CAME FROM JONES, SWITZER HAD BEEN PUTTERING around Norman, Oklahoma, for five years, half-heartedly pursuing business ventures. He constantly reminded friends that he had plenty of money to live on for the rest of his life. At his favorite restaurant, Othello's, he rarely talked football with owner Pasquale Benso, a close pal for a quarter of a century. Instead, they discussed the unfortunate circumstances of Switzer's childhood, or the nightmarish legal shenanigans that had cost him his job at Oklahoma. At Switzer's corner table, nicknamed the Table of Truth because no lies could be told there, a plaque still reads, "Old coaches never die—they just forget how to score."

But today, March 29, 1994, Switzer had already said yes to Jones's offer to coach the Dallas Cowboys and was rolling at 75 m.p.h. toward the sprawling silver city that seemed to stretch all the way to the Oklahoma line.

As he aimed his white BMW south down Interstate 35, he felt depressed. Switzer had been to Texas many times for social adventures. He liked the music, the women, and the night life, and he even appreciated Dallas's deal-maker mentality. He liked the fact he was going to work for his millionaire buddy, Jerry Jones, the owner of the Dallas Cowboys. But he didn't like leaving the security of Norman after twenty-seven years. Since being forced to resign as the Sooners' head coach in 1989, he had found peace at home. A man who once loved to run the bars had been getting comfortable on the living room couch.

"Hell, I've actually settled down some the last five years," he had told friends.

Now he was a marked man headed into enemy territory. It felt like he was driving into the jaws of a monster. Dallas hated his guts. Switzer decided not to tune in the talk radio stations, knowing they were already bashing him. Twenty years ago, when he was in his mid-thirties and his Sooners had won two straight national championships, he had loved to drink, dance, and romance across Dallas, kicking some big egos along the way. Now, at age fifty-six, he wondered why he was still chasing rainbows. Did he really need one more last call?

It wasn't long before Switzer began to have creeping doubts. Hidden behind that wide smile was a man having second thoughts. It had all happened so fast.

"As I crossed the Red River, I started thinking about my friends and the business commitments back home," he said later. "I started getting depressed. I had planned to do a lot of things with my younger son as far as getting him ready for college football. All of a sudden that was going to change. When it hit, everyone thought that I was on top of the world. But believe me, I didn't feel that way when I drove into Texas."

"I couldn't sleep," he said. "And fatigue just added to my depression. So when the next morning rolled around, I turned around and looked at my attorney Larry Derryberry and said, 'Are we doing the right thing?' Here's the thing. I was happy with my life. A lot of people get out of coaching and realize that is all they know how to do. I wasn't that way. I was happy. I really didn't have to work. I had money in the bank, a good income, and money for my kids."

During the three-hour drive from Norman to Dallas, Switzer also thought about the irony of his reunion with Larry Lacewell, who had been one of his closest friends two decades earlier. For the past two years, Lacewell had been the Cowboys' director of college and pro personnel. The picture of Lacewell and Switzer working side by side for America's Team was certain to spark controversy.

Their relationship actually extended back to the mid-fifties, when they played in the same high school district in southern Arkansas. Switzer was a linebacker and center for Crossett High. Lacewell was a halfback for the Fordyce Redbugs, who claimed another illustrious alumnus in Paul "Bear" Bryant. (Lacewell's father coached Bryant in the forties.) Lacewell often called Switzer "my high school hero."

At Oklahoma in the 1970s, Switzer and Lacewell's Sooners won two national titles and six Big Eight championships. Lacewell was named defensive coordinator in 1969, and Switzer was promoted from offensive coordinator to head coach in 1973. They brought the glory years back to Oklahoma football. It was an intoxicating time of partying, drinking, and womanizing.

"When I was drinking a lot, I used to say that you should never give up the moment," Lacewell said recently. "Here was a good ol' boy from Arkansas, driving a Cadillac and a Lincoln, and I was on top of the world. You couldn't have found a happier person."

The friendship died suddenly in 1978. The two were coaching in the Hula Bowl, an all-star football game for college seniors. One night in the hotel, Lacewell discovered that Switzer was having an affair with Lacewell's wife. They engaged in a brutal fist fight in the hallway of the hotel. Upon returning to Norman following the game, Lacewell resigned his post, ending a relationship that had helped the Sooners mount a brilliant run of winning seasons.

(Fourteen years later, during a six-week libel trial brought by *Dallas Times Herald* reporter Jack Taylor against Switzer in 1992, the coach would testify that he had indeed had an affair with Lacewell's wife. He also testified to having written a $25,000 check to Lacewell to ensure that he didn't discuss the matter with reporters. The trial pretty much ended in a draw—no money changed hands, but the judge directed each party to stay away from the other's business.)

Lacewell and his wife separated for several months. His friends described him as being a "broken man." But he returned to coaching at Arkansas State. Not long after Switzer was forced to resign at Oklahoma in 1989, he called Lacewell and apologized. The two had several meetings in Norman to patch up their differences.

Lacewell is now philosophical about it. "Seventeen years is a helluva long time," he says. "I mean, time goes on. If people make a mistake, you just hope that time can take care of it. I've made mistakes and I hope that someone would look at me the same way that I've looked at him. People change and people go on. It was seventeen years ago. It's over with. It's all water under the bridge. All of it."

Switzer is hesitant about discussing the matter. He says simply, "Lacewell and I have put our problems behind us. I made sure of that. Today, I consider Larry Lacewell my friend and my confidant."

In the spring of 1993, it was Lacewell who broke the news to Switzer that a split was imminent between Jerry Jones and Jimmy Johnson. The two were attending a party in Dallas during Troy Aikman's charity golf tournament and sitting at the same table with Johnson and Jones. Lacewell invited Switzer out into the hallway to talk.

"Larry told me a year to the date before the blowup that the fuse was lit and that it was burning and it could happen," Switzer says. "We were having a few pops out in the hall. He said, 'The relationship between Jimmy and Jerry is not what it seems to be. Barry, a lot of people think this is Camelot. But it really isn't.'"

The fairy tale was fading away. As the chasm widened between the two JJs, Jones was spending more and more time with Switzer in Oklahoma. He began to drop hints that he might just bring his former college buddy back into coaching. But until March of 1994, Switzer never really took Jones seriously. Then, before he knew it, he was crossing the Red River, heading south into Texas.

BUT ALL OF THAT WAS BEHIND SWITZER AS HE TURNED OFF THE LBJ Freeway onto MacArthur Boulevard in Irving, Texas. He had come too far to turn around. The next day, at the news conference announcing his hiring, Switzer looked like a man holding the winning $40 million lottery ticket as he settled into his seat behind a pile of microphones. All three local network affiliates carried the news conference live. While Jones was clearly irritated by the line of questioning—and the insinuations that Switzer was merely a yes-man for the owner—the bootlegger's boy bounced in his chair, smiled, laughed, winked, waved, and at one point shouted, "We got a job to do—and we gonna do it, *bay-bay*!"

Reactions to Switzer's arrival were mixed throughout the Cowboys' complex. Before making the hire, Jones had grilled Lacewell on Switzer's strengths and weaknesses. He never once mentioned the tender subject of Switzer's affair with Lacewell's wife.

"I told Jerry Jones some good things about Barry Switzer," says Lacewell. "But I also told him some negative things about Barry Switzer. A lot of people said that I recommended Barry for the job. I didn't. And when all was said and done, I was still surprised that Barry Switzer was the one Jerry wanted to hire. Very surprised."

An hour before the news conference was to begin, Lacewell sat in his office. His stomach was churning. He needed someone to talk to, so he called quarterback Troy Aikman.

"I can tell you right now," Lacewell told him, "that I have this very huge knot in my stomach. I don't know if I can live with this. I just hope that everybody will stop talking about our past in the next couple of months."

As Jones and Switzer prepared to meet the press, the Cowboys' owner flashed one of his wide, crooked grins. He turned to Switzer. "I looked at myself in the mirror this morning and this is the best that I have felt about myself in a long, long time," he told his new coach.

Reflecting on that statement, Switzer says, "I really now understand what he meant that day. He had been treated like shit by Jimmy. The things he had been subjected to were not good. He just made a decision that he was going to do it. And he went out and did it. Now, he has to live with it."

★ ★ ★

IN THE WEEKS PRECEDING THE PHONE CALL FROM JERRY JONES, Switzer had been troubled by something his brother, Donnie, had said. For the better part of his life, he'd experienced trouble focusing on extensive projects. He was also worried about a temper he couldn't always control.

"Donnie was talking about his son having an extreme case of Attention Deficit Disorder," Switzer says. "And he said, 'Barry, I have observed and seen some of the same things in you that I have seen in my son for years. There is no question in my mind that you have a deficiency. It's a chemical imbalance.' He said, 'You probably need to be tested.'"

Donnie Switzer, a lawyer from Vinita, Oklahoma, is a close friend and confidant of his brother. Barry takes any advice from Donnie seriously. In fact, Switzer was reading a book about Attention Deficit Disorder when he received the first call from Jones in Orlando about taking the Cowboys' job.

As he read, Switzer began to place check marks in the margins. Among the phrases he checked was "Poor impulse control, low stress tolerance with overreaction to the stress." Two others he marked with checks were "Poor organization with poor task completion," and "Extreme mood swings in response to events in external environment, or short, excessive temper."

Switzer discovered that Attention Deficit Disorder is a biochemical and neuropsychological disorder. The mind is often unable to screen external and internal stimuli. A person with ADD often can't be as focused as they would like to be.

As he considered his brother's advice, Switzer remembered his childhood, when he was often unable to concentrate on schoolwork.

"Back when I was in grade school, I never heard one thing that the schoolteacher said to me," he says. "I daydreamed all of the time. I looked at other things. I did that all the way through college. Except when I knew that I was going to have a test or a final or something. Then I would go into hyper-focus. I would go cram. I could block everything out and go to work. That's one of the tendencies of people with Attention Deficit Disorder. They know how to overcompensate when they really need to focus. In college, I jacked around for three years. Then I really buckled down and got things done my senior year when I made a three-point average."

As he continued to read about ADD, Switzer decided to take an eighteen-question test for the disorder.

"I honestly took some time to answer those questions because they had some depth to them," he says. "I self-evaluated and really thought it out. Of the eighteen questions, seventeen were yes answers, with one maybe. The book said that if you have more than twelve yes answers, then you need to be tested medically for deficit disorder. I knew it was time to do something about it."

When he arrived in Dallas on the afternoon of March 29, Switzer had little time for his personal life. But the issue of ADD was still on his mind. A few days later, he called team psychiatrist Dr. Mark Unterberg, one of the most respected men in his field. Besides his large private practice, Unterberg had worked with several players, coaches, and front-office personnel over the years.

After an hour-long interview, it was Unterberg's opinion that the coach displayed many of the symptoms of ADD.

"I described a lot of the situations to Mark," says Switzer. "He finally told me, 'You are a prototype. Let's put you on a low dosage of Ritalin.' I agreed that we needed to do something."

Switzer figured several days would pass before he felt the effects of the medication.

"But it didn't take long to take hold," he says. "I remember sitting here at the desk the exact moment that it kicked in. It took the edge off everything. I wasn't excitable anymore. I wasn't jumping from one thing to the other. I could finish a task. I could listen to someone. I could tell almost immediately that it was working. I slowed down. I sat there and stared at someone. I remember reading in the book about a woman who took Ritalin for the first time. She said she could remember the exact moment that she slowed down. She said that she had been on a treadmill all of her life. She said all of a sudden she slowed down. I had the same exact feeling. Everything slowed down all of a sudden."

Of Ritalin, Unterberg says, "It is part of the amphetamine family. So, in effect, you get what is a paradoxical response from people with the deficiency. If you give it to someone who doesn't have ADD, you would get an increase in hyperactivity. But it will slow people down who have the disorder. It stimulates the part of the brain that is not working properly. With that part of the brain now actually working normally, the person will appear to be calmer."

Indeed, Switzer appeared to be much more relaxed as he began his work with the Cowboys. He rarely raised his voice with players. They described him as "laid back," not a description he was used to hearing. Lacewell, who had known him for almost forty years, says Switzer almost seemed to be running in slow motion.

"In some way, he's just not the same guy that I used to know," Lacewell says. "He even walks slower. I was used to a guy who was a lot more hyperactive."

For the Cowboys' players, the contrast between Switzer and Jimmy Johnson was the difference between night and day. Switzer was armed with positive reinforcement from the start. He walked the hallways of the Cowboys' complex cracking jokes. Players who had been chastised for years by Johnson now were feeling a friendly hand patting their backsides.

One afternoon at Valley Ranch, the enigmatic Charles Haley discovered that his dominoes had been tossed in the trash. Trainer Kevin O'Neil had warned the players not to leave dominoes lying around the conference room. A livid Haley confronted O'Neil and threw a tantrum in the trainer's room. He abruptly left the premises and drove to his home in nearby Coppell. An hour later, Switzer drove to Haley's home to calm him down. It wasn't the first time that Switzer had gone out of his way for a player. When Haley had come down with flu-like symptoms earlier in the season, Switzer had personally delivered medicine to his home.

Skipping practices had been strictly taboo with Johnson, regardless of the reason. However, during the '94 training camp, Switzer allowed Mark Tuinei, Bill Bates, Alvin Harper, and Dale Hellestrae to miss complete workouts due to "personal reasons."

The day before the NFC title game in San Francisco, Switzer was trying to decide where to hold a "walk-through" practice. It had been raining throughout the day and the field at Candlestick Park had turned into a quagmire. So he opened the issue up to the players to vote on where to practice. The players decided it would be better to hold the final workout in a basement banquet room of the team's hotel. Many were shocked that they would be given a voice in the matter.

"They said that I couldn't have personal relationships with my players and still win football games," Switzer says. "Well, I'm not double-dating with them. I'm not going to their homes every day. But I like going into a work place where people have smiles on their faces. I would rather have harmony than to have that kind of tension. Jimmy didn't do it that way. All he did was stomp around on the sidelines and scream and holler. It's like Dixon Edwards told me one day. He said, 'Coach, Jimmy Johnson never even knew my name.'"

Switzer could be a jolly figure around the locker room. He was the friendly uncle who always had time to play checkers. Switzer even got a laugh during a Monday night game when safety James Washington and several Giants' players had been scuffling behind the end zone just before half-time. Washington grabbed a photographer's monopod and brandished the long piece of steel like a club. "What were you going to do, James?" Switzer asked him after the game. "Line 'em up and take all of their pictures?"

Switzer has a chicken-fried wit that sometimes gets him into trouble. At one point, Switzer was following Jones down one of the long hallways of Valley Ranch, hoping to have a brief conversation. But Jones was escorting four members of the NAACP to his office. The Cowboys had just announced a plan for more front-office minority hirings.

Reaching Jones's office doorway, Switzer tried to peek inside.

"Oh," said Marylyn Love, Jones's assistant. "Jerry's in there with the men from the NAACP."

"Is that right?" Switzer said. "What's he doing? Timing them in the 40-yard dash?"

His Tuesday news conferences were carried live on Dallas's all-sports radio station, KTCK. Along with the assorted "hells" and "damns," Switzer sometimes let a "son of a bitch" slide in front of a live TV or radio mike. The announcers went so far as to set an over-under on the number of cuss words Switzer would let slip over the next thirty minutes.

Stepping to the lectern for his November 21 news conference, the rookie coach didn't realize that the radio mike was already "hot." Sportscaster George Riba of WFAA-TV began to rearrange the microphones on the lectern. Riba was placing a long wireless microphone with a black wind screen into position when Switzer blurted, "Hey, George, that looks just like a dildo." Pausing, Switzer added, "Well, it kind of looks like an old dildo, George." Both statements made it onto the air.

Many folks in Dallas didn't cotton to Switzer's four-letter lingo. The *Dallas Morning News* received several letters about the expletives.

★ ★ ★

EARLY IN THE COWBOYS' 1994 SEASON, SWITZER FOUND HIMSELF having to wage war against the widely held notion that it was Jones, not Switzer, who was now coaching the Dallas Cowboys. Problems had started within days of Jimmy Johnson's firing in March, when the owner had moved his practice field gear into the private locker room that had been assigned to the head coach. Switzer was left to dress with the assistant coaches.

The perception problems continued during Switzer's first mini-camp that spring, when Jones started acting like one of the coaches. Getting dressed for practice, Jones traded his power suit and tie for coaching apparel, complete with a Cowboys' cap and a parka that sported a Cowboys' star on the front. He made certain to stand right next to Switzer on the sideline, creating the impression of a two-headed Cowboys' coach. Jones would never have tried this kind of stunt around Johnson, who would have blown a fuse if he had. He concluded the mini-camp by running pass patterns for the Fox network cameras.

With Johnson as head coach, Jones had merely seemed meddlesome. But the owner hungered to display his football acumen. He hadn't spent $140 million to sit behind an executive desk, figuring out more ways to market the most marketed team in NFL history. Jones wanted to be a football guy—and he wanted badly to be respected for his powers of pigskin perception. He desperately wanted to be embraced by the team he had emptied his bank account for. After all, he'd been the co-captain of the 1964 national championship team at Arkansas. He knew something about winning football.

Switzer didn't feel the need to distance himself from Jones. In fact, he felt obligated. For five years, he had been gathering dust on his living room couch. Because of the scandals he left behind at Oklahoma, Switzer had been blackballed from the college coaching inner circle. Only the University of Arkansas, where he had played and coached, had showed a passing interest. NFL owners hadn't called because they figured his only expertise was with the wishbone offense, now outdated even on the college level.

Feeling that the Cowboys had misconceptions about Jones, Switzer lectured the team a few days after hitting town in early April. During the meeting he told them that he felt that Jimmy Johnson had poisoned their view of Jones. At that point, wide receiver Michael Irvin stood up and shouted, "You don't know the bullshit some of these guys have been through with this owner." Irvin started walking toward the door. "Wait a minute, Michael," Switzer said, "will you please let me finish?" Irvin kept walking, firing expletives in all directions.

Switzer, the Bootlegger's Boy, was suddenly being perceived as something of a Bootlicker's Boy.

ON DECEMBER 29, WITH THE FIRST PLAYOFF GAME STILL TEN DAYS away, Switzer snapped. There had been too much locker-room debate about who was running the Cowboys—Barry or Jerry. Switzer had been called Jerry Jones's puppet since the day he'd arrived. Now, he felt haunted by the image.

The latest trouble had started just minutes before kickoff of the regular-season finale against the Giants, when he had reversed his plans and decided to start Troy Aikman. Aikman had a sore knee that needed rest. But the quarterback had pleaded with both Switzer and offensive coordinator Ernie Zampese to let him play a quarter or two. Since it had already been announced in the Giants press box that backup Rodney Peete would start, the press was surprised when Aikman trotted onto the field for the first series.

Jones had stood close to Switzer in the locker room while the decision was made to start Aikman. Again, Switzer worried, the team had gotten the wrong idea. Trainers later told him that several players were speculating that Jones had called the last-minute switch to Aikman.

Five days later, a still-upset Switzer lifted his elbows from his desk at Valley Ranch, balled his hands into fists, and began to punch at the air. His eyebrows arched and his teeth clenched. His face was turning the color of Oklahoma's home jerseys—crimson red.

"Jerry doesn't make any coaching decisions," Switzer snapped. "He never has made any decisions. But if and when he does, he's going to have to pay me several fucking million dollars because I'm going north of the Red!"

Switzer was still loaded with venom as he walked into a team meeting later that day. He opened the meeting by throwing a full can of Coke across the room. The auditorium fell silent.

"I want you mother fuckers to know," Switzer began, "that hey, 90 percent of you fuckers I can get rid of! Don't ever question who makes the decisions around here. Those statements about Jerry coaching the team, or making the decision on Troy, were stupid statements made by immature people. That's ALL! I guess it's time that I get hold of some of you people, to let you know who is the BOSS around here!"

Switzer's tirade could be heard well into the parking lot. Players were stunned at the outburst. Some, at first, didn't know what he was talking about. A few days later, Aikman told a reporter, "Until you just told me, I really didn't know what he was really mad about. But I will say this. I'm glad that he got mad about something."

A screaming Switzer was the polar opposite of what they had gotten used to. "It was so quiet in that room when he started yelling," said veteran safety Bill Bates, "that you could have heard a pin drop."

Several hours after the fiery speech, Switzer was back at his desk, still fuming over the locker-room rumors, and with the talk that Jones was running the team.

"Just because Jerry walks in there and we start talking, it doesn't mean that he is coaching this team," he said. "All of a sudden, there are a bunch of players back there talking to the trainer and telling him that Jerry told me to start Troy. That's a bunch of bullshit. I want these dumb fuckers back here to know Jerry didn't come out of the goddamn press box to tell me to play him. Dumb fuckers ... As a matter of fact, he went back to the press box thinking that I was going to start Rodney Peete. I just wanted those little termites to know that Jerry doesn't make those decisions. I told them never to question me on this AGAIN."

Even as he finished chewing them out on December 29, though, Switzer was apologizing. Although the players were accustomed to his free way with expletives, he now regretted using some of the harsher ones.

"At the end, he said was he was sorry for using the MF word on us," Bill Bates said later. "He just said, 'Guys, don't get me wrong. I really don't think you're a bunch of MFs.' But here was my feeling. I didn't care if he had to jump and bump his head on the ceiling. We needed that speech. I don't care if Barry was going to be the coach, or if Jerry was going to be the coach. We needed that speech."

Players could remember only two other serious Switzer outbursts. Once during training camp, when several players showed up hung over for practice, Switzer took them aside. "They ran me out of Oklahoma because of bullshit like this," he yelled. "I'm a nice guy. I'm going to treat you nice. But don't jack with me." The second explosion came early in the season when rookie first-round draft choice Shante Carver showed up late for a special teams meeting. Carver, considered an attitude case and a draft bust, had already had several run-ins with coaches. Switzer gave Carver a piece of his mind, expletives not deleted, and told him he'd better straighten his butt out, or words to that effect. Carver was later fined $10,000.

★ ★ ★

THE PREVAILING LOCKER-ROOM SENTIMENT WAS THAT SWITZER HADN'T been tough enough. Over the years, the players had grown accustomed to Johnson's blistering tirades. The pervasive paranoia created by Johnson's unpredictable outbursts had seemed to work. They had won two straight Super Bowls, hadn't they? Something was missing with Switzer and his laid-back style. Some of the players actually missed the crack of the Johnson whip.

Johnson had constantly threatened to cut players. When halfback Curvin Richards fumbled twice during a meaningless blowout against Chicago, the running back was released the day after the 1992 regular season finale. The blowups had started two weeks earlier when Johnson threw a fit on the chartered flight back from Washington after the Cowboys blew a lead and a crucial game to the Washington Redskins. He thought the team wasn't taking the loss hard enough. So irritated was Johnson that he ordered a couple of flight attendants to sit down and demanded that all in-flight service to the players be cut off.

"When Jimmy got pissed off, he put the fear of God in players," Aikman says. "I'm not kidding you. Some of those guys he was yelling at were scared to death. They would almost pee in their pants. They knew he would cut them in a heartbeat."

Three weeks before the end of the season, the Cowboys were leading the Denver Broncos 17-13 at half-time. But Johnson was so enraged with the lack of production by defensive end Charles Haley that he led the defensive end into a hallway outside of the locker room and threatened to cut him on the spot.

"If you think I give a damn what Jerry Jones thinks, then go ahead and keep playing like this," Johnson snarled. "Because when we get back to Dallas, if things don't change, I'm going to cut your ass."

Haley, who had only two sacks all season, had two in the second half.

Sports psychologist Don Beck, director of the National Values Center in Dallas, observes, "Jimmy is Machiavellian. He believes in pulling the puppet strings and having that kind of control. He is very ambitious and has a strong need to control. Jimmy's thinking is that you must get better, better, better. Barry's thinking is that if you're a talented athlete then we'll just kind of put you together and get out of your way."

Of Johnson's constant run-ins with players, Beck says, "Jimmy can have no alliances, no governments. He can have no bonds that obligate him. And therefore he can't be obligated to his veteran players. Barry is so different. He has many bonds with his players."

TROY AIKMAN WAS ONE OF THE PLAYERS WHO FELT THE MOST BURDENED by the change in coaching styles. Even with a 12–4 record at playoff time, the season had been virtually joyless for him. Everyone in the locker room could see that. Even as the Cowboys prepared for a divisional round playoff game against Green Bay at Texas Stadium, the atmosphere didn't feel right.

"I've been told since training camp that I'm unhappy," Aikman said.

"Well, maybe that's so. I don't know. I just know it's been a tough year on this football team, both emotionally and physically. Maybe we did miss Jimmy. The way that Jimmy wanted to get things done was very consistent with the way I wanted to get things done. When Jimmy was here, things were very easy for me. I saw eye to eye with the football coach. There were no real frustrations."

By the end of the season, Aikman had chewed on just about everyone. He became so angry on the practice field three days before the Green Bay game that he ripped off his helmet and began unleashing a Switzer-size load of expletives. The reason: A receiver who was supposed to run a seventeen-yard route had cut it short by four yards.

"I found myself yelling and screaming a lot more this year and showing a lot more frustration than I had in the past, probably because I had frustrations built up inside of me that Jimmy in the past would have released for me. Without Jimmy being here, I just had to get the frustrations out myself."

To help blow off steam during practice, Aikman would often punt a football into the distance. Aikman was kicking footballs so frequently during the 1994 practices that teammates began to worry he was going to start doing it during games. What bothered him the most was that players were not getting disciplined.

"If I were the coach of this football team, I can guarantee you that there would be three guys I would cut from this football team right now," he said. "Athletes and people who are professionals should know what their jobs are. But that is not necessarily the case. It doesn't happen that way with football teams, at least the ones I've been around. That is why the head coach must assert himself. I love Barry Switzer. But what he's doing is not working with this football team right now."

The philosophies of the coach and his star player began to clash from the first day of training camp in Austin. Switzer told the players that it wasn't his job to police the entire team. So he passed along some of the responsibility to team leaders like Aikman. To some, it seemed like a cop-out.

"If I have to police the players, if I have to be an asshole like Jimmy Johnson, then I'm going to be hated around the locker room," Aikman said. "I'm not going to have the respect of my teammates and therefore there is no way I can be a leader in that situation. Barry put me in a bad situation."

Like Aikman, running back Emmitt Smith was not fond of the more relaxed atmosphere. Although Smith had supported the hiring of Switzer, he eventually questioned his motivational tactics. "With Jimmy, he was going to cut your butt if he got mad at you," Smith told ESPN after the NFC championship game loss. "Two things were going to happen. You were either going to stop sleeping in the meetings, or you were going to try harder. Ninety percent of the time, it worked out well. You got better. With Barry, it was just too laid back."

★ ★ ★

BY THE TIME THE 1994 POST-SEASON ARRIVED, SWITZER HAD PROBABLY heard enough about his casual and laid-back coaching style. He had kept his cool in the face of media critics and cynics. He had barely blinked when former 49ers' coach Bill Walsh called him a "ceremonial coach" and said the assistant coaches were running the team. It didn't seem to matter that Pulitzer Prize-winning columnist Dave Anderson of the *New York Times* had described him as "this thick slab of tooled leather."

Even Johnson, now a Fox TV commentator, had been sniping at him through the media, questioning his commitment to the team.

Jimmy had ripped Barry for not riding herd over the Cowboys the night before the September 11 game against Houston. Switzer had flown on Jones's Lear Jet to Conway, Arkansas to see his son Doug play quarterback for Southern Missouri, returning around midnight.

"That shocked me," Johnson said of Switzer's trip. "Not even showing up for the meetings. He doesn't think that he needs to burn the projector until midnight. A couple of players have told me they better not be criticized for not focusing when their coach doesn't focus, either. One of the players said to me, 'What difference does it make? Switzer doesn't do anything anyway.'"

One afternoon near Christmas, Switzer gazed across his desk and said, "What did I ever do in life to have Jimmy Johnson doing these things to me? I was always nice to Jimmy. What did I do to Jimmy Johnson for him to say these things?"

Ironically, in 1967, Switzer had recommended Johnson for his first assistant coaching job in college football. Now, though, Switzer was sitting in Johnson's old office, with his elbows on Johnson's old desk and coaching Johnson's old team. Shortly after arriving on the job, Switzer had opened the office refrigerator to find Johnson's beer still chilling away. Jimmy's ghost was everywhere, and he wasn't about to let Switzer enjoy the job he'd taken from him.

Johnson's bitterness toward Switzer ran far deeper than most realized. In the fall of 1993, Switzer had called Aikman to ask if he could bring his son, Doug, to Dallas for some passing instructions. Aikman said yes. Even though he'd transferred from Oklahoma after only two seasons, he felt no animosity toward his former coach. Aikman said he'd work with Switzer's son at the Cowboys' complex the next day after practice. When Johnson had learned that Switzer was coming onto his turf, he asked Aikman to change his plans. Aikman met Switzer and his son at another location.

At the time, Johnson had told Aikman in a biting tone, "I don't want Barry Switzer thinking that I like him any more than I do."

When the two were coaching in the college ranks, Johnson was obsessed with beating Switzer. Johnson had been kicked around by the Oklahoma Sooners while he was head coach at Oklahoma State. But things changed when he moved on to Miami. The Hurricanes were leading 3–0 against Switzer's teams.

Before Miami played Oklahoma in 1985, Johnson became so possessed with winning that he called Michael Irvin aside and said, "If we win this football game, I can assure you that you will be taken care of for the rest of your life."

Ironically, Aikman was the Oklahoma quarterback, and he had the offense moving against Miami in the first quarter. When he ran forty-three yards for a touchdown, Johnson started ranting and raving on the sideline. Johnson told defensive tackle Jerome Brown, "I want you to go out there and break Troy Aikman's leg."

Aikman did suffer a broken leg that day, although he said it was a clean hit. Miami won the game.

★ ★ ★

ONE OF SWITZER'S FAVORITE POST-GAME SLOGANS IS, "THEY SPILLED their bucket out there today." This is his way of saying the team totally expended its energy and emotion. Did Switzer "spill his bucket" for the Cowboys during 1994? Several times during the season, he dropped hints that he would happily quit the Cowboys and return to his couch in Norman if he ever grew tired of coaching. *Sports Illustrated* reported that Switzer began to think seriously about getting out of coaching after the third game of the season, when the Cowboys lost an overtime game to Detroit. Switzer said the report was inaccurate, but he also admitted that he no longer had a deep passion for coaching.

"It was just like I told Jerry on the day that he hired me," Switzer says. "I'm not thirty-five years old anymore. I am not starting out all over again. I don't feel that I have that much to prove, that I have that much to accomplish. I am human. And I'm at the twilight of my career. Therefore, I want to win to be successful. But I don't need to prove myself anymore. I don't have to go out and show somebody something. I don't have that in me anymore. It's not important. I keep a perspective on life. There are just more things that are more important to me now. Like my family."

Clearly, this was not the same Switzer who had jump-started the Oklahoma Sooners with his motivational fire in the 1970s and led them to three national championships.

Some of the players wondered if Switzer was serious enough to be the coach of the Dallas Cowboys. Others wondered if he knew what he was talking about. He rarely seemed to know much about the upcoming opponent and could barely recite the names of three or four players on the other team. Referring to the NFC East division race, he called it "our conference." He often seemed detached and rarely seemed to know much about the upcoming game plan. Before the Cowboys played Philadelphia, Switzer told a gathering of reporters that the defense had no plans of using a "spy" formation against quarterback Randall Cunningham, known for his running and scrambling. But defensive coordinator Butch Davis would use three "spy" packages against the Eagles quarterback during that game.

Fox play-by-play man Pat Summerall spent a lot of time around the Cowboys during the 1994 season. He attended most of Switzer's news conferences and co-hosted a weekly television show with Troy Aikman. On Switzer's first season in the NFL, Summerall said, "I thought he started off bewildered and it got worse."

Dallas-based agent Steve Endicott, who represents wide receiver Michael Irvin, says, "When Michael and those guys start talking about Barry, they say he doesn't know what he's doing. They laugh at the guy. They make fun of him and his coaching. He doesn't even know the teams in the division. He doesn't know any names of the players around the league. But, at the same time, they like the guy. Kind of hard to believe, isn't it?"

Many of the Cowboys feel that it was Switzer's lack of drive and loose discipline that eventually caused them to sink in San Francisco. It could be argued that the team was not mentally prepared to play, since the Cowboys had three turnovers in the first five minutes. In his postgame analysis, Johnson surmised that the workouts leading to the game hadn't been physical enough. That could have been the reason for the turnovers, he argued.

One veteran player had a different opinion. "If Barry Switzer had spent as much time coaching this football team as he spent trying to get jobs for his friends, there is no way we wouldn't have gone to the Super Bowl," he said.

Football is driven by emotion. Johnson's way of motivating was by wiring the locker room with tension. Switzer preferred to see smiles. Was motivation the missing factor? If so, was it Switzer's fault, or should a veteran team be able to motivate itself? Or was San Francisco just the better team?

"All Jimmy did was constantly try to create a crisis," Switzer says now. "I don't have to do that to get results. I don't believe in staging a dog-and-pony show. You want to know the truth? The players really don't care who the coach of this football team is."

That, of course, is open to debate. If the Cowboys remain on track and win another Super Bowl under Switzer, a ceremonial coach will do. For the moment, though, they still haven't forgotten Jimmy Johnson in Dallas. And until Switzer makes them forget Johnson, he'll never feel completely at home south of the Red River.

CHAPTER 10

Image Is Everything

EVEN THOUGH THE COWBOYS HAVE PLAYED IN THE LAST THREE NFC championship games, have won two of the last three Super Bowls, and are among the most financially successful franchises in all of professional sports, Jones still gets strongly mixed reviews around the country and around the league. He was widely criticized for firing Tom Landry when he bought the team. He was considered a meddling owner while Johnson was head coach, and an egomaniac when he fired him. In many Cowboys fans' minds, he was permanently awarded the trophy for "Greediest Owner in Sports" when he shoehorned more seats into Texas Stadium, began charging tens of thousands of dollars for seat options, and then raised ticket prices again for the 1995 season. The fans might have overlooked his actions if the team had won a third consecutive Super Bowl but that, of course, didn't happen.

Roger Staubach has been an occasional Jones ally, but also understands the public's negative perception of Jones.

"His image is not overwhelmingly good," Staubach says. "I think there are a lot of people who respect Jones for putting his money on the line and building an operation that has been as successful as it has. But some of the things he's done have been at the expense of employees. The team is ticked off at him. Fans don't like him because he put in extra seats and charged a premium. Sometimes you'd like to say to him, 'Hey, why do you do these things? What are you going to gain?' Jerry Jones deserves a lot better image-wise. But he's just not getting it because of some of the negative things that he does on the side."

★ ★ ★

Jones arrived in Dallas with his spurs jingling. "Why do things conservatively?" he said. "Why not try to hit a home run every time?" Unfortunately, the high-risk, wildcatter philosophy that had served him so well in the gas and oil fields backfired during his early dealings with the media. It seemed that every time Jones opened his mouth, he inserted his foot.

It wasn't long before he referred to the Dallas Cowboys Cheerleaders as "the pick of the litter." Then fourteen cheerleaders quit the squad when Jones lifted the team's bans on the use of alcohol during cheerleader events and the dating of Cowboys players. The women didn't want the Cheerleaders' squeaky-clean image compromised. Jones eventually reversed his field and convinced the fourteen cheerleaders to come back, but he had suffered yet another public black eye.

Other gaffes would follow. Jones appeared on Brad Sham's radio show on KRLD with the owners of the local basketball, baseball, and soccer franchises. A caller asked about the variety of duties of a pro sports owner. "The difference between you fellows and me," Jones blurted to the other owners, "is that your balls are round." A stunned silence was followed by hysterical laughter from everyone on the show, including Sham.

Jones found himself having to work overtime on damage control. The public viewed him as a hoghat-wearing hillbilly from Arkansas, a fiddle-playing primate who had wandered down from the Ozark Mountains. If there's one thing that Texans hate worst than an "Okie"—a person from Oklahoma—it's an invader from

Arkansas. "People around here seemed to perceive his actions as an assault," says long-time Dallas psychologist Franklin Lewis.

Part of Jones's image problem stems from his willingness to change his position or his story depending on the needs of the moment. *Dallas Morning News* columnist Frank Luksa has been writing about Jones since the day he arrived in Dallas. Luksa says, "If he told me the sun was going to rise in the morning, I would want it notarized, photographed, witnessed, and fingerprinted."

The fact that Jerry Jones makes contradictory statements, and that he isn't always true to his word, hardly makes him unusual among sports executives, owners, or coaches. Still, Jones's record puts him among the leaders in the "most likely to mislead" category.

Since the Saturday Night Massacre in 1989, when he fired Landry, Jones has backtracked on many of the statements he's made to the media. For example, on February 25, in front of more than 200 reporters, and with live cameras rolling from all three Dallas network affiliates, Jones said, "The facts are that I wouldn't have been an owner if Jim Johnson wasn't the head coach."

Almost six years later, Jones sat in his executive office at the Cowboys' complex and said, "I have often been asked if I would have bought the team if Jimmy Johnson had not been available. I don't have to speculate on that. I know that I still would have. There is no question that I would have bought the team anyway, even if Jimmy weren't coming."

Less than two weeks after buying the team, in a speech to the Greater Little Rock Chamber of Commerce, Jones described an argument that he had with then-president Tex Schramm that almost led to a fist fight. Jones claimed that Schramm had started to crawl over the desk at him. Jones told the gathering, "I said, 'Tex, I'm forty-six, and you're sixty-seven. Don't come over that desk at me.'"

Schramm denies the incident ever happened. "Again, there goes Jerry making up more stories," he says.

After firing Coach Tom Landry on the day he bought the club, Jones expressed remorse at his handling of the matter. He told the media, "It was the most inadequate that I had ever felt in my life. And if you could grade that conversation from Jerry Jones, I got an 'F.'"

However, at the same Chamber of Commerce luncheon in Little Rock, Jones said that Landry, at age sixty-four, was just too old to coach anymore. "A man who is sixty-four years old can't communicate with twenty-two-year-olds anymore. It doesn't take a rocket scientist to figure that out. You've got too much of a gap there."

In 1992, Jones told *Dallas Morning News* columnist Randy Galloway, "I'm much more of a traditionalist than Tex Schramm. Tex gave the NFL imaginative thinking. He also kept the Cowboys on the cutting edge. Me, I'm more of a traditionalist." This couldn't have been further from the truth. Even though Schramm had an innovative side, he worshipped tradition. Jones, on the other hand, showed a blatant disregard for Cowboys' customs when he radically changed the Cowboys' trademark white jerseys during the 1994 season, after stating that the old jerseys carried "the traditional value of the old Yankees' pinstripes."

Less than a week after beating Buffalo in the 1994 Super Bowl in Atlanta, Jones was asked by a *Dallas Morning News* reporter about the potential for a breakup with Jimmy Johnson. Jones said at the time, "It's not serious. Our relationship is the very best it's ever been. It has a lot of substance."

Two months later, Johnson would be fired. Recalling the firing several months later, Jones said, "Apart from us winning the Super Bowl, it really shouldn't have surprised anybody, given our relationship, that I would fire Jimmy. Anybody who really knew what Jimmy was doing knew that we wouldn't last."

Long-time Dallas sportscaster Brad Sham, who did the play-by-play on Cowboys' broadcasts for nineteen years, questioned the integrity of both Jones and Switzer during a pre-game commentary during the 1994 season. Sham was coming to the defense of broadcast partner Dale Hansen, who had been both verbally and physically pushed a little harder than he'd expected by Barry Switzer during a preseason TV interview at the Cowboys' training camp. Switzer was upset that Hansen had reported on the radio that a rift was developing on his coaching staff. "What Jerry Jones and Barry Switzer say, and what they mean, aren't always the same thing," said Sham. He was immediately fired from Jones's weekly television show in Dallas. Lingering hard feelings were part of the reason that he moved from the Cowboys' broadcasts to the Texas Rangers baseball broadcasts seven months later.

As sports psychologist Beck says of Jones, "He's guilt-free. What he says today is for today only. He can change tomorrow. Whatever he has to say right now is justified in his own values system."

CLEARLY, JONES IS DRAWN TO PUBLICITY LIKE A MOTH TO A CANDLE. ESPN sportscaster Roy Firestone has interviewed Jones several times and has never been turned down on any request.

"It's like a drug with him," he says. "It can be addictive. And Jerry Jones, believe me, is addicted to the spotlight. I think that the guy would love to be a movie star, in the same way Ted Turner would like to be Clark Gable. Turner grew his mustache and moved to Atlanta for that reason. Jerry Jones would love to be Elvis. There is truly a desire to be on the big screen."

Jones takes on all comers. Sam Donaldson. Barbara Walters. *Time. Newsweek. Sports Illustrated. The Sporting News.* ESPN. CNN. No other NFL owner has ever been bathed in such a large, bright spotlight. In December 1994, ABC named him one of their "Ten Most Intriguing People of the Year."

Firestone has interviewed hundreds and hundreds of sports figures for ESPN's "Up Close," a forum for lengthy, personal interviews. Often, his specific goal is to elicit tears from his subjects—and Firestone, a smart, extraordinarily smooth interviewer, usually gets them. In late December, he spent more than an hour with Jones in his executive office. As his cameras rolled, Firestone repeatedly prodded Jones about his ailing father, Pat Jones, who at the time was thought to be on his deathbed. This time Firestone didn't get the tears he was looking for. But that didn't deter him from praising his subject. "I am as much or more fascinated with Jerry Jones as anyone that I've interviewed over the last two years," he says.

Television sportscaster Dale Hansen of Channel 8 WFAA-TV has been perhaps the most visible person in the Dallas–Fort Worth market over the last ten years. He has been at odds with the Cowboys since the summer of 1994, following a confrontation with Coach Barry Switzer. But Hansen still follows Jones closely, and often socializes with him.

"The guy is just crazy about the spotlight," Hansen says. "That's why when Jimmy Johnson was getting all of the credit, they didn't get along. These guys just didn't realize that this is a helluva big spotlight. I just wish they could have sat down and figured out a way to split it up."

The Cowboys' 1993 highlight film was debuted at the annual kickoff luncheon held before the 1994 season. The event is attended by more than two thousand Cowboys fans, most of them businessmen, who pay for the privilege of rubbing shoulders with their gridiron heroes. In the original version of the thirty-minute video, Jimmy Johnson was widely quoted and shown in several sideline shots. But that version was replaced by a new one after Johnson was fired four months before the season. In the final version, produced by NFL Films but approved by the Cowboys, Johnson's face barely appeared. In the final cut, Jones made more appearances than some of his star players. From prowling the sidelines to cheering in his luxury suite to being interviewed about the Cowboys' Super Bowl victory, Jones hogged the show.

Returning to the dais after the screening, Jones laughed, then said, "I guess I should apologize for being the most valuable player in the highlight film."

After viewing the video, Associated Press football writer Dave Goldberg wrote, "You get the impression there are two reasons the Cowboys won the Super Bowl—Emmitt and Jerry."

Is Jones's obsession with the limelight merely a case of full-blown vanity, or just good business sense? Surely, he is not the first successful owner to recognize the value of marketing and self-promotion. The man who preceded him as the club's general manager, Tex Schramm, was one of the best in the business. Once told by a veteran reporter that he reminded him of a young Schramm, Jones replied, "I take that as a very high compliment." Schramm, too, kept his vanity parked on center stage.

But the speed with which Jones has moved into the public eye is mind-boggling. Before he bought the Cowboys, Jones was a rich but obscure oil-and-gas man from Arkansas. He had never appeared in any medium larger than a Little Rock TV station or one of the local newspapers. Barry Switzer, who has known Jones since 1960, recognized long ago that Jones was destined to grab headlines and to dominate the airwaves. Somehow, show business was in his blood. "The guy is a just total extrovert," Switzer says. "He could be Robert Preston in *The Music Man.* Jerry likes the lights and the glamour. He really does. And he handles it well and carries it well and there is nothing in the world wrong with that."

Jones doesn't just welcome attention. He runs out into the middle of the freeway and flags it down. During the annual NFL draft, he allows ESPN cameras into the draft room, also known as the War Room, to capture every grimace and nervous twitch. While time counts down for the Cowboys to make their first-round selections, Jones takes center stage. He paces. He gathers his coaches and scouts around him, plotting strategy like Eisenhower before D-Day. He grabs the phone and rapidly dials the offices of another NFL team, presumably to cut a last-minute deal. Although there is no microphone in the room, you can sense that something momentous is happening. All the while, he keeps one eye on the red on-air light of the ESPN camera. "You can be sure," says a former employee who has spent a lot of time in the War Room, "that Jerry is always watching the red light on that camera. When it goes on, he springs into action."

Says Cowboys' director of scouting Larry Lacewell, "Jerry is known to get a little carried away. But you've got to love his energy."

Firestone says, "When Jerry is on camera, he cares about everything. Most people don't even think about it. But he cares about the lighting. He cares about how his hair is going to look on television. He has asked me to stop the tape to redo something he didn't like. Call it vanity. Call it whatever you want. He's got it. He knows that his image is as important as substance. Jerry Jones has taught us that more than Andre Agassi."

During a playoff game against Green Bay, Jones allowed a *Sporting News* reporter and photographer into his luxury box to capture his every emotional low and high. Firestone followed him around and sat in his box above Candlestick Park during the NFC title game against San Francisco.

Jones is also fascinated by celebrities. In 1990, actress Elizabeth Taylor sat in his luxury suite and called the coin toss for the Cowboys before a game at Texas Stadium. Of course, the coin had to be re-flipped—it's the visiting team's call. But Jones knew the image of Liz on his arm was one that would reverberate far beyond the sports shows.

The Cowboys' owner got into trouble with Jimmy Johnson in 1992 when he invited Prince Bandar bin Sultan, Saudi Arabia's ambassador to the United States, down to the field at Texas Stadium as the Cowboys were beating the Chicago Bears in the regular-season finale. Jones and Bandar are close friends; they share a passion for oil, gas, money, and the Cowboys. Bandar also happens to be one of the most powerful men in the Middle East. But Johnson wouldn't know Prince Bandar from Bart Starr.

That day was truly a moment in the sun for Jones. Leading Chicago late in the game 27–0, his Cowboys were on their way to the playoffs, and eventually to their first Super Bowl under the Jones-Johnson regime. As he reached the field, the Cowboys' owner paraded in front of the fans, bellowing "Cah-boys! Cah-boys!" while pumping his fists high into the air.

While the Bears were scoring a couple of late touchdowns, and halfback Curvin Richards was losing a fumble, Jones and the prince continued to cavort and celebrate on the sideline. Jones figured that it would be okay to take his friend into the locker room after the game. It was his team, wasn't it? But he didn't foresee two problems. One, the prince had a large entourage of security guards. Two, Johnson was in a foul mood after his team's sloppy finish.

Says Jones, "I really didn't think all of the security people would have to go into the locker room. I didn't anticipate it. But there was a large crowd outside the locker room. And the prince's people were getting a little nervous."

So the entourage piled into the Cowboys' sweaty locker room just as Johnson was unloading one of his loudest, nastiest tirades of the season. Johnson was not pleased at their intrusion. Later, Johnson and Jones would have a nose-to-nose shouting match after several drinks in the owner's luxury suite. "Jimmy was pissed that I brought all of those people into his locker room," Jones says, grinning. "But he didn't have to be that big of an asshole about it." It was just one more spark leading to the blaze that eventually torched their relationship.

Prince Bandar bin Sultan is just one member of Jones's celebrity fun house. Others who have watched games from the luxury suite include actor Charlton Heston, megamillionaire Donald Trump and his wife Marla Maples, talk-show king Rush Limbaugh, the Reverend Jesse Jackson, and country and western singer Reba McEntire. Limbaugh and Jackson were both invited to the Green Bay game, but Limbaugh couldn't make it. Imagine the argument that might have ensued between those political opposites.

Of Jones's collection of celebrity friends, sports psychologist Dr. Don Beck says, "When Jerry parades out his friends like Liz Taylor and Donald Trump, it's like trophy collecting. It's like the husband who ditches his wife for the pretty young thing that he can put on his arm."

What does this passion for attention say for the man? Johnson once said, "Jerry is the most egotistical man who ever walked the face of the earth. It's scary." It should be noted, though, that Johnson himself rarely dodged the spotlight. He vigorously tried to elbow Jones out of the public eye on more than a few occasions.

With Johnson out of the picture, Jones now leads the publicity parade. Switzer stands by his side, smiling and happy for his long-time buddy. He knows how much the attention means to Jones.

Clearly, Jones was born to be in the center ring. This thirst for attention is why he gladly swapped his privacy back in Arkansas for a place in the public eye—an eye that can turn discerning and cruel. Buried deep in his psyche, there may be other reasons for craving the spotlight. Is that a confident swagger the public sees, or a facade? Is the smile genuine, or is it hiding something? When Jones peers into the eyepiece of the TV camera, is he ever *not* selling something to the public? Or is he trying to sell himself on something—like self-confidence?

"Almost every cocky, egotistical, arrogant, camera-hogging person that I know has this incredible insecurity," says Hansen, who's known a few. "You really have to strip away some bullshit to find it. But it's there with Jerry Jones. It really is ... See, Jerry may have the money to buy financial security. But you can't always buy self-confidence."

Some friends and insiders say that Jones's love for lights and cameras is linked to his lust for power. Those who get along with Jones know how to stroke the man and his ego. Dealing with Jones's ego has been compared to a friendly game of catch in the backyard. If Jerry lobs you a compliment, you lob one back to him. For every kudos he tosses your way, toss one back at him. Those who have risen to power with Jones, and have survived, know the game. Jimmy Johnson didn't. He refused to play the game.

What does it take to get along with Jones? That questioned was posed to his partner, Mike McCoy. "First of all, you must have a desire to succeed," McCoy says. "And you must also have a willingness not to be number one. Jerry will demand to be number one a lot of the time. If you can swallow that, you'll work great with Jerry. It is partly ego. It's partly style. There's nothing wrong with ego, as long as it's directed correctly. It can be good or bad. There are no presidents without egos. Jerry's ego and self-pride have driven him to work harder."

It is clear why McCoy is still a business associate and Johnson is not. "You can say that I've been willing to share the good and the bad with Jerry," says McCoy. "His more notable ex-business partner did not."

★ ★ ★

ABOUT A MONTH OR SO AFTER JONES BOUGHT THE COWBOYS, HIS image and popularity had deteriorated to the point that they couldn't possibly get any worse. One afternoon, Cowboys' marketing director Greg Aiello received a phone call from James Francis, an aide to former Cowboys' owner H. R. "Bum" Bright. Francis had also run the successful political campaigns of two Texas governors, Bill Clements and George W. Bush, along with the campaign of U.S. Senator Kay Bailey Hutchison. Francis had been traveling in political circles for years. He clearly knew something about image and its power. And he knew that Jones's mishandling of the media had been a ruinous mistake.

Francis began the conversation by telling Aiello, "You've got to get this guy some help. They're going to kill him if he doesn't get some help."

Aiello agreed. After some discussion, the two decided that Jones should be trained by Fairchild and LeMaster, a media consulting firm in Dallas. They dealt primarily with individuals from the private sector who were diving headfirst into the public fishbowl. Jones was a perfect candidate for their tutoring. Then it was Aiello's job to tell Jones of their plan and get him to sit still long enough to learn how to handle the media.

Jones saw the need for drastic action instantly. A few days later, a rare but heavy snow was falling in Dallas as Aiello drove Jones to the offices of Fairchild and LeMaster. Lisa LeMaster met the two at a side door and smuggled Jones into the office. The offices of Channel 5, KXAS-TV, were right next door. LeMaster wanted to make sure that Jones wasn't spotted by reporters. Jones's media tutelage would remain a secret—at least for a while.

"The energy level of the guy was unreal when he walked in," LeMaster says. "He really was a great student. He's very bright. I remember him standing up and folding his arms and saying that he really understood what we were talking about. We were proposing a different way of thinking. Here was a man who had never been counseled on how he would be questioned by reporters."

Mostly, Jones is known for his talking. But there is another side of him that is rarely seen in public—a man who listens.

"When Jerry is on the learning mode and learning curve, he is a great listener," says agent Leigh Steinberg, who has been trading ideas and theories with Jones since 1989. "The world thinks of him as having an opinion on everything and talking all of the time. It's easy to miss his ability to listen because we just don't see it very much."

Jones listened as LeMaster lectured him on how to address the "real audience."

"Jerry didn't think of himself as talking to an audience when he was being interviewed by the beat reporter or the columnist," she says. "You have to think of it as a three-way conversation between the reporter, the fan, and the subject. Most people being interviewed just believe that they have to satisfy the reporter. I asked him who the most important person was. And he realized it was the fan."

That lesson spawned the phrase that he still continues to use—"Certainly for our fans." He began to realize that if he was going to improve his image, he needed to keep the fan in mind when he was talking to the media.

By August of 1989, Jones was ready to test his media schooling with a tricky oral final. In a bold move, he decided to face ABC-TV's Sam Donaldson live from the 50-yard line at Texas Stadium. Donaldson was appearing before a live audience in New York, with Jones responding via a satellite hookup from the middle of the field. It was the second show to be aired on the new series entitled *Prime Time Live*. From his opening address, it was clear that Donaldson was going for the jugular.

"So how does it feel to be Conan the Barbarian, Mr. Jones?" began Donaldson, referring to the bungled Landry firing.

"Sam," Jones replied with a smile on his face, "Coach Landry is a great coach. I wouldn't have bought the Dallas Cowboys if not for the great respect that I have for Coach Landry." At that point Donaldson interrupted and moved on to his next question. Jones would be cut off several times in mid-thought or mid-sentence.

Just a few weeks earlier, Jones had said, "I didn't pay Troy Aikman all of that money just to look good in the shower," referring to the rookie quarterback's $11 million contract. Most reporters considered it to be nothing more than one of Jones's many non sequiturs. Donaldson, however, grabbed it like a pit bull and refused to let go.

"You've been quoted as saying that you don't just hire good athletes," Donaldson said. "You've said that you hire athletes who look good in the shower, like Troy Aikman. Does Troy Aikman really look that good in the shower, Mr. Jones?"

Jones paused and grinned, and then said, "Sam, Troy Aikman looks good in the shower, and he looks good down on the football field."

Arching his bushy eyebrows, Donaldson said, "What do you do, Mr. Jones, go down and check the showers?" With that, the studio audience in New York burst into laughter. Trying to remain composed, Jones said, "Sam, I've been in a lot of showers, and played on a lot of football teams." With the laughter rising in the background, Donaldson bid his subject good night. At least the embarrassing interview was over.

A curious thing happened after this event. Over the next few days, public sentiment toward Jones began to shift, at least in Dallas. Columnists who had been bashing him took a more positive tone. The radio talk shows were not nearly as critical.

"The stories the next day were about how mean Sam Donaldson had been to Jerry," LeMaster says. "All of the talk shows were about how brutal Sam had been. And the fans, at least in Dallas, really didn't like it. I thought it was the turning point for Jerry."

Says a long-time Cowboys' employee, "It was like the people in Dallas still thought Jerry was an asshole. But at least he was their asshole. And they didn't like an outsider like Sam Donaldson treating him that way." Jones was becoming accepted by Dallas—at least to an extent.

Although Jones would stumble again, from that point forward his public image steadily improved. During the difficult season of 1989, Jones learned more about media, hype, and image control than most public figures do in a lifetime. He had to. He loved being at center stage too much. He had too many words bubbling out of him to either cap or censure them. He insisted on being the lead story, and his colorful manner and quotable style were irresistible to reporters.

The question, of course, is whether Jones, through courting the media and rarely saying no to interviews, has really revealed himself. Or has he successfully hidden his insecure side? Is Jones the most innovative executive in the history of sports? Or is he still Jethro from Arkansas?

"Any effort to portray him as a gomer, or a hillbilly, is not only ill-advised, it is inaccurate and stupid," warns Firestone. "He is anything but stupid and he is extremely savvy." Jones may never be completely accepted by his adopted state and city—or forgiven for the brutal firing of Landry the Legend—but his popularity has taken huge jumps since the Saturday Night Massacre. And his careful manipulation of his image has enabled him to successfully stride the boards of the biggest stage there is—as perhaps the most successful and recognizable sports owner in history.

IN SPORTS, OF COURSE, ONE OF THE SUREST WAYS TO SPRUCE UP A dilapidated image is to put a winner on the field. And with his team's playoff victory over the Green Bay Packers on the eighth day of January, 1995, the rehabilitation of Jerry Jones was nearly complete.

Hours earlier, the Cowboys owner had been so uptight that he had rushed down to the field from his luxury suite in the first quarter to holler at an official who, he believed, had blown a call. During the tirade, he walked a thin tightrope over the NFL rules. One wrong step could have resulted in a 15-yard penalty. But on this day, Jones was oblivious to protocol. He even stepped across the sideline stripe near the 30-yard line and onto the playing field to vigorously shake his finger at the official. "Dammit, we're playing for the Super Bowl here," he yelled at the official. No other NFL owner had ever rushed the field to protest a call. But Jones does things his own way.

Now, high above the stadium in his luxury suite, an animated Jones stood face-to-face with the Reverend Jesse Jackson. The two were verbally rehashing the highlights of the game. Their noses were almost touching. To an outsider, they might appear to be the odd couple. But during the last several months, the two had talked often over the phone. At the behest of Jackson and the NAACP, Jones had made scattered front-office hirings and promotions of African-Americans. The Jackson-Jones relationship had become so friendly that Jones now called Jackson "Jess."

Then Jones yelled, "Let's go," and burst through the door of his luxury suite. Waiting outside was a covey of stadium security guards and Irving police officers. Head down and arms pumping, Jones stormed past the black-shirted crew before they could figure where he was headed. Some half-jogged to keep pace with the high-speed owner in the dark suit and high gloss dress shoes. More security guards seemed to magically appear—like a phantom army—from the shadows down the hall. By the time Jones bounded down the stairs and emerged at a trot in the parking lot, the security phalanx had escalated to presidential-escort numbers. Earlier in the day, a Texas Stadium official received a death threat directed at Jones. An irate caller—apparently a big Jimmy Johnson fan—had vowed to kill the owner if the Cowboys lost. But Jones was not worried. It was only one of many threats made on his life during the previous six years. Besides, the Cowboys had easily beaten the Packers and were headed to the NFC championship game—with Barry Switzer, not Johnson, as their coach.

With his armed blockers leading the way, Jones charged like the old fullback he is into The Corral, a huge, circus-sized, blue-and-white tent assembled on the parking lot, where Cowboys' rowdies party after the game. More than an hour had passed since the final gun, and the crowd was well-juiced. The Corral, an invention of Jones, boasted the chaotic atmosphere of a circus drunk on tequila. A country-and-western band was banging out a song by Garth Brooks. The $6 frozen margaritas were selling faster than they could be blended. Jones's unannounced appearance was greeted with a wild cheer. Fans were groping toward him and yelling "JER-REE, JER-REE!" But they could not penetrate the wall of guards.

The man of the hour strode onto the stage. The band yielded the microphone to him, and Jones paced the stage like a lion stalking its prey. During times like these, Jones had the look of an evangelist. Not a polished, controlled Billy Graham, but the kind of fire-and-brimstone, arm-thrusting preacher who travels the dusty back road circuits and shouts, "What has the devil done for ya LATELY?" to a tentful of eager worshippers. Instead of good-time religion, though, Jones was selling football—and himself. His passion was evident in his piercing eyes. The spirit was upon him. Say Hallelujah, Brother Jerry!

"Do you think the Dallas Cowboys should show up to play those big ol' bad-assed 49ers?" he bellowed into the microphone, sending high-pitched feedback squawking across the room. "I've had my ass kicked so hard that I've bled through the nose," he said. "And believe you me, that is never going to happen again."

Whipped into a frenzy, grown men and women leaned over the edge of the stage, sloshing beers and margaritas, trying to touch the sanctified one. But the guards maintained a tight and rigid line. Some fans waved pieces of paper to be autographed. A woman stretched on tiptoe to hand him a pen and a pair of red panties. "I wanted Troy's autograph," she yelled. "But you're pretty cute. I'll take yours instead!" Jones smiled crookedly and winked, then waved politely and said, "Maybe another time, darlin'."

As he left the stage, he yelled to no one in particular, "To hell with Jimmy Johnson." But he couldn't be heard above the roar of the crowd, which was now a single, hungry monster. The guards were beginning to look worried. Together they began pushing through the crowd as they escorted Jones back toward daylight. Jones tried not to look fazed. But his face was glowing. He had just weathered the most critical day of his football career. He had showed the world that America's Team could win without Johnson. This victory belonged to the owner of the Dallas Cowboys. It was a feeling worth all of the millions he'd paid. The boy who bowed to the ladies in Rose City was now proving that he, too, knew football.

★ ★ ★

IN THE END, JONES FEELS THAT HE SHOULD BE JUDGED AGAINST THE bottom line—whether he is able to turn the Dallas Cowboys into another in his string of mega-million dollar successes. As his son Stephen Jones told the *Sporting News*, "Money is how businessmen measure success. In a way, accumulating money is a way of keeping score. Jerry may not need any more money. But if he doesn't make it, in his mind, he has failed." By this yardstick, Jones is well on his way to one of the biggest wins of his career.

"Tex (Schramm) told me in September of 1988 that I shouldn't buy this team," Jones says. "He said, 'You can't make any money buying this football team.' That first year, I was worried. With all of the visibility problems I had right off the bat, along with the unsound economic times, I was thinking about saying, 'To hell with the cheese. Just let me out of this trap.'"

His financial advisers warned Jones that his losses could be devastating. Not only was the Dallas economy in a recession, but the NFL didn't have a collective bargaining agreement. NFL commissioner Pete Rozelle was retiring. The NFL owners were fearful that their next television contract would include large cuts. The advisers predicted that by 1992, Jones would be losing $25 million a year.

Indeed, in 1989 the Dallas economy was unpredictable. Analysts didn't know if the area would pull out of the real estate and petroleum nose dives that had started during the early 1980s. When the Cowboys had moved to Valley Ranch in 1986, there had been grand plans for building elegant restaurants, a high-rise hotel, and a Cowboys' Hall of Fame. But with the economy crumbling, many of the original developers went belly up.

Now, though, as you drive down the steep hill on MacArthur Boulevard entering Valley Ranch, you can see condos and apartments and houses stretching far into the distance. The economy has rebounded—and so have the Cowboys.

"I know this son-of-a-bitch could be losing $25 million a year right now," Jones told the *Sporting News* in early 1995. "And I could be the laughingstock of the rest of the world. But some good things happened. The economy and the TV contract took off. If that hadn't happened, there is no way the Cowboys could have pulled out of it."

The Cowboys' financial ledger portrays one of the greatest turnaround stories in all of sports. The team lost $9 million in 1988, the year before Jones bought the team, and continued to struggle financially throughout the first year of his ownership. During his first four years running the Cowboys, however, Jones more than doubled the team's revenues. The Cowboys have averaged more than $30 million in profits per year over the last three years. During the 1995 season, his seventh with the team, revenues are projected to more than triple.

The Cowboys' franchise alone is now worth over $200 million. Since the team cost Jones $60 million, its value has more than tripled in six years. Add the stadium revenues, and Jones's properties are now worth over $300 million. That's especially amazing when you consider that original owner Clint Murchison Jr. purchased the team in 1960 for only $600,000.

Jones is clearly proud of the Cowboys' financial performance. According to *Financial World* magazine, the Cowboys have been the most valuable team in all of sports the last three years. No other NFL team has produced a larger profit or seen its overall value soar like the Dallas Cowboys. If the Cowboys can continue to win Super Bowls at a fairly consistent rate, Jones is sure to remain the top dog among major league sports owners.

At times, Jones's passion for profits seems obsessive. According to several financial and investment sources, Jones's net worth is approaching $1 billion. Recently, he invested $35 million in a West Texas oil-drilling deal with geologist and oil field partner Mike McCoy. The two are taking these multi-million-dollar petroleum plunges on a regular basis across the United States and Canada. As Jimmy Johnson says, "The first thing Jerry thinks about when he wakes up is how he's going to make more money. Then he thinks about how he's going to keep it all."

Jones disagrees. "I'm not saying that I deserve medals or anything like that," says Jones. "But when people tell me, and I hear it all of the time, that Jerry is in this thing just for himself, and for the purpose of just making money, then I laugh. That is very convenient and nice, and just as wrong as it can be. You have to make such a reach to buy these clubs. So you need other alternatives for making money."

He loves his success, but he hates to hear that he is perceived as an owner who cares only about money. He especially hates to be called greedy by Johnson, his ex-coach. Granted, Jones did Johnson a tremendous "favor" back in 1989 when Johnson divorced his wife of thirty years. Jones paid the $1 million divorce settlement—but with a couple of stipulations. First, Johnson had to sign all of the money he received from radio and TV contracts over to the Cowboys. Second, he had to both wear and endorse Cowboys apparel free of charge. All in all, Jones probably made his money back and more.

In fact, Jones turns emotional when he's told that the public thinks he's greedy.

"I'm not in this thing to make money," he says, clearing his throat. "If I sold the Dallas Cowboys tomorrow, I could find much better ways to make money. I could invest that money. In five years, it would be worth ten times what it was. You could line up ten financial experts and they would tell you the same thing. Hell, I could put it in the bank and make $30 million a year. What people don't realize is that I love football and that I love the Dallas Cowboys. Shit, I'd cut my nuts off for the Dallas Cowboys." No doubt there are Cowboys' fans who would like to hold him to his word.

CHAPTER 11

Honky-Tonk Man

"It wasn't God who made honky tonk angels."
—*KITTY WELLS*

"JERRY JONES IS THE GO-GETTINGEST GUY THAT I'VE EVER SEEN IN MY life," says Cowboys' coach Barry Switzer, flashing a broad, knowing smile. "And he is physically tough, too. He can hang out as late as anyone I've ever seen, then get up as early as anyone. He plays as hard as anyone I've ever seen for his age. He's unbelievable. Maybe he seems that way to me because I've partied some all my life, and now I can't keep up with him anymore. Jerry's had some practice—and I think that he's probably getting better and better."

Those who have partied with Jones know that he moves at a blinding speed. Just one night around the Cowboys' owner and you realize that he plays as hard—perhaps harder—than he works. As another Cowboys' employee says, "Drinking with Jerry Jones can be as hard as working for him." Chicken magnate Don

Tyson says, "When Jerry comes to work, he is a hundred-per-center. When Jerry comes to drink and play, he's a one-hundred-and-ten-percenter."

Jones calls this life in the fast lane "honky-tonkin'." Hank Williams sang about it in such classic songs as "Honky Tonkin'" and "Honky Tonk Man." Among his most famous lines was, "I could never pass a honky tonk, and there's one on my way home."

Those are words that Jerry Jones lives by, too. As he once told a writer for the *Dallas Times Herald*, "I like to stay out late. I enjoy the music and the camaraderie. I play hard. I like to dance and I like to be around pretty women. But you won't see any pairing up. There's the potential for someone to make something out of that."

No one knows (or really cares) what goes on behind closed doors—or after all the honky tonks have closed down for the night. But Jerry Jones lives full time in the public eye—conducting even his "private life" on a very public stage. He is well known for "playing hard"—making the rounds of the "honky tonks" with business associates, celebrities, and attractive women. His hard-partying approach to life is inescapably part and parcel of his personality, his image—even his management style.

THE JERRY JONES STORY IS A TEXAS-SIZED ONE WITH ROOTS IN AN Arkansas soap opera. The portrait that friends, former friends, and acquaintances paint of Jones during his heyday in the 1970s and '80s in Little Rock is one of a hard-partying free spirit who loved to gamble—and who somehow found the time to work hard enough to make the hundreds of millions of dollars it took to buy the Dallas Cowboys.

Although Little Rock boasts almost a quarter of a million residents, it can feel like a small town. Gossip travels fast in Little Rock. Although Jones's name rarely appeared in the media during his pre-Cowboys days, he maintained a high profile around town. His money and his status as a former Razorback star gave him instant recognition and respect wherever he went.

Even President Bill Clinton is entangled in Jones's past. Jones carried on both a social and political relationship with Clinton during the mid-1970s—when Clinton was governor of Arkansas. Even though Jones is a staunch Republican, he often contributed to Clinton's campaigns for governor. As recently as 1989, both Bill and Hillary Clinton attended a fund-raising homecoming for Jones sponsored by the Greater Little Rock YMCA. In spite of their political rivalry, the Clintons and Joneses were openly friendly toward each other that night, smiling and joking with each other during the evening.

Jones's connection to the Clinton family goes even deeper. Jones introduced Roger Clinton, the president's brother, to Molly Martin, his soon-to-be wife, at a party in Little Rock. They were married in Dallas in 1993.

Beyond the high-profile social scene around Little Rock, Bill Clinton and Jerry Jones also ran in the same late-night circles. They were often seen around Little Rock at some of the same bars and restaurants, including Cajun's Wharf, one of the city's hot spots.

Relations between Jones and Clinton soured in 1990, when Jones encouraged his close friend Sheffield Nelson to run against Clinton as the Republican candidate for governor. Although Jones had moved his family to Dallas in 1989, he remained connected to Arkansas through Nelson's campaign. He traveled to his native state at least once a week and contributed heavily to the effort to unseat the incumbent governor.

Before the election, Jones, on Nelson's behalf, hired a private investigator in Little Rock to tail Clinton on some of his nighttime excursions. In 1991, during the Cowboys' training camp in Austin, Jones bragged to reporters that the investigator had turned up evidence concerning Clinton's affairs with several women. "He even led our guy to Gennifer Flowers," Jones said. Just a few months later, as Clinton was campaigning for the White House, Flowers claimed that she'd carried on a long-standing affair with him. Former U.S. Congressman Tommy Robinson, who was a member of Clinton's original cabinet in 1979, said that Jones and Clinton have a common bond when it comes to women. "Jerry and Bill are cut from the same cloth," he says. "They both love to chase pretty women." Flowers also has been seen by several eyewitnesses in Little Rock, and later in Dallas, with Jones.

★ ★ ★

It wouldn't have been the first time that Jones had been seen in public with an attractive young woman. Just as the stories about Clinton and his womanizing in Little Rock have been circulated widely, so have those about Jones and his circle.

Robinson, who ended his friendship with Jones in 1990 over political and financial disagreements, says "Jerry has always been a womanizer. It is his Achilles heel. People have always asked me how he got away with it... Well, Jerry is a bullshit artist. He thinks he can talk his way out of anything. And he got his womanizing from his dad. Jerry was around it growing up in that environment in Rose City. His dad was one of the biggest womanizers you'll ever see. Jerry learned from the master."

Jones has often said that when Pat Jones ran Modern Security Life Insurance Company in Springfield, Missouri—where Jerry Jones was executive vice president—he would base his hiring decisions on a potential salesman's speed and expertise at seducing women. Sports psychologist Dr. Don Beck, who is familiar with Jones's night life, says, "He likely inherited his thrill-seeking personality from his father. He is searching for approval—and he may very well be searching for approval from his father."

Fred Marshall played quarterback and was a teammate of Jones on the University of Arkansas's national championship team in 1964. Marshall has known Jones since they were freshmen together in 1960. He also helped manage Jones's various petroleum interests in Little Rock from 1981 through 1983.

"I think that it's just a known fact that Jerry loves women," Marshall says. "Back when I was working for him, there were always women around—whether it was at 35,000 feet in his airplane, or in some bar. There was always drinking and there was always fun and there were always women. I can't be specific because I can't remember their names. And what he did behind closed doors, I don't know. He never invited me in there."

THE EXPLOITS OF SOME OF JONES'S FRIENDS OFFERS A PICTURE OF THE hard-partying atmosphere in Little Rock during that era. One of Jones's buddies was Dan Lasater, a Little Rock businessman and investor and a highly successful thoroughbred race horse owner. Lasater and Jones often traveled to New York—or to the local racetrack—together. Lasater raced many of his horses at Oaklawn Park, a racetrack fifty miles southwest of Little Rock. He won three straight Eclipse Awards, racing's equivalent of an Oscar. It was no secret that Lasater was living the fast life around Little Rock in the 1970s and 1980s. Parties at his office and other spots around Little Rock featured attractive young women and readily available cocaine. In 1994, Lasater told CNN, "I was giving cocaine at parties to friends and partners." While there's no evidence—and there should be no implication—that these friends and partners included Jerry Jones, Lasater has admitted to using cocaine with Roger Clinton, as well as giving it away to the soon-to-be president's brother. (Roger Clinton later served prison time on a charge of trafficking the substance.) Lasater has also said he loaned Roger Clinton $8,000 to help pay off his cocaine debts.

In 1986, Lasater was convicted in federal court of purchasing cocaine for his personal use. He served a year in a federal penitentiary. During his 1986 trial, he testified that he'd never trafficked in the substance, but said that he'd given it away in large quantities to his friends and acquaintances on several occasions.

GAMBLING HAS ALSO BEEN AN IMPORTANT PART OF JONES'S LIFESTYLE. In fact, if the National Football League had known of some of Jones's sports gambling activities in the 1970s and 1980s, his confirmation for ownership might not have been as swift or as painless.

Before a potential new owner is approved by league owners, the league's security investigators check out his background. The investigators look into the candidate's personal and professional life, including his marital status, his past use of drugs and alcohol, and possible illegal gambling activities. One potential investor, part of a group that tried to buy the Cowboys from Clint Murchison, Jr., was disqualified by the league in 1984. The league determined that the man had a past history of "dangerous association with gamblers."

One person the security investigators didn't question while checking out Jones was Joe Calva, a long-time sports and horse-racing bookmaker in North Little Rock who has been in and out of trouble with the law for more than thirty years.

Calva was a friend of the Jones family almost from the day that Pat Jones moved his family back from Los Angeles to North Little Rock in 1945. In fact, Calva and Pat Jones had both grown up in Scott, a small cotton-farming town outside of North Little Rock. For a short time, Calva was Pat Jones's partner in a Little Rock life insurance agency. His first recollection of meeting Jerry was at a fish fry in North Little Rock in the late 1940s.

"We used to all meet at the Old River Club down near Scott," he remembers. "We'd have chitlin' suppers down there. I've known Jerry for a long time. Jerry is just a blueprint of his dad. They were exactly the same." Calva says that Pat Jones placed wagers through him on football games and the horse races.

For more than twenty-two years, Calva owned and operated the Checkmate Club in North Little Rock, a smoky singles bar in the basement of a former church. Located in the aging downtown area near the Arkansas River, the Checkmate featured live music and stayed open until four in the morning. The bar often drew shoulder-to-shoulder crowds, especially on weekends. It was also known for several years as a meeting point in North Little Rock for drug deals. Patrons often smoked marijuana in the restrooms and even on the dance floor.

For more than thirty years, Calva made quite a bit of extra cash on the side as a bookmaker. He accepted bets on most professional and college games, along with wagers on the horses at Oaklawn Park. Bets often were either paid or collected at the Checkmate.

One of his betting customers, Calva says, was Jerry Jones. According to Calva, Jones was a regular at the Checkmate during the nineteen years that he lived in Little Rock. He often showed up with a regular crowd of friends, including Sheffield Nelson.

"Jerry would make bets of a few hundred to several hundred to maybe a thousand [dollars] or more on football," Calva says. "He liked the college games. But what he really liked was the horses. He would always bet across the board (win, place, and show)."

Robinson confirms Jones's betting. "Jerry didn't necessarily bet to make money because he had all of the cash you could need anyway. But if he saw a point spread out of whack, say, St. Louis favored over the Cowboys, he'd bet $500 or $1,000, maybe more, just to show the bookmakers they were wrong. He was pretty regular on his bets on the Dallas Cowboys."

Jones's application for ownership might have been treated differently if the league had known of his betting on NFL games. According to a NFL official, "If it was known a prospective owner had bet on NFL games, and there was solid information, it would have been troubling," the official said. "Betting on games by prospective owners is a strict violation of NFL rules. There would have been some serious questions."

In the 1980s Calva pleaded guilty to a misdemeanor charge of bookmaking, paid a $7,500 fine, and was given a year of probation. In 1982, Calva came under federal investigation for placing wagers across the state line. Although he was never indicted, Calva said he was warned by a FBI agent in Little Rock. "That agent told me he'd be back to get me," Calva says. "Sure enough, they came back. And they got me." Convicted in 1990 on drug conspiracy charges, he also pleaded guilty to money laundering. Calva says he was operating an illegal bingo parlor above his night club. The Checkmate, now closed, was seized by the federal government after Calva's conviction.

After spending more than two years in the federal correctional unit in Millington, Tennessee, Calva was released in August 1993. He is now retired just outside North Little Rock.

★ ★ ★

WHEN JERRY JONES ENTERED THE INTENSE MEDIA SPOTLIGHT THAT surrounds the Dallas Cowboys, he didn't leave his honky-tonkin' ways behind. Once his day spent selling, marketing, and running America's Team comes to an end, Jerry Jones flips off the office lights and heads for the bright lights. That's when the good times start to roll.

Jones is more fond of Dallas's upscale trendy bars than its dimly lit roadhouses—where a blue-collar crowd drinks long-neck beers, the action is hot and sweaty, and the floor is littered with peanut shells. In Dallas, he socializes with a squeaky-clean mon-eyed crowd in high-toned places where Mercedeses and Jaguars are parked outside and where jukeboxes have long been forgotten.

Some of his nighttime prowls through Dallas lead him to the live music spots along Belt Line in Addison, into the glittery young country dance clubs of North Dallas, or the trendy bars in the McKinney Avenue Uptown area. You might find him dancing at the Broadway Grille one night, or at the very hip 8.0 the next. You might also find him in The Library, the intimate piano bar inside the stately Melrose Hotel on Oaklawn Avenue, or across the street at the Star Canyon Restaurant, one of Dallas's most elite and expensive eateries.

Another of his regular stops is The Mansion on Turtle Creek, perhaps Dallas's finest hotel and restaurant. It's where the party really began for Jones back in 1989, where he and Jimmy Johnson, along with their wives, stayed while the sale of the Cowboys was finalized.

Wherever he goes in Dallas, Jones is treated like the King of the Cowboys. There may be a curfew for the players, but not for Jerry and friends. He has literally been the toast of Dallas and anywhere else Cowboys fans congregate since his team won its second Super Bowl.

"Here is a man who loves to be loved," says KRLD-AM radio talk show host Jody Dean, a Jones friend and supporter. "He'll buy a round even if it's in Austin Memorial Stadium (seating capacity—80,000)."

Jones is a very rich, very powerful, very charismatic man who likes to have a good time. Because Jones is the highest profile owner in American sports, and because the Cowboys won two Lombardi Trophies in the 1990s, he is often overwhelmed by autograph seekers—and just plain seekers.

"When Jones walks into a bar, he just takes over the room," says popular WFAA-TV sportscaster Dale Hansen, who regularly bar-hops with the Cowboys owner. "He loves people hanging on him. He loves the attention of being Jerry Jones. He goes into the bar, shakes hands with everybody in the room, buys drinks for everyone in the room, and flirts with every woman in the room. But who really knows what he's doing? You can imagine. But who really knows?"

DURING THE SUMMER OF 1994, JONES AND HANSEN WERE MAKING their fourth stop of the night, bar-hopping around Austin, when they realized that last call was approaching at 2 a.m. The lights started going up. Jones leaned across the bar to order one more round. He was brusquely informed that the place had just closed.

"Okay," Jones said, cocking an eyebrow and winking at the bartender. "If you're not gonna serve us, then here's the deal. I'm going to buy this goddamn bar right here and now, and you're gonna be the first fucker to go."

A few minutes later, after negotiating with the bartender, Jones leaned over to Hansen and said, "Go to the bathroom."

"Huh?" Hansen said. "I don't need to go to the bathroom."

"Just go to the bathroom, Dale, dammit," Jones said, winking. "I'm telling you. Go to the bathroom."

What Hansen found waiting in the rest room was far more interesting than the usual stalls and urinals. "I walked in and the bartender was sitting there on a stool, mixing drinks right in the bathroom," Hansen says. "He just set up shop and went to work. I went to the bathroom about six more times that night."

Not only did Jones manage to keep the drinks flowing, he convinced several of the patrons to hang around. It wasn't the first time, nor would it be the last, that the Cowboys owner would threaten to buy the bar just to make sure it wouldn't close.

"About 4:30 in the morning, I decided it was time for me to go to bed," Hansen says. "I looked out on the dance floor, and Jones was out there dancing like crazy with about twenty other people. I woke up the next day at three in the afternoon with a hangover that would kill the average bear. Jones got up that morning at seven and did *Good Morning America*, or something like that. I don't know how he does it. He's got more energy than any man should be allowed to have. When it comes to partying, he is on the NFL level. I think I'm pretty good. But I'm just a small-time NAIA college team compared to him."

JONES HAS A TEXAS-SIZED REPUTATION WHEN IT COMES TO PARTYING and womanizing. More often than not, you will find Jones dining, dancing, or drinking with at least one attractive female on his nighttime excursions. More often than not, that attractive female will not be Gene Jones, his wife of thirty-four years.

"Jerry Jones likes good-looking, young, attractive women hanging on his arm when he's flirting and hanging out in the bars," Hansen says. "There are worse things. There are worse marriages. Hell, I like young attractive women hanging around me, too."

Not everyone in Dallas approves, though. Cowboys' quarterback Troy Aikman, who admires Jones, says, "I have nothing but respect for Jerry Jones as a businessman and as a football person. But when I hear about and see some things that he does in the bars at night, I have some serious questions about him."

Former Cowboys' wide receiver Drew Pearson was a partner in a nightclub called Drew Pearson's 88, a bar in North Dallas that often featured live music. Jones could be seen there frequently, dancing and drinking and schmoozing with the customers. "Some of the things he used to do in my club were disgusting," Pearson says of Jones's hard-partying style.

Jones sometimes irritates women he doesn't know by pinching them on the rear end. One evening in June of 1993 he was sitting at a table near the front door of 8.0 in Dallas. As a couple passed, Jones reached up and pinched the woman's rear end. Little did he know that the woman, Marla Mantle, was the wife of David Mantle, the son of the late baseball great Mickey Mantle. She was also six months pregnant at the time. Knowing that her husband would be enraged, she didn't tell David Mantle what had happened until the next day.

JONES IS OFTEN SEEN IN PUBLIC WITH SUSAN SKAGGS, AN ATTRACTIVE sales and marketing employee at Texas Stadium who is twenty years his junior. Skaggs was at Jones's side in the lobby bar of the Hyatt Grand Cypress in Orlando when Jones revealed his plans to fire Jimmy Johnson and hire Barry Switzer.

It is no secret that Jones and Skaggs have had more than a boss-employee relationship, although Cowboys' employees—who fear for their jobs—rarely talk about it. Jones and Skaggs have been seen dining, drinking, and dancing at bars and restaurants throughout the Dallas area for the last three years. Since she was hired by the Cowboys back in 1991, Skaggs has often traveled to the team's away games. Skaggs also travels with Jones to NFL marketing seminars and meetings, even though her duties are not directly tied to the football club.

Skaggs started working for Texas Stadium in 1991 as the marketing director of the Texas Stadium Market Place, a doomed attempt to create the world's largest flea market. The project ended up costing Jones more than $4 million. But Skaggs was promoted to marketing director at Texas Stadium. She handles special events at the Stadium, including the annual Cinco de Mayo celebration and a country and western festival sponsored by a local FM radio station.

Although Skaggs's duties are directly related to Texas Stadium, she doesn't report to Bruce Hardy, the Stadium's long-time general manager. The only person she answers to is Jones, whose offices are more than ten miles away at the Cowboys' complex in Valley Ranch. Skaggs also outranks Hardy in terms of salary—she makes $100,000 a year, $30,000 more than Hardy.

Like several other employees, she is allotted four season tickets, which she then passes along to a car dealer in return for the use of an automobile. It's a custom that most of the employees follow. Before Jones bought the team, these tickets for auto dealers were generally situated on the 50-yard line. That kind of placement guaranteed that the Cowboys' employees could drive high-priced foreign cars.

But in 1990 Jones moved these tickets from the 50-yard line down to the 5-yard line. As a result, Texas Stadium employees who hold jobs equivalent to Skaggs's now drive domestic cars valued in the $15,000 to $20,000 range. Skaggs, however, drives a new $40,000 Acura Legend. The reason is that, along with the usual four season tickets, she was also given luxury box tickets to pass along to her car dealer. The arrangement was set up by Jones.

One of Skaggs's duties was helping to organize the Cowboys' first Super Bowl parade through downtown Dallas after the 1992 season. The parade was an unmitigated disaster, thanks in good part to inadequate planning by city officials. Thousands of fans broke through barricades and pushed their way to within a few feet of the motorcade. Most of the Cowboys' players were riding in convertibles. Some were with their families. Many players admitted that they were frightened by the unruly crowd. Fights broke out throughout the downtown crowd and several injuries were reported. Police had trouble controlling the crowd well past nightfall. Television accounts of the violence were carried that night across the country.

Jones chose to spend that evening celebrating the parade with Skaggs at Memphis, a popular spot in Addison known for its live music. Jones and Skaggs sat together next to the front door.

Six weeks earlier, when the Cowboys defeated the Philadelphia Eagles at Texas Stadium in the first round of the playoffs, Skaggs had also accompanied Jones on the celebration trail. One stop that night was the Broadway Grille, another of Addison's live music spots. After Cowboys' games, the Broadway Grille draws shoulder-to-shoulder crowds. This night was no exception.

As Jones and Skaggs stood at the circular bar, the Cowboys' owner talked to several patrons, including Cowboys' defensive tackle Tony Casillas. Soon they were all dancing. Jones is rather unorthodox on the dance floor. He keeps both hands in front of his face, as if he's talking into his cuff links. He appears ready at any moment to break into a Kung Fu move. As a friend in Dallas says, "Try to imagine Andy Griffith boogying. That's what Jerry looks like on the dance floor."

But Skaggs isn't the only young woman Jones is seen with around Dallas after the sun goes down. In a story Jones likes to tell about himself, he once went home after an outing in Dallas with a note from a female admirer in his coat pocket. Gene Jones discovered the note as she prepared to take the coat to the cleaners. When Jones returned home from work the next night, he found his wife still steaming mad. She surprised him with the note and then stood there with her arms crossed. But Jones thought quickly. "Dad-gummit," he said with a nervous chuckle, "that Marylyn Love is always playing tricks on me. Yep, that's her handwriting, all right. I guess she thought she was being pretty funny, leaving this dad-gum note in my coat." Marylyn Love is an assistant to the Cowboys' general manager, and the handwriting, of course, was not hers.

AS COWBOYS' PLAYERS WERE FILING OFF THE BUSES OUTSIDE THE Phoenix Airport Hilton on October 22, 1994, a very young, very attractive woman stood in the hotel lobby, waiting to meet the stars. The Cowboys were scheduled to play the Arizona Cardinals the next day at Sun Devil Stadium in Tempe. The team often attracts huge crowds in hotel lobbies, more so than any other team in the NFL. Amanda Brown (not her real name) was a model from the West Coast, and in many ways not unlike the many other pretty women who stand around the hotel lobbies where the Cowboys stay on the road. She had curly blonde hair and blue eyes, and her short skirt emphasized her deep tan and shapely figure.

As the players began entering the lobby, Brown made it known that her goal was to meet Cowboys' quarterback Troy Aikman. Women seem especially attracted to Aikman because of his money, fame, talent, and rugged good looks. But Aikman has remained steadfastly single and often frustrates potential suitors with his aloofness.

On this day, however, Brown was ready. She carried what is known in the modeling business as a flip card. The front showed a head shot of the pretty young woman. The back showed two poses of her in an extremely revealing bikini—from both the front and back. It also included her vital measurements—height, weight, bust size, waist size, and even the size of her hands and feet.

Working her way through the crowd, Brown couldn't reach the Cowboys' quarterback. But she did meet a few members of the Dallas traveling party, and passed out her pictures. The Cowboys traveling party was soon buzzing with talk about the young woman. That evening, she struck up a conversation with two television cameramen from Dallas in the lobby bar. After several drinks, one of the photographers offered her a sideline pass for the next day's game. One of their conditions was that she help them carry their equipment. She gladly accepted the pass, knowing it might get her closer to the action, and closer to Aikman.

As the threesome conversed, Jerry Jones walked into the bar and began ordering drinks. Even on the road, Jones is quickly recognized. Before long, he was shaking hands, slapping backs, and ordering more drinks. He also quickly noticed the young model. After a few more drinks, Brown was sitting next to Jones, listening to his stories about the Cowboys. To the cameramen's frustration, she left the bar about an hour later with the Cowboys' owner.

The next morning, however, Brown didn't forget about her sideline pass for the Cowboys-Cardinals game. She met the cameramen in the hotel lobby and boarded the media bus to the stadium. As the cameramen had expected, Brown could not have been less interested in helping them. Bob Ackles, at that time the

Cardinals' assistant general manager, noticed her the moment she stepped on the field. "There were a lot of people down on the field watching her," he remembers, "and not many watching the game."

Amanda spent the better part of the afternoon trying to position herself in front of the Fox cameras. "She wasn't so interested in working for us," one of the cameramen says. "She took off, and I don't even remember seeing her after the game."

They wouldn't see her again until two days later.

Each Tuesday during the football season, Switzer and Jones hold separate news conferences for Dallas area reporters and broadcasters. Switzer goes first, answering questions for about twenty-five minutes inside the players' auditorium. Lunch is then served in the players' lounge. As lunch winds down, Jones addresses the media and then fields questions, sometimes for more than an hour. On October 25, many of the reporters who had been in Phoenix two days earlier were shocked when Brown walked into the players' lounge while Jones was speaking. Carrying a lunch plate, she sat down at the head table a few seats from Jones. As Jones spoke, she tried to maintain eye contact with the Cowboys' owner. Mickey Spagnola, a writer for *The Insider*, looked down at his plate and said, "I can't believe this is happening."

When Jones finished his news conference, Brown returned to the owner's office with Marylyn Love. The official word was that Jones had flown her into Dallas for a job interview. She stayed at The Mansion on Turtle Creek, where regular rooms are priced from $320 to $380 a night, and suites run from $495 to $1,350.

That night, Jones was scheduled to give a speech in Houston, forcing him to cancel a few of his afternoon appointments. At three o'clock, he and Brown left Valley Ranch in his black Cadillac. He had told several people at the Cowboys' office that he was taking Brown to the Dallas–Fort Worth International Airport for her return flight to Los Angeles. Almost thirty minutes later, the Cadillac pulled up in front of The Mansion. Hurriedly, Brown ran inside and up to her room, gathered her belongings, and returned to the car.

Instead of going to DFW Airport, though, Jones drove to Love Field, where his private jet is parked at the Jet East hangar. Because the afternoon had turned cloudy and chilly, Brown was wearing a blue-and-white Cowboys' parka with a star on the front. At 4:05 p.m., they boarded Jones' silver-and-blue Lear Jet with the Cowboys' star on the tail. Minutes later, the jet took off for Houston.

After the speech and a night of partying, Jones returned to Love Field at 10:40 the next morning. Amanda Brown remained in Houston, later saying she had had "some business to attend to."

But it wouldn't be long before they were together again. Jones and Brown traveled together to Chicago the following Monday for the NFL owners' fall meetings. First, though, they attended the Monday-night game between the Bears and the Packers at Soldier Field. Played in a driving rainstorm, and with both teams wearing their "throwback" jerseys, the Packers overwhelmed the Bears on a mud-soaked field. Also that night, the Bears retired the jerseys of former Chicago greats Gale Sayers and Dick Butkus during half-time ceremonies.

Making their way around the stadium, Jones introduced Brown to several people, including Sayers and his wife, as the Cowboys' marketing director. As the owners' meetings began the next day in Chicago, Jones was the talk of his peers. But the conversation didn't center on the Cowboys' chances of winning a third straight Super Bowl, or Jones's controversial blueprint to revamp the NFL's revenue-sharing plan. Instead, many owners talked about the attractive young woman with the curly blonde hair and blue eyes. Recalls one prominent NFL executive, "Jerry caused quite a stir at those meetings with that woman. But it wasn't the first time."

AUSTIN, THE TEXAS STATE CAPITAL, IS KNOWN FOR ITS LUSH, UN-TEXAS-like beauty, its laid-back lifestyle, the rows of bars along Sixth Street, and a booming music scene that has churned out countless recording artists. Since 1990, it has also been known as the summer home of the Dallas Cowboys—during the team's six-week training camp.

Set in the lake-riddled Hill Country of central Texas, Austin, "the San Francisco of the Southwest," doesn't move at Dallas's frenetic pace. But it has embraced the Cowboys like adopted sons. Cowboys' coaches, players, executives, and even members of the media get VIP treatment just about anywhere they go in Austin after dark.

Since the Cowboys were awarded a franchise in 1960, the team had always held its summer training camp far away from Dallas. The time-worn theory was that players and coaches were better able to concentrate away from the day-to-day distractions of family life. Until Jones moved the team to Austin in the summer of 1990, the Cowboys trained 1,200 miles from Dallas in Thousand Oaks, California.

While getting out of Dallas may create a better working environment, it also loosens the reins for fun-seekers. Just as former Cowboys president Tex Schramm loved the after-hours scenes of southern California, Jones is the leader of the pack when it comes to partying in Austin. The fun begins shortly after the end of the afternoon practice and often doesn't end until dawn. You can normally count on Jones to run with the crowd from start to finish.

The main congregating point for front-office personnel, the media, and even some players in the summer of 1994 was the Copper Tank, located on Fifth Street, just around the corner from the heavy foot traffic of Sixth. It's a classic Austin bar with a wooden floor and David Allan Coe on the jukebox—but the Copper Tank also provided genuine down-home VIP treatment for anyone involved with the Dallas Cowboys. In fact, security personnel would greet Jones's limousine at the front door, then make certain that Jones's party could enter and leave the bar safely without interference from the crowd. A section was always cordoned off for the Cowboys' party during the six weeks the team was in town. The group didn't even have to bother with long lines at the public restrooms—they were permitted to use the employees' facilities.

Young, attractive females were a regular fixture at the Copper Tank, especially at Jones's table. As a friend of Jones says, explaining the attraction, "A lot of these women are looking for the ego screw. Everyone in Austin is looking for a hero. If they can't find a player, who better than Jerry Jones, who probably has the Cowboys' star embroidered on his underwear?"

★ ★ ★

THE JONES TRAINING CAMP ENTOURAGE WAS PARTYING AND DRINKING heavily one night in July 1994 at the Copper Tank. As usual, a section of the bar had been cordoned off for them. The night was gaining momentum when a tall, stunning blonde wearing a short skirt walked into the bar. Almost every head in the Copper Tank turned as she moved through the crowd and joined the group from Dallas.

She sat down at one of the corner tables. Jones pulled up a chair next to her. Her name was Kristi Hoss, and she was there to interview Jones for a syndicated morning-drive FM radio show broadcast from KLOL in Houston. She was armed with several questions for Jones about Houston Oilers' owner Bud Adams, who is largely regarded as a buffoon in Houston now that the team has fallen upon hard times. Hoss's intention was to stir up what might be called in Texas as a "spittin' match" between Jones and Adams. Instead, she would stir up something far more controversial.

Hoss, whose on-air moniker is Lucy Lipps, is a sidekick on *The Stevens and Pruett Show*. In the radio business, Stevens, Pruett, and Hoss are known as "shock jocks"—smaller-scale versions of the nationally-syndicated Howard Stern. Their job in general is to satirize, criticize, and poke fun at people in the spotlight. On the show, Lipps is known as "the skirt with the dirt."

On this night, in spite of the introductions, Jones apparently didn't realize whom he was talking to.

"He was already three sheets to the wind when I got there," Hoss says. "He reeked of tequila. As a matter of fact, he sat down and ordered more tequila. He had four shots right there in front of him. He tried to grab me around the waist. I'd start to get up and he'd pull me back down, or he'd pull me onto his lap."

Hoss claims that Jones made several passes at her.

"He kept saying, 'Darlin', you are just way too beautiful to be on the radio,'" Hoss says. "He said, 'You are the epitome of the Texas beauty queen. You have the most beautiful legs I've ever seen. Why don't you come on and be a Cowboys' cheerleader?'"

Hoss says that Dale Hansen soon realized that Jones was in trouble. Hansen was familiar with *The Stevens and Pruett Show* and had, in fact, been a target of their humor more than a few times when they worked at a station in Dallas. "Dale Hansen kept telling Mr. Jones that he should calm down," Hoss says. "He told the guy, 'You're going to get lambasted on the radio tomorrow morning, Jerry, if you don't stop this shit right now.'"

Hansen says he remembers Hoss coming into the bar—and confirms her encounter with Jones. But he says he doesn't remember warning Jones about his remarks or his actions.

"She was so good-looking that, hell, yes, I remember her coming in the bar," Hansen says. "She was about a seventeen on a scale of one to ten. But I don't remember saying anything like that to Jones. I am in no fashion calling her a liar. I know that she trashed the Cowboys, Jones, and me for me being drunk the next morning on the radio. But I just don't remember giving Jones a warning about her."

Before going on the air the next morning, Hoss talked to her lawyers about what she was planning to say. She says they told her that since Jones's actions took place in a crowded bar where there were plenty of witnesses, there was no legal obstacle to her telling her story.

What Hoss said that morning about Jones, Hansen, and the rest of the Cowboys' party was not pretty. Remembers Hoss, "I proceeded to tell every single detail on the air. I said that Jerry Jones's wife is nuts for staying with him. I said that if I were married to the lowly son of a bitch I would have divorced him a long time ago and taken his money. He is gross. He has bad teeth. And he is a gross old man."

The next morning, however, KLOL received a phone call from a Cowboys' executive who threatened a lawsuit. Hoss says that the Cowboys threatened to pull their advertising from another station in Dallas, KEGL, that carries the show. She also said the Cowboys threatened to warn other sponsors about what they considered to be reckless reporting.

Three weeks later, KEGL did pull *The Stevens and Pruett Show* off the air. But the cancellation also coincided with an ownership change at the station. An official at KEGL recently refused to comment on why the show was pulled, saying he was not familiar with the events of the previous summer.

Hoss, who spent the next four weeks in Austin, said she was instantly banned from the St. Edward's University campus where the Cowboys spend training camp. Hoss laughs as she remembers, "I went in to see Jerry Jones as 007—and I came out as a 911."

However, her experience with the owner of the Dallas Cowboys was nothing out of the ordinary, especially in Austin. At the same bar just a few weeks later, Jones spotted a young attractive woman sitting with KRLD sports reporter Rob Geiger. Like Hoss, she was wearing a short skirt. According to Geiger, Jones leaned over him, grabbed the woman by the wrist and whispered into her ear, "Have you got any panties on under that short skirt?" Leaving the bar several hours later, Jones again leaned over Geiger, grabbed the woman's hand, and whispered into her ear, "Give me five minutes with you and I'll send you to heaven."

DRINKING, PARTYING, WOMANIZING, AND LATE-NIGHT CAROUSING IS not unusual in professional sports. In fact, it has been common for decades among teams that go on the road for five, six, or seven weeks to train for an upcoming season. While the teams go through their morning workout, the sideline is often filled with hung-over front-office personnel, reporters, and broadcasters. A single woman who often traveled in NFL circles in the summer of 1994 says, "I know now that I would never marry anybody in sports. Those guys—and I'm talking about players, coaches, executives, everybody—they get away from home and they start running wild with women and booze. You never know what's going to happen on any given night."

Unlike many of the decisions he made after he bought the Cowboys, Jones's night moves fit in perfectly with Cowboy tradition. The night life wasn't much different in Thousand Oaks, California, where the Cowboys trained from 1963 through the summer of 1989. About the only person who stayed in his dorm after the workday was over was Coach Tom Landry, and maybe Roger Staubach.

A running joke in Thousand Oaks was that everyone except the players had a sunrise curfew. Schramm, the club's president and general manager for twenty-nine years, once joked, "I want to know why there isn't a curfew for the front office."

A classic Cowboys' training camp legend tells how one night in the summer of 1981, after the bars had closed, Schramm and several others headed for one of their regular hangouts, the home of a local cocktail waitress. As the temperatures dropped into the fifties, several men and women undressed and waded into a large hot tub in the back yard. Some of the guests wore their underwear. Some wore bathing suits. Others wore nothing at all.

As the drinks flowed and the laughter spilled into the cool summer night, the Cowboys' party was unaware that a jealous ex-husband lurked in the shadows. Men around Thousand Oaks resented the Cowboys because local women often dropped whatever they were doing to party with America's Team. On this morning, the man's ex-wife was sitting in the hot tub just to the left of Schramm.

No one in the hot tub was aware that the jealous ex-husband had crept within a few feet of the hot tub—until he leaped from the darkness and bashed Schramm over the head with an aluminum lounge chair. To his instant horror, however, Schramm's attacker discovered that the man sitting to Schramm's right just happened to be former All-Pro tight end Mike Ditka.

In 1981, one year before he left the team to become the head coach of the Chicago Bears, Ditka was coaching the Cowboys' tight ends. The forty-two-year-old Ditka was still in playing shape. He still jogged five miles a day and had the muscular physique of some of his Cowboys' players. Just two years earlier, he had broken a clipboard over the helmet of a Pittsburgh Steeler as he was trying to make a tackle near the Cowboys' sideline. He had also challenged the entire Cowboys' receiving corps to a fist fight for what he considered to be a halfhearted effort during 110-yard wind sprints. Ditka faced Drew Pearson, Tony Hill, Butch Johnson, Billy Joe DuPree, and Doug Cosbie. None of them wanted to fight.

On this crisp California evening, Ditka would display the fierce temperament that earned him the nickname "Iron Mike." Leaping from the hot tub, Ditka hit the jealous ex-husband with a flurry of punches that sent him scurrying off into the darkness. A buck-naked Ditka chased the man for several blocks, loudly promising further bodily harm if he ever returned.

Back at the Cowboys' camp the next morning, Schramm had to explain the large cut and bump on his forehead. At the advice of vice president Joe Bailey, Schramm told reporters that, while washing his feet in the bathtub, he had slipped and fallen forward, striking his head on the metal faucet. Few people around the training camp, however, were buying Schramm's story.

Putting aside the animosity that developed after Jones bought the team, he and Schramm have a lot in common. Both love to drink. Both love the spotlight, and are almost maniacally driven to win. In this last aspect, at least, Jones has proven that he is a true Cowboy.

More than two years ago, Jones surprised his wife at Christmas by giving her a five-acre tract of land in the fashionable Highland Park section of Dallas. The tree-lined tract at the corner of Preston Road and Armstrong Parkway sits along Turtle Creek in one of the city's most exclusive areas—part of the old-money corridor of Dallas. By gutting and remodeling a home that had belonged to Dallas oilman Bill Saxon, the Joneses made a statement. They were aligning themselves with the rich and the famous who have deep roots in Dallas.

But while workmen toiled for months on the Jones mansion, which had hidden staircases, hand-carved wine racks, and closets the size of bedrooms, rumors of a Jerry-Gene divorce were rampant. Dallas socialites say they had been seeing less and less of the couple at charity events and other functions.

"You know, he's really been divorced for two years," Hansen says sarcastically. "Really, though, I started checking out the rumors myself because I heard that Gene was going to get part of the team. I asked Jones about it. And he went home that night and said, 'Gene, baby, are you divorcing me? I can't go anywhere without hearing that you're divorcing me.'" Jones has denied to Hansen that the couple is considering a divorce.

In March 1995, Skip Bayless received a phone call during his popular morning sports talk show in Dallas on KTCK-AM radio. The caller said he'd heard from several reliable sources that the Joneses were splitting up. He said he'd heard that Gene Jones had contacted a realtor to buy herself a new home in Dallas.

"This is how people think," Hansen says, rolling his eyes. "Jerry Jones is in the bar at two o'clock in the morning. Therefore, he is getting laid. Therefore, he is getting divorced. I know a lot of people talk about it. But that's just something that Jerry Jones and Gene Jones will have to work out."

WHY IS JERRY JONES'S PERSONAL LIFE AN ISSUE? WHY SHOULDN'T HE BE treated like any other solid citizen who likes to play as hard as they work? For one thing, Jones has placed himself squarely in the public eye. His high-profile job—and the high-profile way he handles it—puts him under the scrutiny of his competitors and the media twenty-four hours a day. But when darkness descends, Jones doesn't retreat into the shadows. He doesn't run and hide. He clearly loves the attention and the perks that his visibility and success have brought him.

Never forget, though, that Jones is always selling something. From ripe watermelons at a storefront fruit stand to network affiliations out of an air-conditioned suite, he has proven himself to be the perfect salesman. Today, he is selling you silver-and-blue gladiators, he is selling you on the Cowboys' image, he is selling you America's Team and the myth of American sports—and he is selling you Jerry Jones. And like every product you pay good money for, it's important to know just what you're getting.

Radio talk show host Jody Dean has been making the post-workday rounds with Jones since he arrived in Dallas in 1989. To understand the complex Cowboys' owner, Dean says you must first accept the sum of his disparate parts.

"He is a con-artist, womanizing, hard-drinking, snake-oil salesman who you end up liking in the end," Dean says. "I can tell you why. Jerry Jones is the rainmaker. He rode into town on a real dry day. And he dazzled everyone with the force of his personality. Even though you know there isn't a lot of science behind the divining rod, there is nothing more likable than the rogue who has hold of it. Jerry Jones is brassy. Jerry Jones is brash. He is the living, working personification of balls."

CHAPTER 12

Maverick

WHEN JERRY JONES STRIDES INTO AN NFL OWNERS' MEETING, HE CAN expect a remarkably divided reception. His allies include Raiders' owner Al Davis, the original maverick, dressed in black and white and looking like a senior member of the Harley Davidson crowd. Many of the new-generation owners, who've either written enormous checks to join the exclusive circle or are up to their eyeballs in debt, also side with Jones. They're thankful to him for the monster TV deal he put together with Fox, and they hope his profit-making magic will rub off.

But an icy wind blows from the other side of the room. The older, more traditional owners like Cleveland's Art Modell, Kansas City's Lamar Hunt, New York's Wellington Mara, and Pittsburgh's Art Rooney don't trust Jones, and rarely speak to him. They whisper and harrumph behind his back.

According to one NFL source, Modell has told many fellow owners, "I hate the son-of-a-bitch."

The conservative right wing of the NFL is made up of traditionalists. Some, like Mara, have roots that go all the way back to the fledgling NFL days of the 1920s. His father, Timothy J. Mara, bought the Giants in 1925. Wellington Mara began working for the club over sixty years ago, in 1933. The traditionalists believe that Jones, if given his way, will eventually wreck the league.

"Our league is based on a set of principles," Mara says. "And thank God that we had the people back forty, fifty, and sixty years ago that had the foresight to make the rules that they did. We had better stand by the rules. If we don't, we're going to end up just like baseball with all of their problems."

MANY OF THE LEAGUE'S TRADITIONALISTS ARE UPSET THAT JONES refuses to play by their rules. In one much-ballyhooed incident during the 1994 season, he was fined by the league office for allowing too many star-studded friends to stand close to the team down on the sidelines of Texas Stadium. Jones now jokes about the $10,000 fine. "I thought to myself that maybe we should send our coaches to the dressing room so we could make more room for Marla Maples and Charlton Heston," he says, grinning.

The Cowboys were also fined for concealing a thumb injury to quarterback Troy Aikman. Aikman banged the thumb on his throwing hand on the top of a teammate's helmet on the next-to-last play of a Friday practice about forty-eight hours before the November 13 kickoff against San Francisco. Jones met with Switzer and trainer Kevin O'Neill after practice that day. The three agreed that the injury wasn't serious enough to be listed on the twice-weekly NFL report, so the league office wasn't notified. The next day, as the team's chartered flight headed to San Francisco, Aikman told several teammates that the thumb injury was especially painful. Word began to leak to the media.

That night at the team's hotel, Aikman met with the Fox Network broadcast team of Pat Summerall and John Madden.

"He told us that if he had to play a game that night, he couldn't have done it," Summerall said later. "He was just in too much pain. It was very clear that he was bothered by the thumb."

As the kickoff approached, the Dallas coaches were on pins

and needles. During the pre-game breakfast, they talked about the possibility of switching to backup quarterback Rodney Peete for the biggest game of the regular season. Offensive coordinator Ernie Zampese paced the locker room floor. But Aikman threw with enough velocity during pre-game warm-ups that the coaches decided to let him start the game.

Aikman threw three interceptions and the Cowboys lost 21–14. Aikman didn't blame the sprained thumb for the interceptions, but said he had trouble throwing the ball deep. He said a few passes got away from him because he couldn't grip the ball properly.

On Monday, members of the Dallas media began calling the league office to complain that Jones had intentionally left Aikman off the injury list. An inquiry by the league office was conducted by vice president Joe Browne. Jones insisted that the Aikman injury was not serious enough to report. But he never told the media, or the league office, that he had intentionally failed to report the thumb sprain.

A few days after the game, Jones said, "We just didn't want San Francisco knowing about it. Why should we give them a competitive edge when we didn't have to? Besides, I would do it again. I don't believe in the injury rule in the first place."

Stanley Marcus, the co-founder of Neiman-Marcus and one of Dallas's preeminent business leaders over the last fifty years, knows a few things about marketing. When Jones defied the league by concealing Aikman's thumb injury, Marcus wrote in his weekly column for the *Dallas Morning News*, "Mr. Jones' response to the football commissioner—defiantly declaring, 'We'll do it again, no matter what the leagues says about it'— was reminiscent of the attitudes of some of the early Western settlers. In essence, Mr. Jones was saying, 'How dare you question me—the man who restored the Cowboys to a position of preeminence.'"

Jones had once again stepped outside the league boundaries—and received only a slap on the wrist for it.

★ ★ ★

ONE OF THE SUREST WAYS TO ANGER THE NFL OLD-BOYS NETWORK IS to hit them where it hurts—in their wallets. From the traditionalists' point of view, Jones's biggest crime is his plan to take a jackhammer to the league's revenue-sharing system, which has existed almost from the day the league was founded in an automobile dealer's showroom in 1920.

To the traditionalists, Jones's attack on the plan strikes at the league's foundations. At present, 77 percent of all revenues from television, tickets, and merchandise are shared equally among the twenty-eight NFL teams (thirty in 1995, when Charlotte and Jacksonville begin play). The revenue-sharing formula helps keep weaker teams competitive, and makes it possible for a team from tiny Green Bay, Wisconsin not only to survive, but thrive. None of the other major sports leagues can boast of having a team in a city where the population is less than 100,000. Consider that in the Dallas-Fort Worth metroplex alone, there are seven cities larger than Green Bay.

One of Jones's top priorities is to keep a larger share of the league's merchandising revenues. Why? Because the Cowboys are a lean, mean selling machine.

The Cowboys are to pro football in the 1990s what the New York Yankees were to baseball in the 1950s and early 1960s—head and shoulder above the rest of the league in popularity and prestige. Not only have the Cowboys been voted the most popular team in sports in every poll taken since 1992, but they have unparalleled media exposure. Just check your radio dial. The Cowboys' radio network numbers 151 stations from Maine to Hawaii, including thirty Spanish-language stations on either side of the United States–Mexico border.

During the 1994 season, the Cowboys accounted for 30 percent of the NFL's more than $100 million in retail merchandise sales. The San Francisco '49ers ranked a distant second at 8.1 percent of sales. Clearly, the Cowboys are the World Champions of caps, t-shirts, and gimcracks.

At a recent league meeting, Jones stood up and explained to the owners that he had cut a separate marketing deal with the J. C. Penney company to sell an exclusive Cowboys' jacket. He encouraged the other owners to cut their own deals. However, the NFL's Finance Committee quickly pointed out that the deal was out of bounds, and Jones was forced to cancel it.

In early August 1995, Jones announced a ten-year contract worth more than $40 million between Texas Stadium and Pepsi-Cola—in defiance of the National Football League and its long-standing policies. Three-years earlier, the NFL had contracted with Coca-Cola for the exclusive promotional rights to NFL logos.

During a press conference, Jones admitted that he was challenging the economic structure of the NFL. "This is a direct hit on the Coca-Cola deal with the league," he said. "Ultimately, all logos, the helmet and the star associated with the Cowboys will be handled by the Dallas Cowboys and not the marketing arm of the NFL. That is not a popular stance to take with other members of the NFL."

Jones said that he would continue to honor the general concept of the league's revenue-sharing policies—including the arrangements covering television money. But he said that he planned to cut his own marketing deals that would be independent of the league's revenue pools.

Jones's lucrative agreement with Pepsi is bound to increase the tension between himself and other NFL owners. To his league peers, it confirms that Jones is no longer a team player.

"At best, something like this is short-sighted and self-serving in terms of the Cowboys's interests. At worst, it's very unfair and destructive," NFL commissioner Paul Tagliabue told *Dallas Morning News* columnist Frank Luksa.

"My legacy in this league is that I'm going to be the one that unshackles the merchandise sales," says Jones. "Who knows their individual markets better than the individual clubs?" If he gets his way, the Cowboys would pocket nearly $30 million annually instead of the mere $3 million they receive now.

THE COWBOYS HAVE ALWAYS BEEN AMONG THE LEAGUE'S BEST AT exploiting their team's popularity. When Jones assumed control,

the Cowboys had played twenty-one of the last twenty-two
Thanksgiving day games. Taking on this game in 1966 was one of
Schramm's many marketing brainstorms. At the time,
Commissioner Pete Rozelle felt the league was imposing by asking
the Cowboys to play every year on the holiday. But Schramm told
the commissioner not to worry. For almost three decades now,
the Cowboys have had the late afternoon national television audience to themselves. While the country is digesting turkey and
dressing, the Cowboys are raking in the TV ratings and selling
more merchandise.

Kansas City owner Lamar Hunt has spent years trying to
break up the Cowboys' Thanksgiving deal. He wants to have the
game rotate around to the other teams. Hunt would also like to
break the Detroit Lions' sixty-one-year hold on the holiday games
(they play on the earlier half of the Thanksgiving network dou-
bleheader). But NFL owners tabled Hunt's motion at the league's
spring meetings last March.

Jones, of course, is fighting for more than tradition when he
clings to the Thanksgiving game. The merchandising bonanza is
one nobody could have foreseen thirty years ago. In 1994, with
the nation watching, and the biggest shopping day of the year just
twenty-four hours away, he debuted a new double-star special
edition jersey. He had to do an end run on the league office to
make the sale, but he pulled it off.

Initially, Jones had been ordered by the league office to provide a year's notice before introducing new jerseys. Jones argued
that the jerseys were not really intended to replace the old ones,
but were special-edition jerseys to be used only on "special occasions"—for example, Thanksgiving. The league gave its permission.

A few days before the game, Jones called a news conference
at the Cowboys' complex to unveil the new jerseys. More than
thirty reporters showed up. Television stations and production
companies sent thirteen minicams.

Always the showman, Jones appeared on NBC's pre-game
show with sportscaster Jim Gray. Jones was dressed in shoulder
pads and Troy Aikman's special edition jersey. Later, Jones would
wonder why many of his critics considered the TV appearance so

self-serving. "I really thought it was pretty funny," he says, cracking his wide grin.

Once again, Jones was accused of being a shameless huckster. But the Cowboys' owner had the last laugh. Because of the team's enormous national appeal, the jerseys started selling out in stores all over America. And, contrary to Jones's announced plan to use the jerseys only on special occasions, the Cowboys wore the jerseys—providing valuable advertising—in six of the final seven games of the 1994 season.

Informed that more than 137,000 of the jerseys had been sold in one week, NFL commissioner Tagliabue says, "Playing on Thanksgiving is one of the benefits the Cowboys have enjoyed for many years. It doesn't have to be that way. It is not one of the things the Cowboys have made attractive. It's one of the things that the league has made attractive. Jerry may underestimate the value of the things that he has going that have been provided by the league, especially with the Thanksgiving day game. I'm not saying the Cowboys won't continue to play on Thanksgiving. But some other teams have had some pretty good success on Thanksgiving, too. The Giants could sell the same number of jerseys if we put them on the Thanksgiving game as part of the Macy's parade."

Several sources inside the NFL have said that Jones accepted a $1.1 million bonus from Apex Inc., the NFL's primary sports apparel manufacturer, for switching jerseys. Two owners seeking anonymity say they will ask the league office to investigate the bonus. They want to know if the money Jones received falls under the league's revenue-sharing plan. If so, Jones would have to split the bonus money with twenty-nine other teams.

Always the entrepreneur, Jones tinkered with the idea of introducing a new blue double-star road jersey in 1995. In a complete break with tradition, the Cowboys will also wear the blue jerseys for three 1995 home games.

A FEW OF THE OWNERS HAVE ALSO ACCUSED JONES OF BOTH BREAKING and exploiting long-standing rules regarding revenue from ticket sales. They are disturbed that since 1991 Jones had been charging new season ticket-holders seat for "options" without sharing those revenues with the rest of the league.

In 1991, Jones created a new company, called ProSeat, that began to charge Cowboys' fans between $1,500 and $15,000 each just for the right to purchase a seat, depending on the location of that seat. For more than three years, Jones pocketed all of the profits from this venture—until the league called for an audit of the Cowboys in April of 1994.

Shortly before the start of the 1994 season, NFL commissioner Paul Tagliabue informed Jones that he would have to pay $12 million—34 percent of the money he'd made off the ProSeat deals—to the other owners to comply with NFL rules. The league's decision went unreported by the media. Jones is currently paying off the $12 million bill on an installment plan.

Thanks to the NFL formula for player compensation, the payments immediately affected the NFL's salary cap, which jumped $400,000 per team just weeks before the start of the 1994 season. "The money that Jerry had to pay back to the league caused the cap to jump about $200,000," a league official said when asked recently. "The other $200,000 came from other revenues that hadn't previously been calculated."

Clearly, the driving force behind the Cowboys' merchandising phenomenon has been aggressive marketing and success on the playing field. The foundation was laid by former general manager Tex Schramm, the leading sports marketing guru of his time, but Jones believes that his energy level and workaholic drive have boosted the Cowboys even farther above the crowd. Says ESPN's Roy Firestone, "I've never seen an owner of any sports team work harder than Jerry Jones. I've never seen one who spends more time making sure that a positive spin is put on every story involving the Dallas Cowboys. The man is a true workaholic."

Jones believes that revenues should not be completely shared—that the Cowboys should get a bigger piece of the pie.

"If I work my butt off to make sure that I get something done, then why should I have to share it with everybody else?" Jones asks. "Is the NFL's way the American way? I hardly think so."

Jones also believes that since he's spent more than $90 million of his own money and borrowed the rest against his assets, the league shouldn't put any limits on how he makes money off the Cowboys. Jones virtually emptied his pockets for the Cowboys and the lease at Texas Stadium (at a total cost of $140 million). Jones feels that he took risks and stared down the devil—and now he wants the rewards he feels he deserves. If he wants to put seats on top of the goal posts, so be it. If he wants to stop cutting the Green Bay Packers a share for his double-star special-edition jerseys, that's just how he does business.

MANY OF THE OTHER CLUBS FEEL THAT JONES IS JUST GREEDY. Although the Cowboys have led the league in merchandise sales for the last three years, they have made a long climb from near the bottom of the standings since Jones took over the team. Again, one of his most vocal critics represents one of his team's fiercest on-field rivals. "There were times over the last ten years when we were number one," says 49ers President Carmen Policy. "We never felt that we should capitalize on it to the point where we should rearrange our sharing proposition relevant to properties. But as soon as Jerry gets on top, he wants it all. Maybe we can all learn something from Jerry about making a buck. But in San Francisco, we just don't operate on that quick-buck mentality."

Jones knows he faces a fight over his proposals. Consider this terse response to Jones's plan from NFL commissioner Paul Tagliabue: "There will not be a change in revenue sharing as long as I'm commissioner of the National Football League."

Modell, who has owned the Cleveland Browns for more than thirty-two years, becomes red-faced when Jones's plan for ending revenue sharing is broached. "He'll never get away with it," Modell snaps. "Never."

Modell sees Jones's plan leading to bigger problems down the road. "We can't have owners going out and cutting their own separate deals," he says. "Pretty soon it would tear down the entire revenue-sharing plan." He believes that if teams control their own licensing, the lucrative national television contracts that the league has been able to command will gradually disappear.

"NFL licensing is the basis for many national advertising campaigns," he points out. "And those ad campaigns are ultimately the basis for our TV revenues." Under Jones's plan, an owner could start joining up with his own sponsors. There is little question that the advertising heavyweights would flock to the Dallas Cowboys and not to the Tampa Bay Buccaneers. There is little debate about which team the beer companies would choose.

Sixty-five percent of the league's revenues come from its $4.4-billion-dollar TV contract, easily the largest in sports. If Modell is right, adopting Jones's plan could lead to the end of the NFL's big-money era.

THE LEAGUE'S OLD BOY NETWORK HAS ALWAYS BELIEVED IN "GETTING along by going along," and resents Jones's willingness to go his own way in search of bigger profits.

As NFL president Neal Austrian told the *Sporting News*, "He might be putting his priorities in the wrong order. The league is only as strong as its weakest link. For him to think that he can put the Cowboys above anybody in the NFL doesn't make a whole lot of sense."

Carmen Policy says, "I can tell you this. Jerry Jones is definitely scaling a mountain that will not be easy to climb. I think that he is perceived right now as a fellow who marches to his own beat. He is not perceived in the league as a consistent team player. When it comes to money and earnable income on a local basis, he is without question a proponent of laissez-faire. You won't find Jerry Jones walking around yelling, 'Long Live the League.'"

Tagliabue also questions Jones's priorities when it comes to league matters. Jones sits on two of the league's most powerful boards—the competition committee and the broadcast committee. He was appointed to both by Tagliabue. But the commissioner wonders if Jones's heart is totally consumed by the Cowboys and his own business interests.

"We have those who are consumed with winning on the field with their teams," he says. "That's good. But we don't want people to consider the league a low priority."

NFL owners and executives ask themselves two questions about Jones: Is he merely a self-serving owner who would sell the league down the river if it meant a bigger profit for him? Or is he actually trying to elevate the league by constantly building and improving the Cowboys, and by exploring new avenues for generating revenue? Tagliabue is not completely sold on the latter.

"Sometimes you wonder where Jerry Jones is going with things," he says.

JEALOUSY COULD BE A BIG PART OF THE PROBLEM. CONSIDER THAT IN the last eighteen months Jones has been called both "the Godfather of the salary cap" and "the Godfather of the Fox Network television deal" on sports pages across America. The Fox deal brought team owners a $1.6-billion-dollar bonanza at a time when losses were expected. They will make an extra $8 million per season because the Fox Network stepped up to the plate. In what sounds like a replay of Jones's disputes with Jimmy Johnson, Tagliabue denies that Jones was the force behind the deal.

"He was not the driving force behind the salary cap," Tagliabue insists. "He was not the driving force behind the Fox network deal. Neal Austrian had a lot to do with the Fox deal. Jerry was just one of five members on the television committee that put together the Fox Network deal. I read about his great accomplishments. But to say he was the driving force of all of these things is quite an exaggeration."

According to Tagliabue, then-commissioner Pete Rozelle first approached the Fox Network back in 1987, two years before

Jones got his franchise. Tagliabue personally spoke with Fox executives in 1990.

"It was a long process of getting the Fox deal done," he says. "Jerry is a good negotiator and he was good to have on the committee. But like I've said, he was just one of five members on the committee."

Asked if Jones could be considered an NFL power broker, Tagliabue says, "It depends on how you measure power. If power is developing a consensus and putting together a program, Jerry is among the many in our league who has done that. But he is just one among many."

OTHER OWNERS MAY BE JEALOUS OF JONES'S HIGH MEDIA PROFILE. The man is a master of the sound bite. As the workday ends during league meetings some owners head for their hotel rooms. Others head for the bar. Jones angles for the lights of the cameras. In truth, reporters make a bee-line for Jones because he speaks more than the company line, whether it is self-serving or not. Chances are he will deliver a one-liner or two worth saving for the ten o'clock news or the morning newspaper.

"He never met a camera he didn't like," says Modell. After the public unveiling of the Cowboys' 1993 highlight film, Jones apologized to the crowd of about two thousand luncheon guests because his face had appeared so often in the video.

The Cowboys have always been the most publicized team in sports. NFL Films dubbed them "America's Team" all the way back in 1978. But records for print space and air time have been shattered in the six years since Jones bought the team. Take, for example, the December 12, 1994 issue of *Sports Illustrated*. The magazine devoted forty-five full pages of pictures and print to the Cowboys. That same month, Jones was promoted by ABC's Barbara Walters as "One of the Ten Most Fascinating People in America" during an hour-long show aired in prime time. Another gusher for Jones was the cover of the *Sporting News* on March 13, 1995. The cover headline: "JERRY, JERRY QUITE CONTRARY".

It's the "contrary" side that has many league owners and officials worried.

IN SPITE OF HIS HARD WORK AND FLAIR FOR MARKETING, JONES HAS done a poor job of selling himself, especially to the other owners around the league. Once considered one of the bright rising stars of the league, he is now held at arm's length by most. Some of his co-owners believe he is simply greedy. Others call him Brother Jerry because he reminds them of a crooked television evangelist.

"When I think of Jerry Jones, I think of a snake-oil salesman," says Policy. "I also think of a gunslinger. I also think of a wildcatter from the oil fields. The situation he is creating right now in the NFL is ripe for conflict. He does experience resistance in a lot of things that he does. Jerry's personality is a strong personality. And that highlights and accentuates the differences that exist between him and the other owners. He often pushes too hard and it grates on other owners. Believe me."

Others put a more positive spin on Jones's behavior. Al Davis, the original NFL maverick, was asked if Jones had followed in his footsteps. "I'll say this about being called a maverick," he said. "I think it has a very positive connotation. It describes someone who moves things and makes things happen."

Denver owner Pat Bowlen told the *Sporting News*, "Jerry's not a maverick. He's just out to turn a buck for his football team."

CHAPTER 13

The Once and Future King

THE RED JOGGING TRACK LOOPS AROUND THE GRASS PRACTICE FIELDS and winds through some leafless cottonwood trees before turning right and passing in front of the Cowboys' weight room. It was well past dark on this cool late February night, and the club's practice facility was quiet. Lights from the empty weight room shone onto the track. A quarter-mile away, a silhouette was barely visible, chugging up a hill. With arms pumping and head bobbing, Troy Aikman was on his final lap around the track, breathing heavily and blowing steam into the chilly night.

Three weeks had passed since Aikman had been knocked down nineteen times at mud-caked Candlestick Park, and the Cowboys had been knocked out of the playoffs by the San Francisco 49ers. The physical bruises were mostly gone. But the mental ones hadn't healed. They tend to linger with athletes as competitive as Aikman.

Losing is like death to the Cowboys' quarterback. His team-mates worry about his dark moods following defeats in big games. When the Cowboys' season had ended January 15 in the NFC title game, the flight home seemed to last forever for Aikman.

With the memory of San Francisco still painfully fresh in his mind, Aikman was the only player working out at the Cowboys' practice complex three weeks later. Watching San Francisco steamroll San Diego in Super Bowl XXIX had merely fed his frustration. Now there was something more pressing on his mind. It had been eating at him since Arizona linebacker Wilber Marshall had delivered a brutal blow to his head during the opening drive of a late October game. The blitzing Marshall had gone airborne, flying headfirst at Aikman like a human missile. He rammed the crown of his headgear into Aikman's chin and face mask. After the collision, the Cowboys' quarterback was virtually unconscious on his feet. He had bitten cleanly through the center of his tongue. Blood pouring from both sides of his mouth, he had managed to call one more play in the huddle, throwing a perfect looping 15-yard touchdown pass to Alvin Harper. Then Aikman staggered to the sideline and never returned. For the second time in the last nine months, he had been knocked out of a game with a concussion.

Now, as he finished his jog at Valley Ranch, Aikman pondered the sixth concussion of his NFL career. As he sat down to cool off at a table inside the players' lunch room, he sighed and began to talk about his post-concussion syndrome. "I don't want this to come off wrong," he said, choosing his words carefully. "But I find myself at times forgetting things. I don't know if it's like anyone else forgetting things. Or if it's the result of being hit in the head too much. I forget having entire conversations with people. I know that sounds like somebody drinking too much. But that's really not the case at all. I'll run into somebody I know someplace, and they'll start reminding me of a conversation that I had with them. And I won't be able to remember that conversation."

A concussion is often described as a bruise on the brain. Concussions have driven several players out of football, including former Cowboys' quarterback Roger Staubach. From high school football through his final year with the Cowboys, Staubach endured twenty concussions, five during his final season. At the recommendation of a trusted doctor, he gave up football long before he was physically or mentally ready to go. Another player who left the game early was Chicago fullback Merrill Hoge, who, after suffering a series of concussions, quit in mid-season in 1994 at the advice of doctors in Pittsburgh. Former Jets' wide receiver Al Toon retired after his twelfth concussion. He still has trouble processing information. He is often sensitive to bright light, can't stand noise as subtle as a computer's buzzing, and often has memory blackouts.

The memory loss is what bothers Aikman the most. During the 1994 NFC championship game, when the Cowboys defeated San Francisco, he was struck in the head by defensive tackle Dennis Brown's knee. On the sideline, a team physician who suspected he'd suffered a concussion asked this standard question: Where are you? Aikman told the doctor that he was in Henryetta, Oklahoma, which is where he grew up more than 150 miles away. Aikman has no memory of that day, and has trouble even remembering what he was doing forty-eight hours before kickoff.

Aikman spent the night in a hospital near downtown Dallas. As his agent, Leigh Steinberg, remembers, "The city of Dallas was awash with celebration. You could hear people yelling and cars honking. But Troy was sitting in a darkened hospital room, unable to remember that he'd played."

Aikman asked Steinberg question after question about the game he couldn't remember. Five minutes later, as his memory lapsed once more, he asked the same questions. Finally, Steinberg started writing standard answers, like the game score and the fact Dallas was headed to the Super Bowl, on a piece of paper. "He couldn't hold the explanation for more than five minutes," Steinberg says quietly. "It was eerie."

By the end of the 1994 season, Steinberg decided he'd seen enough. NFL players had suffered more than ninety concussions during the '94 season. Among his other clients who had suffered a series of concussions was San Francisco quarterback Steve Young. In February 1995, Steinberg organized what he called the

Concussion Conference in Newport Beach, California. He invited several doctors, trainers, and head injury specialists to California to explain to players (mostly his clients) the effects of concussions. The topics covered included recognizing the symptoms, gauging the effects of multiple concussions, and analyzing their impact over time.

A few days after returning from the conference, Aikman was in a somber mood as he talked about the impact of his numerous injuries. Besides surviving six concussions, Aikman underwent back surgery after the 1992 season. Two knee injuries have also cost him playing time. He has missed fifteen starts in six years due to injuries. "I could be done in two years," he says. "Who knows how long? I will say this. Injuries, whether they are head injuries or a back injury, will knock me out of the game before I'm ready to go. I have begun to realize my own mortality and to understand that I'm not as invincible as I once was."

Here is the simple truth about Aikman's rash of concussions: One more could end his career, even before he celebrates his thirtieth birthday in November 1996. As he says, "I've been able to study the situation and I understand the long-term effects. I understand now that concussions could have a direct effect on Alzheimer's disease. At least, that's still being studied. What I want to do is live a normal life when I'm through with football. If that means walking away early because of all of those head injuries, then I'll do it."

To study Aikman's history of injuries is to understand how fragile the Cowboys' grip on greatness really is. A team that has won two of the last three Super Bowls could be one concussion away from an 8–8 season. Jerry Jones is fully aware how damaging another Aikman concussion could be. He recently told Dallas talk show host Norm Hitzges, "Aside from the quarterback, there just isn't another player among the forty-seven that makes that big of a difference. Now, I'm not demeaning anyone here. But everyone besides the quarterback is just part of the team."

★ ★ ★

THE ROAD AHEAD FOR JERRY JONES AND HIS COWBOYS COULD BE AS treacherous and crooked as an two-lane Arkansas back road.

The Cowboys and the 49ers now have the most spirited and the most avidly watched rivalry in the NFL. Dallas versus San Francisco has the prestige of a big-time heavyweight title fight, with each contest as hotly contested as the Frazier-Ali "Thrilla in Manila." They have met in the last three NFC championship games, with Dallas winning twice. They will even stage their own undercard by playing a regular-season game November 12, 1995 at Texas Stadium—their sixth meeting in the last four seasons.

Carmen Policy, the 49ers president, makes no secret that his team has become obsessed with beating the Cowboys. Every personnel move is tailored in some way to better match up with Dallas. "We keep one eye and both ears on the Dallas Cowboys at all times," he says. "I don't think that anyone would disagree that the Dallas Cowboys are the team that we're going to have to fear. I think we will be playing them again in the NFC championship game. And I look forward to seeing Jerry Jones in that situation again."

But the rivalry isn't confined to the playing field.

ON THE DAY AFTER THE 49ERS BEAT THE COWBOYS IN THE NFC championship game on January 15, 1995, Policy nearly flew through the roof of his executive office in Santa Clara. He was reading post-game quotes in the morning newspapers, hoping to find the Cowboys finally giving the 49ers the respect he thought they deserved. Instead, he read that Switzer and Jones were blaming their 10-point loss on officiating and the condition of the Candlestick Park playing surface.

"Absolutely no class," he said. "No class at all. I will say this about Barry Switzer. He has a lot to learn about being a coach in the National Football League." Weeks later, Policy still had a bitter taste in his mouth when the owners met in Dallas.

"We were extremely gracious when we were beaten by the Dallas Cowboys," he said. "We said that we had been beaten by this well-coached and very disciplined and very talented football team. To have those kind of remarks surface from the Cowboys just irks you. They said it was an atrocity to play a championship game on a field like that when, in fact, the field was better than it was two years earlier when we played a championship game at Candlestick. Furthermore, championship games have been played in worse conditions. They played the 1981 game at twenty below (in Cincinnati). What about the Ice Bowl between the Cowboys and the Packers (played at sixteen below)? I just thought it was incumbent upon a team that had enjoyed the status of a champion to conduct themselves accordingly. The Dallas Cowboys and Jerry Jones didn't conduct themselves accordingly."

AS THE STAKES GROW EVEN HIGHER, SO WILL THE LEVEL OF ANIMOSITY. In the past two years, the media has focused on the growing hate between the two front offices. Jones versus Policy may become bigger than the game itself. Jones is clearly the most publicized of all NFL owners and front-office executives. But Policy's status has been elevated by his success at signing high-priced free agents while almost miraculously keeping those huge salaries squeezed beneath the salary cap.

Free agency and the salary cap have helped reconfigure the NFL's equation for winning. While the Cowboys suffered large roster hits after the 1993 and 1994 seasons, their main rivals, the San Francisco 49ers, were less depleted by free agency. Jones has accused San Francisco 49ers president Carmen Policy of cheating. Policy retorted that Jones didn't know how to maximize his money and personnel under the new rules. (In Texas, this kind of heated give-and-take is called a pissing match.)

"Two years ago, Carmen Policy was still trying cases in court," Jones said recently. "He couldn't even spell 'football.'"

When told of that remark, Policy laughs. "It has been six years since I was in the courtroom. And, yes, I will say that six years ago I wasn't fully apprised of whether the football was blown up or stuffed. But I will say this. Football is a people business and a money business. And I was able to learn how to handle the people, the economics, and the salary cap. So, yes, I now know that the football is blown up."

Many NFL observers say that the 49ers won the 1994 NFL championship in the previous off season. With Policy wheeling and dealing, the club went to work on the NFL's recently implemented salary cap, trying to reduce their payroll from $47 million in 1993 to the NFL limit of $34.6 million in 1994. In the process, they raised red flag after red flag among their competitors. While the 49ers seemed to be cutting payroll, they also were adding top-notch players like New Orleans linebacker Ricky Jackson, Dallas linebacker Ken Norton, San Diego linebacker Gary Plummer and, yes, even Mr. Neon himself, cornerback Deion Sanders, who turned down a $17 million offer from New Orleans.

Somehow, Policy convinced Jackson to sign for $162,000 and Sanders to sign for $1.1 million. But both contracts contained enormous incentive clauses. Jackson, in fact, collected $868,000 as a reward when the 49ers made it to the Super Bowl. Sanders stands to make $2.5 million in a promotional deal from Sega Genesis, the computer game company, if he is willing to stay in the Bay Area, close to the company's headquarters. As the 1994 season approached, players virtually stood in line outside Policy's office to have their contracts re-jiggered. Somehow, most of the star players walked away with huge smiles on their faces.

All of this, of course, led Jones to cry "foul." By November, the 49ers were being investigated by the league office—their salary cap strategy was suddenly under a microscope. But the NFL found the 49ers' monetary game plan to be as clean as a referee's whistle.

Which led to even more frustration for Jones.

"They are mortgaging their future," the Cowboys' owner says. "While we're keeping our powder dry, and our feet up under ourselves, they're living with a credit card mentality. It just won't work over the long haul. I can tell you that right now."

Clearly, Jones detests the idea of having been outsmarted by anyone. The 49ers did win round one against the Cowboys by beating them twice in the first year of the salary cap. But the race is no sprint. The current collective bargaining agreement, which includes the salary cap, runs through the 1998 season. By then, it will be clear if the 49ers violated their credit limit, or if Policy truly understands the game's economic boundaries better than Jones.

"When Jerry talks about the credit card mentality, he is dead wrong," Policy says. "If his evaluation is correct, then there are about fourteen teams out there who have mortgaged their futures more than we have. The reason that I'm taking as strong an attitude as I am is because I am pretty proud of the job that we did. We had the longest road to travel to get under the cap. We were the team that was supposed to be decapitated by the cap. It presented the most competitive situation for us. We have done it. We won."

Fans in both San Francisco and Dallas believe that Policy won and Jones lost. Jones has been held accountable on the Dallas-area call-in sports talk shows. He has repeatedly been called "cheap" by his own fans. In the first year of the salary cap, the overall perception was that the 49ers showed more imagination and, therefore, were able to out maneuver the Cowboys, who had held a sizable lead in talent heading into the 1994 season.

Carl Francis, an executive with the NFL Players Association, told the *Wall Street Journal*, "While other teams were blaming the salary cap for having to get rid of players, San Francisco was showing that if they want to sign a player, they can find a way to do it."

Policy has recalibrated the business dynamics of the NFL, with a free-agency plan that knocked the Cowboys and Jones off their huge pedestal. But just like anything else he gets into, Jones believes the fight is never over until he has won.

"We beat them in two straight championship games, and the 49ers felt like they had to level the house and start all over again," he says. "We stayed with our game plan. I will tell you right now that we will win in the long run. We have to win in the long run. There's really no other way."

★ ★ ★

As much as Jones hates the thought of being outmaneuvered by Policy, he's also had his hands full trying to keep the Dallas dynasty intact. Clearly, the Cowboys have their greatest assets in place. Troy Aikman, Emmitt Smith, and Michael Irvin represent a tremendous team core. But one of football's clichés claims that small things make the biggest difference, and the Cowboys do seem to have been whittled away at the edges.

The 1994 draft produced a first-round bust in defensive end Shante Carver, a potential starting tackle in Larry Allen, and not much else. The 1995 draft has been panned by most critics. After the 1995 draft, *Dallas Morning News* NFL writer Rick Gosselin wrote, "One AFC board rated six of the ten draft choices as free agents [unlikely to be drafted]. Another AFC board rated seven of the Dallas picks as fifth-rounders or worse. One NFC board rated six Dallas picks as sixth-rounders or worse. Another NFC board rated six Dallas picks as fifth-rounders or worse."

The *Sporting News* gave the Cowboys a "D" grade for their draft picks and wrote, "[The Cowboys] have developed an allergy to tough decision-making."

Since Johnson's departure, the official line is that the Cowboys have made draft decisions by committee. Jones has tried to sell the idea to the media that he, along with Switzer and scouting director Larry Lacewell, now make the draft decisions. But this is merely a smoke screen. In truth, Lacewell is responsible for gathering and disseminating the draft data. But the final call on almost every draft decision goes to Jones.

Along with draft failures, the Cowboys have suffered heavy losses to free agency since the NFL's new system kicked in following the 1993 season. As the 1995 season begins, the Cowboys are missing two starters in the offensive line, along with wide receiver Alvin Harper, linebacker Ken Norton Jr., defensive end Jim Jeffcoat, defensive tackle Jimmie Jones, and safety James Washington. Every one of these players was a key component on the last Super Bowl team. Perhaps the biggest overall loss came after the 1994 season when center Mark Stepnoski, who is deeply respected by his teammates and players around the league, signed with the Houston Oilers.

Switzer proudly notes that the Cowboys were the only NFL team ranked in the top twelve in all six of the league's major statistical categories in 1994. But there were many signs of erosion in their status. Under Johnson, the Cowboys consistently had the best special teams in the league. In 1994, they fell to fifteenth overall and didn't have a single rookie on special teams, something Johnson would never have stood for. Special teams coach Joe Avezzano often was credited with the team's superb special teams play. But since Johnson's departure, it has become clear that Avezzano may have been overrated.

The Cowboys' coaching staff was once a talented, well-defined unit. But over the last three years, the team has lost two defensive coordinators, Butch Davis and Dave Wannstedt, to head coaching positions, along with Norv Turner, who had proven himself as one of the best offensive minds in the game before leaving the Cowboys to become the head coach of the Washington Redskins.

The mixed signals coming out of the Cowboys' front office were never more evident than when Davis left the team after the '94 season to become the head coach at the University of Miami. Jones wanted to name linebackers' coach Jim Eddy as defensive coordinator. Switzer preferred to promote defensive line coach John Blake. But they compromised on secondary coach Dave Campo to lead the defense.

His critics say that the Cowboys are feeling the aftereffects of Jones's efforts to run the team single-handedly. It hasn't helped that he continues to say publicly that he feels qualified to coach the Cowboys. Perception is everything, especially around a football locker room, where gossip runs the 40-yard dash in 4.1 seconds. One veteran player says, "Jerry needs to stay off the practice field, and off the sideline, or he needs to put a whistle around his neck. We know who's calling the shots. And it's not Barry."

During the upcoming campaign, Switzer's greatest challenge will be convincing his players that he, not Jones, is coaching the

Cowboys. The principal reason Switzer got off his Oklahoma couch to coach the Cowboys in 1994 is because his good buddy Jerry Jones wanted him to. As the Cowboys prepared for the 1995 season, he showed signs of a man headed toward retirement.

Switzer has been encouraged by several people to take charge of the Cowboys. Troy Aikman went to his office after the NFC championship loss to San Francisco and virtually begged Switzer to kick butt and take control of the team. But nothing seems to have changed. The 1995 season will decide his fate as the Cowboys' coach.

It hasn't helped that players, fans, and the media continually compare Switzer's style to that of Jimmy Johnson. For example, the atmosphere on the team's chartered flight returning from the 1994 loss to San Francisco was far from morgue-like. The beer flowed. Players wandered the aisles. They talked loudly about everything besides football. Several hit the Dallas bars that night after the flight touched down at DFW International Airport.

A year earlier, any partying on the flight home would have been squashed by Jimmy Johnson. Following a heartbreaking loss to Washington in 1992, Johnson went off like a roman candle during the return flight. Instead, Switzer sat quietly in his first-class seat. His behavior was true to his laid-back approach to his first NFL season. Aikman would later say, "Hopefully, the loss in San Francisco did knock some of the swagger out of this football team. Maybe it brought it back to its blue-collar roots, where it really all began, and it might just get this team doing the work that it did in the past."

Jimmy Johnson's style was to whip the assistant coaches into line. In turn, his coaches would whip the players into shape. Thanks to Switzer's laid-back style, along with key defections among the coaching staff, the power base at the top of the Cowboys' organization is crumbling. Has that lack of discipline trickled down to the players? Just check the bars around Dallas. You can see that Cowboys' players are starting to run out of control.

★ ★ ★

Several Cowboys' players had been partying the night after a road win over Arizona at the Iguana Mirage, a large, gaudy dance club on Greenville Avenue. The bar regularly cordons off a large section for players and their friends. A popular drink among Cowboys' players is Dom Perignon, which runs over $100 per bottle. Instead of sipping the expensive French champagne, though, Cowboys' players drink it straight from the bottle, as most people swill beer. After scoring two touchdowns in the fourth quarter to beat the Cardinals 28–21, the players were in a partying mood. Several admitted they had been drinking heavily on the chartered flight from Phoenix to DFW International Airport. Players are supposed to be served no more than two beers per chartered flight. But that rule is loosely enforced, especially after victories.

That night, tackle Erik Williams, a man who speaks so softly he barely can be heard, crashed his Mercedes 600 SL into a concrete retaining wall. The fact is that after drinking heavily with his teammates, Williams lost control of his car on a sharp turn. He had been racing wide receiver Willie Jackson while talking on his cellular phone. His car struck a guardrail and skidded, plowing across a grassy area before ramming head-on into the retaining wall. Police estimated that he had been traveling in excess of 75 m.p.h. Williams suffered a broken rib, a torn ligament in his right thumb, a wrist sprain, and multiple facial cuts that required plastic surgery. He also sustained two torn ligaments in his knee. A week later, he pleaded no contest to a misdemeanor drunk driving charge. His blood alcohol level was .17 percent, well above the .10 percent legal limit. His playing future was in doubt.

Under league rules, since Williams was not injured while playing football, Jones had no financial obligations to him. But Jones quickly forgave Williams, and even agreed to pay him the remainder of his salary along with his hospital bills. "I have a hard time being punitive on a mistake in driving," Jones says. "That has happened to every family and every person there is. The risk of life and how close he came to losing life is a good message to the youth in our community." A mixed message, apparently, since Jones has in effect rewarded Williams for his actions.

The Cowboys' owner also excused his players for their heavy drinking, saying, "It's just a fact of life that they're young men. It's just a fact of life about the physical shape they are in. They can have a couple of beers and, with the condition they are in, it won't have nearly the impact that it might have if they didn't have the size and the exercise they do."

After pleading no contest to drunk driving, Williams said, "It slowed me down a lot. A lot of guys come into the league and believe that they are invincible. They tend to go overboard. Maybe I did. But I won't again." However, six months later, Williams and a friend were arrested and charged with sexually assaulting a 17-year-old girl at his home north of Dallas. Williams reached an out-of-court settlement of a civil lawsuit with the young woman. However, in early July a Collin County grand jury decided not to indict him on a criminal charge of sexual assault. Williams has publicly vowed to be more careful about the people he associates with. He continues to rehabilitate his surgically repaired knee. At first, team doctors didn't expect him to be ready for the start of the 1995 season.

The same night, rookie defensive end Shante Carver abandoned his overturned truck on the northbound Central Expressway. He later called the police to say that his car had been stolen. Carver later recanted that story, admitting he'd been driving the vehicle around 3:30 that morning.

Heavy drinking and raucous partying are, of course, nothing new to Cowboys' players. In the 1960s, quarterback Don Meredith and his teammates were legends around Dallas for their boozing and pot-smoking. As ex-Cowboy Pat Toomay once wrote, "Any way to anesthetize the pain of playing for (Tom) Landry and playing with injuries." In the 1970s, wide receiver Bob Hayes went to prison for trafficking in cocaine. But nothing could match the early 1980s, when the Cowboys were called South America's Team by insiders for their use of cocaine. Five players were linked to an FBI investigation. Although the players were later cleared, cocaine was still widely used by some players.

However, there are no signs of cocaine use in the newest edition of the Cowboys. League-wide mandatory drug-testing may have something to do with that. But it is a heavy boozing team. Many players also seem to be infatuated with topless dancers. Granted, they didn't develop these vices on the day Switzer arrived in Dallas to coach the team. But Switzer, the Bootlegger's Boy, is starting to receive criticism for his players' behavior. When he coached at Oklahoma, the school was known as Renegade U. Jerry Jones may well decide that America's Team needs to develop a more upright and upstanding reputation to play a role in his megabucks marketing campaigns.

IN THE MEANTIME, JOHNSON SITS POISED LIKE A JACKAL ON THE NFL sideline. He will observe the 1995 season from the Fox Network studios. As he did in 1994, Johnson will dissect every move made by Jones and Switzer. Johnson loves to make headlines by verbally slicing up his former boss and Switzer.

Where is Johnson headed after the 1995 season? Most likely to San Francisco to become the next head coach of the 49ers, according to inside sources. Johnson might have had the job in 1995 if George Seifert hadn't coached his team to an easy win over San Diego in Super Bowl XXIX. Carmen Policy and owner Eddie DeBartolo, Jr. are prepared to offer the job to Johnson if Seifert succumbs to coaching burnout. They believe the timing would be right for Seifert to step down after the 1995 season— opening the door for them to hire Johnson. Johnson has already informed the 49ers they are one of four teams he would like to coach. The others are Miami, Tampa Bay, and the new NFC team that replaces the Rams in Los Angeles.

Johnson would fit in perfectly in San Francisco. Sources claim that Policy is ready to virtually turn the football operation over to him, and Johnson craves control. Former 49ers' coach Bill Walsh was the most powerful coach in the NFL before leaving the 49ers at the end of the 1988 season. A Johnson move to San Francisco also helps feed the 49ers–Cowboys hate-fest. Policy has developed an intense dislike for Jones over the years. Hiring Johnson in San Francisco, and then watching him embarrass his former boss, would be very satisfying to the 49ers president.

Johnson will have to clear one obstacle before returning to the NFL as a head coach. League security officials have been keeping track of his heavy gambling activities in both Nassau and Las Vegas. He's also made numerous trips to the Crystal Palace Hotel and Casino in Nassau, which is an hour-long flight from Miami, and frequent stopovers in Las Vegas at Caesar's Palace during trips to the Fox studios in Los Angeles.

While Johnson's gambling is not illegal, the frequency of his trips to casinos and the size of his wagers have concerned league officials. He often plays up to $20,000 per hand at the blackjack tables, and routinely plays four different hands at $5000 apiece.

During his five-year tenure as the Cowboys' coach, Johnson was warned by NFL officials to limit his trips to casinos. They suggested that he make no more than two trips a year to gambling establishments. Instead, he made several trips to Nassau and Las Vegas casinos to play blackjack even while coaching the Cowboys. When the Cowboys played a preseason game in London during the summer of 1993, Johnson spent several nights in the casinos playing blackjack. One night, he took his entire coaching staff along. He made several $1500 bets for members of his staff.

An NFL official says of Johnson's gambling, "When Jimmy was coaching, there were some conversations with the Cowboys about him being in the casinos so often. If someone has a gambling problem, then it could become a problem for the NFL. It couldn't prevent him from coaching again, unless he was associating with gamblers or gambling activities that could discredit the NFL. More than likely, he would get a warning before coming back to the NFL as a coach."

IF THE COWBOYS ARE TO RETURN TO GLORY, IT WILL BE JONES WHO leads them. He has set himself up as the man who would be King of the Cowboys. He runs the college draft. He makes the personnel moves. During the season, he meets daily with Switzer to go over the performance of players. Jones does everything but wear a whistle around his neck and call the plays. Even his practice field attire occupies the room where the head coach once dressed. The ball game is now his.

Before firing Jimmy Johnson, Jones allowed his coach to flex some muscle and flaunt some power. Jones knew he had to. Johnson was too talented and headstrong to be reined in. Besides, the Cowboys were winning Super Bowls. Johnson had far more freedom than most NFL coaches. But when the power game tilted too far in Jimmy's direction, Jerry felt he had to regain control. When the party turned sour in Orlando in March of 1994 and Johnson declined his toast, Jones saw his opening and ran for daylight. He fired Johnson even though he knew it would hurt his team's chances of becoming the first ever to win three straight Super Bowls.

Today, there is no owner in sports who runs his team from top to bottom more completely. Perhaps Jones was driven by something that his father, J. W. "Pat" Jones told him in 1989 when he bought the Cowboys. Jones recalls, "My father called me one time after I'd been in Dallas for three or four months and said, 'Jerry, I really don't know if you plan to do anything else with your life except the Cowboys. But if you do, I don't care if you do it with smoke, mirrors, or baling wire, you have to be successful there. Goddammit, Jerry, everybody is looking at you. You've got to do it, son.'"

Somehow, Jones came to believe he could win without Johnson, whom many considered the best overall football man in the business. Instead of placing his ego and hard feelings aside, he stepped toward center stage. His thirst for power had become overwhelming, and he lusted for its adrenaline rush. That is why stepping onto the stage of The Corral outside of Texas Stadium in January 1995 was so intoxicating and satisfying. The Cowboys had just won their first playoff game without Johnson. And, as Jones spoke that day, the crowd chanted, "JERR-REE, JERR-REE, JERR-REE!" Jones had been vindicated. The fire in his eyes told the story. He loved it. The owner of America's Team had become wired on winning. And he knew at that moment he was now wearing the crown.

★ ★ ★

AT THE NFL OWNERS' MEETINGS IN MARCH 1994, ABC-TV HAD staged the party at Pleasure Island where Jones, while drinking heavily, happened upon a table of current and former employees. Among them were Bears' head coach Dave Wannstedt, Redskins' coach Norv Turner, former Cowboys' personnel man Bob Ackles, and their wives. At the center of the table was Jimmy Johnson, who boldly ignored his boss when a toast was offered.

In March 1995, the NFL held its spring meetings at the Arizona Biltmore in Phoenix. This year, the Fox Network sponsored one of the nightly parties. Again, the drinks were flowing and spirits were high. Close to midnight, the same collection of people had assembled near the center of the banquet room— Wannstedt, Turner, Ackles, and Johnson. As in Orlando, they were swapping stories. Johnson seemed especially relaxed after a year away from coaching. And, as in Orlando, he was doing most of the talking while the others listened and laughed. Wives and girlfriends stood close by.

A few feet away, sitting at a table with a group of friends, was Jones. Like his former coach, Jones was the life of his own little party. The sting of losing to San Francisco in the NFC championship game had started to wear off. Jones was as gregarious as ever as the party rolled toward midnight.

Wearing a dark suit, San Francisco's Carmen Policy made his way through the room, shaking hands. "Carmen was pretty drunk," Ackles would say later. "In fact, most of us were. But I remember that Carmen had had quite a few. And he was pretty embarrassed the next day about what he did."

From the corner of his eye, Policy spotted Johnson, Turner, Wannstedt, and Ackles. Cocking his eyebrows and fighting off a smile, he approached the group. Policy is a diminutive man who walks with a proud swagger. When he realized they'd spotted him, Policy raised his glass and threw back his head in glee. "Here's to the Dallas Cowboys!" he said, laughing loudly. It was the same toast Jones had made a year ago. Policy even managed to mimic Jones's nasal twang. Much of the room erupted in laughter as the men began to high-five each other. Policy was clearly proud that he'd recreated the scene in Orlando. This time, though, no one cared to notice if Johnson acknowledged the toast.

Just a few feet away, one person in the room wasn't laughing or even smiling. Jones had overheard the joke, which was clearly on him. He stood and began striding toward the door. Head down, elbows out, and arms pumping, he moved quickly into the cool Arizona night. This time he wanted to hide his feelings. This time he wouldn't go to the lobby bar. He wouldn't gather the sports writers around to announce his intentions. The King of the Cowboys had decided to store his anger for another time, another fight. He was down. But the fast-talking Arkansas wildcatter quietly reminded himself as he walked away that he never stayed down for long.

CHAPTER 14

Jerry's World

WITH HIS BLACK-FRAME GLASSES AND CONSERVATIVE SUITS, LAMAR Hunt, the quiet and unassuming owner of the Kansas City Chiefs, could disappear into a crowd. Among NFL insiders, however, he's known as one of the most progressive and innovative figures in American sports. In 1960, Hunt founded and organized the American Football League. During the early 1960s, he introduced the sports revenue-sharing plan that is now one of the cornerstones of the NFL. In 1967, he negotiated the largest merger in the history of sports—between the American and National football leagues. Hunt is the first AFL figure to be elected to the Pro Football Hall of Fame. Some have even credited him with naming the Super Bowl.

Hunt, the son of legendary oil tycoon H. L. Hunt, moved his Dallas Texans to Kansas City in 1963, a year after winning the AFL championship. But he decided to stay in Texas, keeping his offices in one of Dallas's opulent high-rise buildings. Hunt helps run the Kansas City Chiefs from more than six hundred miles away. And one of his favorite pastimes is watching Cowboys' owner Jerry Jones.

"I frequently send newspaper articles about what Jerry is doing to my employees in Kansas City," Hunt says. "When I see the Cowboys do something, or I see Jerry come up with a new idea, I pass along that idea to my people. I don't mind following ideas that others come up with. And believe me, Jerry has plenty of them. I think that Jerry is a very creative person and a wonderful selling person. He is one of the most amazing people I've ever seen in my life."

Jones's newspaper clip file in Kansas City should be spilling over in the next few years. Why? Because he plans to raise the roof—literally—on American sports.

Jones's vision for the Cowboys' future is as expansive as the Texas horizon. Nowhere in sports is there a team owner as ambitious about winning, or as aggressive about exploiting his product above and beyond the playing field. According to Jones's plans, the Texas Stadium complex in Irving will be transformed into a futuristic plaza of theaters and museums, with tours, interactive exhibits, a high-rise hotel, and posh restaurants by the turn of the century. There will even be a tram to shuttle tourists from the nearby Dallas–Fort Worth International Airport. The world of sports hasn't seen anything like the game plan about to be implemented by Jerry Jones.

As the next century approaches, Jones's plans for expansion start big and get bigger. First, he plans to expand skyward. After visiting Toronto's Skydome in 1991, he came home with a plan to install a retractable roof on Texas Stadium. The Cowboys' home, located less than ten miles northwest of downtown Dallas, was built with a partial roof that protected fans from the rain, sleet, or snow, but left the playing field uncovered. Owner Clint Murchison Jr. originally envisioned a stadium that would have both an outdoor and an indoor feeling. Therefore, it was built with a "hole-in-the-roof"—in local legend, the hole through which God watches His Team play.

Under Jones's plan, the eight-acre stadium roof will be raised fifty feet—one-quarter inch at a time—with pneumatic jacks.

Retractable sections will be added to cover the field during cold or inclement weather.

Under the new roof, Jones plans to add a second upper deck with more than 40,000 new seats. The blueprint also calls for lowering the field level by twelve feet so that 6,500 seats can be added on the ground floor. By increasing the overall seating capacity to 104,000 seats, America's Team will have America's Largest Stadium in All of Sports. Jones's ideas for adding seats were born on a trip to Mexico City's Azteca Stadium during the summer of 1994. In spite of a rainstorm and a field that resembled a quagmire, 112,000 paying customers showed up to see a rather boring preseason game between the Cowboys and the Houston Oilers.

Jones is also tired of hearing that Texas Stadium is not fit to host a Super Bowl. The league's reasoning, as it's been explained to Jones, is twofold. First, Texas Stadium doesn't meet the league's requirement of a 75,000-seat minimum. Second, the average temperature for the Dallas area in January is 38 degrees. For Super Bowls, the league has stood steadfastly by warm-weather cities like Miami, Los Angeles, or San Diego—or cities with domes like New Orleans, Minnesota, and Detroit. With more than 100,000 seats, a retractable roof, and air conditioning, the new, improved stadium will certainly increase Irving's chances of hosting a Super Bowl, a Final Four, a national championship game in college football, or possibly a national political convention.

Jones has plans for pumping additional revenue out of all these seats—above and beyond his ProSeat venture. He is considering turning all of Texas Stadium into "club seating." By adding amenities like individual televisions and cup holders, he can justify charging premiums on every seat in the house. One Cowboys' insider estimates that those premiums will average close to $7,000 per seat by the year 2000. Working-class fans, especially those with families, will no longer be able to afford to attend games at Texas Stadium.

Joel Finglass, the Cowboys' director of sales and promotions, justifies the increases by saying, "For a lot of people, the National Football League is the entertainment of their life. If they want to spend the money to get more out of it, they will spend the money. So if the Cowboys can make it more enjoyable, and they can get more out of it, then that [the more expensive seating] is what they will want."

Also included in Jones's monstrous game plan are three grass practice fields and an office complex to be built next to gate 3 of Texas Stadium. Jones plans to either abandon or sell the 80,000-square-foot office and practice facility at Valley Ranch, and to move the entire operation to the stadium. Eventually, as he moves closer to completing Jerry's World, Jones plans to move the Cowboys' summer training camp from Austin to Irving, where revenues are certain to soar. By then, he hopes to have his own high-rise hotel ready, along with several restaurants.

Around Dallas, the project is simply called "Jerry's World"—for obvious reasons. He predicts that the Greatest Show in Sports will attract between three and four million people a year, and they will come from all over the world. Applying one of his chicken-fried witticisms, Jones says, "The day will finally come when the world will look at Texas Stadium and call it 'The Big Boy.'"

GROWING UP IN BALTIMORE, JOEL FINGLASS WAS AN AVID FAN OF THE Jetsons. Thirty years later, he is returning to that space-age world at warp speed. "Everything in your life influences you," Finglass says. "Hopefully, my ideas come from the Jetsons—and not from the Flintstones."

Finglass has been anointed by Jones to transform his ideas for Jerry's World into the biggest side show in all of sports. Finglass wears long hair and looks like a lead guitarist in a rock band. His training in sports marketing and ticket sales hardly suggest the proper preparation for this space-age project. Until Jones started dreaming up all of his "coming attractions," Finglass had never heard of interactive theaters. Now, Finglass says, "I'm just driving the bus. My job is to make sure that all of the right people get on."

Like Jones, Finglass envisions a brave new world. The new entertainment attraction, to be located just outside the stadium, will more closely resemble those at Universal Studios near Los Angeles than those at your everyday theme park of fast rides and shrill screams. Instead of the Earthquake or E.T. ride, visitors will see Cowboys' players converted into stylized cartoon heroes.

The four-story building will house an interactive museum and three interactive theaters. Unlike the Pro Football Hall of Fame in Canton, Ohio, the Cowboys' museum will not be a collection of grass-stained jerseys and grainy game film. There will be a video library, but fans will be able to do much more than just watch Johnny Unitas throw touchdown passes to Raymond Berry. Through computers, they will be able to participate in calling the plays, and choosing Unitas's receiver.

In the new interactive theaters, fans will feel as if they are in the middle of a live NFL football game. They will experience both the emotion and the physical exhilaration that their heroes have known for years. At interactive theater number one, visitors will see Michael Irvin flying just a few feet overhead, his hands extending to make the great catch right in front of their noses. At the second theater, which will be called the round room, they will experience a blind-side blitz by Chargers linebacker Junior Seau. When Seau sacks the quarterback, the entire room will rock violently. At the third interactive theater, viewers will actually control the Cowboys' defense through body language that activates a computer. By crossing their arms and legs, or by turning in their chairs, fans will direct computer simulations of defensive end Tony Tolbert and tackle Russell Maryland playing at the line of scrimmage. All the while, the objective will be to stop the Buffalo Bills from driving down the field and scoring the winning touchdown.

"The thing about the NFL is that you can reach out, but you can't touch," Finglass says. "This might just give you a chance to touch, too."

After touring the theaters, fans will walk down a tunnel into the locker room area. They will stand next to the equipment cage as an actor explains everything (as Jones might say) "from socks to jocks." He will explain the different types of equipment and might even show you Troy Aikman's shoulder pads.

Then the tour will lead to the playing field, where visitors will be able to actually run pass patterns. A big-screen TV will show a video of Troy Aikman taking a center snap, dropping back five steps, then stepping forward and throwing a pass. As the televised Aikman releases his pass, an actual football will come flying out of the computerized screen.

Along with this space age interactive entertainment, fans will get a chance to walk down memory lane. An announcer will direct fans, through the headsets they're wearing, to the place on the field where Tony Hill caught the winning Hail Mary touchdown pass from Roger Staubach in December of 1979.

If Jones and Finglass have their way, long-time fans won't recognize the experience of attending sports events after the turn of the century. Instead of a ticket, they'll enter the stadium with a credit card. Instead of a walk to the concession stand for a hot dog, they'll punch a series of computer buttons that will activate a dumbwaiter that will serve their lunch with mustard on the side. They'll wear a headset connecting them to the quarterback as he calls the plays. They'll have a TV in front of them linking them to all of the other NFL games. They might even have a telephone and a PIN number that will allow them to bet on those games.

Jones assumes an almost God-like perspective when he begins to talk about the once-unthinkable amenities like the retractable roof, air conditioning, and the grass field. With his eyes widening, he almost yells, "I can control the elements. I can put grass on the field. I can use the technology that is there today and I can put in a retractable roof."

He is even more animated when he shifts into his salesman's pitch, because he knows that selling his grand scheme will not be easy. Projected costs for raising the roof and adding the 40,000 seats are somewhere in the $200 million range. Jones estimates that the interactive theaters and Cowboys' Hall of Fame will cost

another $68 million. Irving Mayor Bobby Joe Raper has pro-
jected the entire cost at closer to $350 million. The figure could
even go higher—as Jones is sure to have other plans that he
hasn't yet revealed.

Jones has informed Irving officials that he expects the city to
foot at least half the bill. Since buying the Cowboys, he has
shrewdly cultivated the Irving City Council. But selling this enormous project will require more than a few free trips to the Super
Bowl for council members. For one, Irving is trying to lure both
the NBA Mavericks and the NHL Stars out of Dallas. Some
council members would prefer spending their mega-millions on a
state-of-the-art arena that would include luxury suites—the
nearest things to gold mines in the sports business—that they,
instead of Jones, would control. Irving is trying to out-hustle at
least three other metroplex cities that have been wooing the
Mavericks and Stars.

Other complications to Jones's plan exist. For one, the city's
sales tax is at the state maximum, 8.25 cents per dollar. And
Raper has said he will not ask the citizens to foot the bill for
Jerry's World directly. So the burden may be pushed to the city's
hotels and motels. Raper believes a hotel-motel tax increase could
make the project feasible. But this plan faces a major complica-
tion. For the past several years, Jones has been quietly buying up
eighty acres around Texas Stadium. He plans to build his own
high-rise hotel on the property. Owners of the many other hotels
and motels in the area might be unhappy to learn that taxes on
their services will be financing Jerry's World while they compete
with Jones in the hotel business.

Few people, however, are willing to bet against Jones, the
master salesman, being able to convince the Irving City Council
to foot at least half the bill for Jerry's World and the stadium
expansion.

★ ★ ★

SINCE UNVEILING HIS PLANS IN OCTOBER 1994, JONES HAS BEEN BOTH
applauded for his unlimited vision, and derided as a sports huck-

ster with a pure lust for money. Some have called him danger-
ously greedy. Others say he is on the cutting edge of American
sports, just as Lamar Hunt was back in the 1960s.

Wayne Huizenga is a sports owner who understands Jones's
level of thinking. He owns the Miami Dolphins of the NFL, the
Florida Panthers of the National Hockey League, and major-
league baseball's Florida Marlins. He is also an entertainment
mogul. Before becoming the vice chairman of Viacom, he built
the Blockbuster video rental chain into the monster it is today.

"There is no question," Huizenga says, "that the game of
football is great. The game is the reason people go to the stadium,
right? But there is a lot of time prior to the game and after the
game during which the fans need to be entertained as well. Of
course, there are so many traditionalists who just want to focus in
on the game. There is nothing wrong with the game. But my philosophy is that we should take charge of the [fans'] experience
from the time you get within two miles from the stadium, until
you are two miles down the road after the game is over. The
entertainment factor is so very important."

Of Jones's grand plans, Huizenga says, "Jerry is a strategizer
and a guy who is looking out into the future. He is not just looking
at this year or next year. He is focused and works hard at it. He is
an all-around thinker rather than just being focused on his team."

Even those who are close to Jones are often awestruck by his
dreams. Says WFAA-TV sportscaster Dale Hansen, "He works on
a bigger stage than I ever dream about. It makes you wonder
what will be next after he gets control of the entire National
Football League. How much does he want? I say to him, 'That's
enough, isn't it?' And the next thing you know he wants to have
100,000 people in the stands at Texas Stadium."

Jones's strategy, however, still runs contrary to that of many
NFL owners, who believe the game should stand forever on its
original foundation. This philosophy is prevalent among the "old
guard" owners who have roots that date back to the 1930s and
the 1940s. Jones's Star Trek thinking may be appreciated by the
Wayne Huizengas—but not by the men who still long for muddy
fields, grass-stained jerseys, and Otto Graham's wobbly passes.

To owners from the old school, Jones seems too focused on his own team and unconcerned with the general good of the game. He often comes off as a carnival barker with one eye on the almighty dollar, and the other on the spotlight.

"To get off your butt, you need lofty goals," Jones says, bristling at critics. "If they are not lofty enough, you will not get it done. Furthermore, I don't have dreams unless I have a sense that I can get it done. This project has tremendous potential for what it can do for the Dallas Cowboys. When I think of the Cowboys, I think of a franchise that will be known around the world. Every year, there are fifty million people who either fly in or out of DFW Airport. Each and every one of them has to fly right over this thing and they're going to see it. This is going to be a tremendous success."

In his own way, Jerry Jones is just as much a pioneer as the league's old guard. As the most ambitious and recognizable owner in professional sports, he is bound and determined to make his mark—and his fortune—by fundamentally changing the way the business works. As the old cliché goes, "You can always recognize the pioneers—they're the ones with the arrows in their backs." Only time will tell if Jerry Jones is about to launch a new sports gold rush—or if he'll make his last stand in an NFL ambush.

★ ★ ★

J IM DENT HAS BEEN AN AWARD-WINNING JOURNALIST FOR THE last twenty years. He covered the Dallas Cowboys for eleven years for both the *Fort Worth Star-Telegram* and the *Dallas Times Herald*. He now does a talk show for Prime Sports Radio, a national sports network. A graduate of SMU, he lives in the Dallas area.

★ ★ ★